POLITICS, PRINCIPLE, AND PREJUDICE
1865-1866

LAWANDA COX AND JOHN H. COX

POLITICS,

Dilemma of Reconstruction America

PRINCIPLE,
AND PREJUDICE
1865-1866

STUDIES IN AMERICAN NEGRO LIFE
August Meier, General Editor

Atheneum   NEW YORK   1969

To m. c.
SCHOLAR AND FRIEND

PREFACE

THIS STUDY CONCERNING THE POLITICS OF EARLY RECON-
struction has been a long time in the making. We should
like the reader to know that we undertook this research with no
intent to write a political study but rather in pursuit of what
seemed a quite different problem. We began without questioning
the interpretation of the conflict between President Johnson and
Congress then current and still quite generally held—though recently challenged by a number of scholars, notably Alfred H.
Kelly, Stanley Coben, David Donald, Jack Scroggs, Bernard
Weisberger, Robert P. Sharkey, Irwin Unger, Hans Trefousse,
Eric McKitrick, David Montgomery, Ira V. Brown, and Benjamin P. Thomas with Harold M. Hyman. When interpretations
contrary to those then generally accepted first occurred to us, we
viewed them with skepticism but could not refrain from pursuing
them with vigor. Although in substance a part of the new re-
visionism, our work had its origins neither in contemporary awareness of the civil rights issue nor in the provocative findings of the
new scholarship. Rather, it represents a judgment independently
conceived and examined through a careful scrutiny of primary
source materials. The reader will judge the validity of our findings on the basis of the evidence here presented, but we wish him
to accept our assurance that the study was undertaken without

preconceptions and that we did not set out either to upset a thesis or to establish one.

Our conclusions are in agreement with those of other recent studies, which find that the Radicals did not represent a unity of economic interest or purpose, that their antagonists utilized race prejudice as political capital, and that Andrew Johnson had a large share of responsibility for the break in early 1866 between Congress and the President. In explanation of that tragic impasse, we have found two key factors that heretofore have received little attention: an effort to jettison the old Republican coalition in favor of a Conservative Union party attractive to Democrats in both North and South; and a crystallization of Republican opposition to Johnson over the issue of basic civil rights, short of suffrage, for the freed Negro. We cannot agree that what the Republican North wished of the defeated South was mere symbol; by March of 1866 the peace terms demanded were substantive.

Although Andrew Johnson's record as President was one of failure, we do not see him as a politically inept Chief Executive during the first year of his administration nor as a martyr to uncompromising constitutional principles. Rather, we have found a seasoned political veteran, who with good reason accepted a view of politics then widely current—namely, that the times were ripe for a new or transformed Union party centered about his leadership and his restoration policies. We have also found his position in respect to restoration of the South prior to his break with Congress in March, 1866, more ambiguous than has been generally recognized.

William H. Seward emerges as a central, though not decisive, figure in post–Civil War politics. The fact that Johnson rejected his Secretary's counsel of concession to Republican majority opinion while accepting Seward's national and political goals may have been decisive in bringing defeat to the President and turmoil to the nation. Greatly complicating the political scene was the eagerness of Democratic leaders to control Johnson and the nation's future and their abiding animosity toward Seward and his political lieutenant, Thurlow Weed.

We have not attempted a comprehensive re-examination of the leading Radical extremists, though we believe one is needed; several recent studies point the way to a more understanding evaluation of their motives. From our own work, it is clear that the Radicals were on the defensive during the first year of Reconstruction and in danger of being eliminated as an effective political force. If they emerged as victors, the result was due not so much to their efforts as to the deliberate decision of moderate Republicans. The significance of this decision of the Moderates, in our judgment, cannot be explained away on the basis of political pressure or party loyalty. Though these factors were operative, added to them was a concern for principle and a reluctant disillusionment with the Chief Executive.

Though it was not evident in 1866 that the nation would fail to effect a post–Civil War settlement of moderation or to achieve civil equality for the freed Negro, we have found the roots of that failure firmly established before the elections of that year. Opposition on the part of Andrew Johnson and the Conservatives to effective national protection of the freedman's basic civil rights, short of suffrage, destroyed the opportunity that existed in 1865 and 1866 to achieve reunion and a resolution of the Negro problem with a minimum of conflict and a maximum of good will and permanence.

Since the bulk of historical writing in this field until very recently has emphasized the principles of the pro-Johnson forces and the politics of their opponents, we have tried to call attention to the principles of those who supported Congress and the politics of those who followed the President. We have not meant to imply that concern for either principle or political advantage was the exclusive possession of either camp. In some respects the conflict over Reconstruction policy held the character of classic drama, with one "right" pitted against another—compassion and fellowship for defeated white Southerners against compassion and protection for Negro Southerners. In our judgment, however, the scales of historical justice do not balance evenly.

Two manuscript collections, for the most part but recently open for investigation at the time we first saw them, convinced us of the need for a fresh look at the Northern politics of Reconstruction: the Freedmen's Bureau records in the National Archives, and the Seward and Weed Papers at the University of Rochester. A close scrutiny of the Johnson Papers in the Library of Congress and of contemporary newspaper files has also had a major effect upon our work. The S. L. M. Barlow Papers, which we had been fruitlessly pursuing for years, fortunately were purchased by the Huntington Library and kindly made available to us in the summer of 1960 before their cataloguing had been completed. The collection proved of major importance, and it confirmed with a wealth of fresh detail conclusions already reached. Reference to most of the other manuscript collections that we consulted will be found in the footnotes.

We have incurred debts to librarians and their staffs too numerous for listing. Their helpfulness has been such that we wish to make record of the fact—apparent to all workers in this vineyard —that it is not manuscripts alone that make possible critical research. Of almost equal importance is the freely given knowledge of those men and women who work constantly and intimately with the collections. Of these, we should like to pay a special tribute to Sara Dunlap Jackson of the National Archives and to Margaret Butterfield of the University of Rochester Library.

We should also like to express our appreciation of the grants-in-aid extended in the very early stages of our work by the Social Science Research Council and the American Philosophical Society. The direction of our research took a turn not anticipated when application was made for their assistance; we trust they will not consider this a breach of obligation.

Finally, we should like to make affectionate acknowledgment of the encouragement we have received over the years from our good friend, the late Howard K. Beale. When last we saw him, the summer before his death, he was most insistent that we speedily finish this study. Since he knew something of our findings, this persistent interest in our work was a mark not only of his friendship but also of his open mind as scholar. We do not suppose that he would agree with all of our conclusions, many of which are in sharp contrast to the ones he arrived at some thirty years ago in a study that will always stand as a landmark of American historiography and a point of departure for all serious students of Reconstruction.

LaWanda Cox
John H. Cox

CONTENTS

POLITICS, PRINCIPLE, AND PREJUDICE 1865-1866

1 THE SEWARD LOBBY AND THE THIRTEENTH AMENDMENT

THE IRREVOCABLE ABOLITION OF SLAVERY SEEMS, IN RETROSPECT, SO inescapable a consequence of the American Civil War that even the historical imagination finds difficulty in recapturing the uncertainty, tension, and passion that surrounded the final passage through Congress of the Thirteenth Amendment. True, opponents of the Amendment conceded that slavery was dying or dead—a casualty of war that could not be resurrected. Yet they none the less argued with bitterness and conviction the unconstitutionality, the inexpediency, the futility, and the danger of interment by constitutional amendment. Some even harbored a hope that the doomed institution might linger on for a gentler death. The opposition in the House of Representatives, and indeed throughout the North, was confined to the ranks of the Democratic party. But the Democrats were numerous. They had fought the recent presidential election with the slogan "The Constitution as it is [i.e., with slavery] and the Union as it was." And although they had been cheated of victory at the polls by the victories of Northern armies in the field, the elections of November would not affect the composition of the House until the assembling of the Thirty-ninth Congress. Therefore, in January, 1865, when the Amendment came up for reconsideration, the Democratic opposition again, as in the previous June, held the power to deny it the requisite two-thirds vote of opproval.

Whether the Democrats would exercise that power, no man knew with certainty until the final vote had been taken. When Representative James M. Ashley of Ohio called up the measure for reconsideration on January 6, 1865, its friends were divided in their predictions, but there was a note of cautious optimism.[1] President Lincoln had forcefully but tactfully urged its passage in his December message, arguing that the people had given their decision for the Amendment in the recent elections and that the next Congress would certainly pass it. In his discreet but unequivocal manner he was exercising the power of his high office in behalf of the Amendment—letting it be known that in case of defeat he would call the new Congress into special session, holding personal interviews with border-state members and lame-duck Democrats, probably supplementing Presidential eloquence with an intimation of Presidential favor.[2] But after a few days of House debate, the Democratic opposition tightened; reporters agreed that the measure lacked three or four necessary votes. Ashley did not push for the early decision originally planned, but postponed final debate until the end of the month.[3]

By January 31, the day for decision, the friends of the measure were counting votes hopefully, but there was still "profound anxiety."[4] According to a well-informed report, "they could not tell whether opposition members pledged to vote for it would hold firm when the hour of trial came. One or two did not. One man had gone so far as to prepare a little speech in its favor, but quailed when the hour came. He lacked the moral courage to meet the sneers of his comrades."[5] Courage was requisite for those Democrats who supported the Amendment. They feared ostracism by their party associates, dreaded the bitter label of "abolition disunionist," hesitated before the anticipated anger of their Democratic constituents—those "lovers of the country, friends of 'the Constitution as it is'" to whom they owed election.[6] Those Democrats who spoke out pleaded their devotion to party in the past and their pledged faithfulness to its future; they argued that only by burying the slavery issue could the Democracy once again gain majority favor and public offices. But unconvinced that they had moved their fellow Democrats to understanding, they summoned brave words of defiance. If this act dug his political grave, declared one, he would descend into it with a clear conscience.[7] Indeed, on the final vote only two of the sixteen Democratic "yeas" came from members who had won re-election to the succeeding Congress; the others came from lame ducks, who had little political fortune to hazard.[8]

From the perspective of almost a century, it is difficult to comprehend the widespread distaste for emancipation among Democratic voters of the North. The arguments of their spokesmen appear in retrospect feeble buttresses for the archaic institution of human slavery. But beyond the logic of opposition lay passions more readily understandable. There was the old, accumulated hatred for Abolitionists on the part of those who held them at least as responsible as Southern fire-eaters for disunion and conflict; the bitter accusation of the war-weary that Lincoln was prolonging the war and repelling Southern overtures for peace, in order to secure the Abolitionists' goal; and—just beneath the surface, sometimes emerging to the level of debate—the dark, deep-rooted prejudice of race.

These deep passions had proved to have explosive political potential the previous July, when Southern emissaries were reported to be waiting in Canada and to be properly accredited to make peace. Lincoln had then issued his famous "To Whom It May Concern," stating his readiness to treat with anyone authorized on behalf of Jefferson Davis to make peace on the basis of the restoration of the Union and the *abandonment of slavery*.[9] The popular reaction as it reached the sensitive ears of Secretary of State William H. Seward and his political alter ego, that master practitioner of practical politics, Thurlow Weed, warned of dire consequences. The President's open letter was a "Death distroying [*sic*] Epidemic"; it had "killed" Mr. Lincoln.[10] Lincoln himself may have hesitated, for a new peace authorization was drafted calling only for restoration of the Union, all other questions to be left for adjustment. Lincoln, however, held firm, and the more yielding authorization was not executed.[11] Charles A. Dana, then Assistant Secretary of War, believed that Lincoln would have hopelessly alienated a majority of the Radicals had he omitted emancipation from his terms for peace.[12] Seward and Weed, however, handled the issue gingerly and ambiguously. In his important and widely acclaimed political speech of September, Seward gave what he termed an "explicit" answer on the question of slavery. While rebels waged war, military measures affecting slavery would continue; when they laid down their arms, such measures would cease and all questions including those affecting slavery would "pass over to the arbitrament of courts of law and to the councils of legislation." Seward made no mention of the proposed amendment to which his party and his President were pledged.[13] Little wonder that Hugh McCulloch, fellow Conservative in the Cabinet, appreciatively commended Seward's speech as "captivating and *adroit*"![14]

Shortly thereafter, Seward refused to answer a friendly request for clarification of his remarks about slavery. The Secretary did "not think it necessary" to enter into correspondence on the subject; he had no objection to the publication of the inquiry.[15] Even after Lincoln's December message to Congress, the Administration's most faithful newspaper, the New York *Times*, chose to interpret the President's position as one that would welcome Southern peace proposals without prior commitment on slavery.[16] If leaders of the party pledged to emancipation saw political hazard in supporting peace with freedom, it is understandable that their opponents, bound to the "Constitution as it is," hesitated to support the emancipation amendment. Although the end of effective Southern resistance was in sight by January, 1865, peace was still elusive. There were widespread rumors of peace missions, and there were fears of protracted guerrilla warfare ahead. Despite the argument of the Administration that passage of the Thirteenth Amendment would hasten peace and insure its permanence, many saw noncommitment on the future of slavery as the most effective inducement that could be offered the South for total capitulation.

Beyond the immediate concern for peace lay the fear of reunion accompanied by sudden freedom for the thousands upon thousands of Negro Southerners who as yet knew only the state of bondage. In the House of Representatives Robert Mallory of Kentucky warned his colleagues of the falseness of the argument that the Amendment would put away once and for all the disturbing question of slavery. With slavery, "we know the status of the Negro," but what of the liberated slaves? Were they to remain in the South? Were they to enjoy suffrage? These were revolutionary times and one step would lead to the next. "Now is the time to resist the radical party and save our form of government."[17] And C. A. White of Ohio asked, "What will be the effect of turning loose this mass of people? Where will they go?" Is it proposed, he queried, to make them before the law the equals of the white man, to give them the right of suffrage, the right to hold office, the right to sit upon juries? "Do you intend, in other words, to make this a mongrel Government, instead of a white man's Government?" In the Mississippi Valley, he stated bluntly, "we have prejudices. . . . We cannot eradicate them if we would."[18]

The New York *World*, "exponent of the present attitude and future tendencies of Democratic opinion"[19] and the guidepost for wavering Democratic congressmen, saw the Amendment as a futile gesture unless accompanied by additional amendments that would leave the states shorn of powers on nearly every subject and the Constitution "abolished." It would lead to the destruction of the right of trial by jury in the state in which an offense is committed. There would need be an end to such undoubted rights of the states as those prohibiting the residence of free Negroes, denying them the right to bear witness against white citizens, depriving them of the power to own real estate or inherit and transmit property, excluding them from schools and poorhouses, imprisoning them for debt and then putting the debtors to work at hard labor, arresting adult Negroes under vagrancy laws and binding out their children as those of paupers. To abolish slavery without such additional amendments would leave the Negro exposed to "intolerable oppression." The *World* was arguing not for further amendments but against "hasty action" on the proposed amendment.[20] It had given assurance that "the Democratic party will never give over the battle for the freedom of the states."[21]

A further peril to the Amendment lay in the mutual suspicions of practical politics. On the floor of the House, Democratic members accused Republicans of the lowest political aims in pushing the Amendment. The party in power was seeking to continue the war and an army of office holders; its "leading motive" was to control the government through the Negro, "to fix the destinies of this Union indefinitely."[22] Republicans viewed the Democratic opposition as equally partisan and unprincipled. In their eyes the Northern opposition leaders were laboring to get the South back without exterminating slavery, so that they could "with the South control the government in four years."[23]

So tense was the atmosphere, so uncertain the fate of the Thirteenth Amendment in December and January, that "one vote was then most momentous."[24] To gain the crucial votes needed for passage was the object of an extraordinary lobby. Organized and directed by the Republican Secretary of State, its members were predominantly Democrats. They were men influential in their day and forgotten in ours. Some were so obscure that their very identities remain unknown. The central figures, however, can be identified, and their character and careers are as improbable as their sponsorship and their activities.

The most important member of the lobby, or at least the one whose activities are best documented in the Seward correspondence, was W. N. Bilbo of Nashville, Tennessee. A former Whig whose devotion to the old party he described as one of "superstitious adoration,"[25] Bilbo was a lawyer of prominence in prewar Tennessee. Nashville residents had laughed in the 1850's when he bought up coal lands on the Cumberland Plateau, but he had sold them to Northern capitalists at a good profit. He was also known for his elaborate waistcoats, his long sideburns, and his elegant manners.[26] From his letters, it is apparent that Bilbo enjoyed wide personal acquaintance with Southern leaders and with influential political figures of New York State. He claimed to know every governor of the Confederate states and most members of the

Confederate Congress, and there is more reason to credit than to discount his assertion.[27]

The early years of the Civil War had found Bilbo in Tennessee and northern Alabama, selling supplies of quinine and morphine to the Confederate forces, pasturing Confederate horses, presuming upon his "limited acquaintance" with General A. S. Johnston to recommend a Tennessean for promotion to the rank of Brigadier General, joining with prominent political and business figures of Nashville in a letter to Jefferson Davis urging the appointment of a fellow Nashville citizen to the office of chief collector of the state.[28] In those years he was apparently a loyal Southerner, speaking of his "ardent and unabated solicitude for whatever can promote the success and glory of our arms and the permanent achievement of our independence."[29] He even gave testimony against a suspected Union spy.[30] Yet some time in 1864 he left the South and arrived in New York, "ready to do good service to the National cause."[31] Neither Bilbo's letters, military records, nor State Department archives disclose the occasion for this break with the Confederacy or the nature of Bilbo's early contact with Secretary Seward. There are only obscure references to his "long personal acquaintance" with Seward and the Secretary's "kindness to, and confidence in me upon my return from Richmond in 1864."[32] In a letter to Andrew Johnson, to whom Bilbo wrote as a personal friend, he spoke of having suffered in "Jeff Davis' hellish Confederacy" and of his "intense hatred for Davis and Isham G. Harris," the latter Confederate governor of Tennessee and wartime aide to the Confederate Army of the West.[33]

Bilbo left from New York for Washington in mid-November, 1864, armed with letters of introduction to Lincoln from Simeon Draper, Collector of the Customs, Moses H. Grinnell, prominent New York merchant and public figure, and Bilbo's "old friend,"[34] Horace Greeley, editor of the influential *Tribune*. Each vouched for his loyalty and the importance of his mission.[35] Apparently Bilbo won the desired interview with Lincoln, for he subsequently referred to his introduction to the President by Judge Homer A. Nelson, representative in Congress from New York.[36] Bilbo's services to the Union were quite equal to the honor, for in addition to his intensive activity on behalf of the Thirteenth Amendment, Bilbo aided the cause "by beguiling the so-called Confederate spies and auxiliaries in the City of New York," by furnishing information "of the number, condition, and movement of the Confederate armies," and by "sending to General Sherman then at Savannah a Gentleman whom I brought with me from the South, whom he honored with a position on his staff, to pilot as he did successfully his army from Savannah to Raleigh, N.C."[37] At the war's end, Bilbo continued to give support to the Administration. Before returning to Nashville, he attempted with friends to purchase either the New York *Daily News* or the *World* in order to transform one of these opposition Democratic papers into a Government organ.[38] Back in Tennessee, he labored to win acquiescence in the Executive requirements for reconstruction and to promote appreciation of Johnson and Seward. Apparently honoring a promise to Seward, he also sent long reports on political conditions in Tennessee and other Southern states.[39]

In January, 1865, quite ill but hard at work in New York garnering Democratic support for the Amendment and assisting in the detention of a Confederate messenger, Bilbo was suddenly threatened with arrest as a Confederate spy. He at once wired Secretary Seward:[40]

Some Tennessean has charged me to General Thomas of being a Southern spy and General Thomas has ordered General Dix to arrest me and send me to Nashville at once. Mr. Seward you know this is false. Please see the President and get him to order my release immediately.

General Dix, too, telegraphed the Secretary of State, and Seward promptly wired back assurances of Bilbo's loyalty and added that he was "heartily cooperating with us in promoting the object of all loyal men."[41] The same day an order came by wire from President Lincoln directing General Dix to discharge Bilbo on his parole.[42] Bilbo at once signed an oath of allegiance and continued his labors. With "unfeigned gratitude for my prompt release," he wrote President Lincoln of his successes with Democratic friends and included a self-characterization that is the only personal evaluation of the man that we have found: "I may be justly charged of being impulsive, defiant, and precipitant, but never a hypocrite or spy—*never*, never."[43] Some time later Bilbo described himself as a Southerner who loved "with an almost idolatrous affection the clime that gave me birth," but loved "my country more."[44] Whether his affirmation of loyalty to the Confederacy in 1861 and to the Union in 1865 were equally sincere, can only be left to conjecture. Certainly Bilbo's letters and activities from 1864 to 1866 indicate an ebullient, dedicated man. The only favor he seems to have asked for his services to Seward was a request in 1867 for support of his claim to compensation for the destruction of his property in Nashville by Union forces while he was in the North. In that letter, the last in the Seward correspondence, he referred to himself as in "necessitous circumstances," but he did not elaborate.[45]

In his efforts to influence New York Democrats, Bilbo leaned heavily upon the assistance of one George O. Jones, a man who was as unlikely a midwife to the Thirteenth Amendment as Bilbo himself. Jones was a professional lobbyist, first in Albany and later in Washington, D.C. In Albany, Jones did business for Commodore Vanderbilt of the New York Central Railroad and for "Uncle Daniel" Drew, the notorious speculator, with whom he became a partner in the New York stock market.[46] His professional services at Albany brought him some twenty to thirty thousand dollars annually, but his sense of propriety was outraged by the outright purchase of votes by Vanderbilt and Gould in their struggle for control of the Erie Railroad in 1868. Shortly thereafter he turned his back on the "Vanderbilts, Clarks, Schells, etc." and began to denounce them and railroad corporations generally as the source of corruption among public officials. He called for public regulation of railroads, reduction of their capital stock, limitation on dividends, monthly public statements, and the establishment of rates by a state railroad commission. Called a "striker," a "fool," then a "fanatic," Jones maintained his determination "to start afresh and see if something could not be done to relieve the people from the unjust burdens that have been imposed upon them."[47] He became a devoted stalwart of the Greenback party and ran as their candidate in 1885 for governor of New York, thereby winning 2,130 votes and the affectionate title of "Governor" from his friends. He died in 1895 at the age of seventy, still well known to the New York press and to politicians who spent their evenings at the Fifth Avenue Hotel.[48] Back in the winter of 1864–65, when he aided Bilbo through his intimate acquaintance with New York Democratic politicians, Jones had not yet embarked upon his career as reformer.

In Washington the legislator whom Bilbo found most helpful, though at first he "would not kindly listen to me," was Judge Homer A. Nelson.[49] Nelson was then serving his only term in Congress. A lawyer by training, he had gained his title of "Judge" by eight years of service on the bench in Dutchess County, his home district in New York. He was already well on his way to local distinction as "a prominent member of the bar and a conspicuous and influential member of the Democratic party."[50] Subsequently he served as secretary of state of New York, as a delegate to the state constitutional convention in 1867, as state senator, and as a member of the commission to revise the judiciary article of the state constitution in 1890. Nelson was also a recognized, but unsuccessful, aspirant for the Democratic nomination as governor both in 1872 and in 1882.[51] A loyal Democrat, Nelson's record during the Civil War had not been tainted by suspicion of undue sympathy with the South. He had raised the 159th Regiment of New York Volunteers and then resigned its colonelcy to serve in the Thirty-eighth Congress. There he made "an honorable record as a War Democrat," supporting Administration measures to raise men and money for the conflict.[52] Probably he was a good personal friend of Bilbo, for we know that it was Judge Nelson who introduced the Tennessean to President Lincoln, and that he shared Bilbo's hotel room during the December recess of Congress while the two men were working for the Amendment.

Another helpful New Yorker was Emanuel B. Hart, a former Democratic member of Congress from New York City. Like

Judge Nelson, Hart worked with the lobby both in the metropolis and at the Capitol. His political connections were excellent, for under President Buchanan he had held for four years the strategic post of surveyor of the port of New York.[53] Merchant, lawyer, and philanthropist as well as politician, Hart was remembered by a contemporary as "the leading representative and the best type of the Hebrews of New York, watching the vast charities of his race as their trustee and counselor."[54]

Resembling Hart in that he enjoyed excellent connections with Democrats of the Buchanan administration, but of much less honorable repute, was Robert W. Latham. Latham, also a New Yorker, shared honors with Bilbo as a leader of the Seward lobby. For fifteen years he had been a personal friend of the Secretary's, and one keenly concerned with the advancement of Seward's political fortunes. Annoyed and distressed by his friend's loss of the presidential nomination in 1860, he was in 1864 still hoping and maneuvering for Seward's elevation to the Presidency.[55] He had already performed one semiofficial mission for the Secretary, having helped with the establishment of the West Virginia government and carried back through twenty miles of hostile territory the dispatches that brought news of the Wheeling Convention of May, 1861. For this service, Latham had received a small amount from Seward's son, who acted as his father's personal and official assistant, but made clear his lack of interest in any further favor by way of money or appointments.[56] He had also sent the Secretary political advice for stemming the drift of public opinion away from the Administration in the dark days of August, 1864.[57] Probably Latham's services in connection with the antislavery amendment were requested by the Secretary.

Latham was no novice in lobbying at the Capitol. His past activity had given rise to public accusations of proffered bribery for changed votes. Even more damaging to his reputation had been his close association with John B. Floyd, Buchanan's Secretary of War, whose service ended in scandal and disgrace. As Floyd's business manager, Latham was regarded as the avenue through which confidential information reached New York speculators and army contractors, to their financial profit. He was also suspected of having an interest in other irregularities of Floyd's administration.[58] Called before a House committee investigating the disappearance of bonds held in trust for the nation's Indian wards—an unsavory mystery in which Floyd's name figured—Latham proved a reluctant witness, answering questions cautiously and frequently refusing to answer at all.[59] In 1864 he was an active agent of the Union Pacific Railroad and was associated with its New York contractors, Samuel Hallett and Company.[60]

In his pursuit of votes for the Amendment, Latham enlisted a certain "Colonel Barrett," "Benett," or "Berrett." After a number of false leads and considerable frustration, we have definitely identified the unmilitary colonel as James G. Berret, ex-mayor of Washington, D.C.[61] Berret was the welcoming mayor of the capital when Lincoln took office, but he did not depart that post in the usual course of political events. Rather, he left the mayoralty by what amounted to a forced resignation. His abdication was in fact required and given as a condition for his release from a three-weeks' confinement in Fort Lafayette, where he had been sent upon arrest in Washington, August 24, 1861, on suspicion of disloyalty. Amidst the confusion and near hysteria of the nation's Capital in the early months of the war, Berret's Southern sympathies made him suspect, but it was apparently an inflated sense of the importance and independence of his office that led to his arrest. As the elected mayor of Washington, Berret had refused to take the oath of allegiance required of all Government officials by a recent act of Congress, and asked of him as ex officio member of the local board of commissioners appointed by the President. His arrest was summary, with no charges preferred and no hearing given; within twenty-four hours Berret was delivered to the commanding officer at Fort Hamilton, New York, along with orders from the Secretary of War to keep him in custody until otherwise ordered by the War Department.[62] Some seven months after his release, Lincoln graciously indicated his confidence in the ex-mayor's loyalty by appointing him one of the commissioners under an act of Congress abolishing slavery in the District. Berret declined the appointment but chose to regard it as a vindication of his earlier conduct and an acknowledgment that his imprisonment had been undeserved. These assumptions Lincoln repudiated, holding that the mayor had made a mistake that justified "men having less evidence to the contrary than I had, to suspect your loyalty, and to act accordingly."[63]

Though long in public service in Washington, as clerk in the Treasury office, chief clerk of the Pension Bureau, postmaster, and then mayor, Berret began and ended his political career in his native Maryland, which he served as legislator and as presidential elector.[64] Like most members of the Seward lobby, he was a Democrat. Curiously, Berret was known as a "good and true friend" of Sewards[65] despite the fact that his arrest had been on order of the Secretary of State. Of course, Seward may have had only ex post facto knowledge of the arrest, as was the case with Lincoln. Whoever was responsible for Berret's detention, it was Seward who ordered him released from imprisonment; and the Secretary's action seems to have been at least hastened by the solicitations of a common friend and also by Berret's brother.[66]

There is another matter of interest concerning Berret that may well have affected his role in the lobby. The fact cannot be definitely established, but evidence suggests that Berret made an important connection with the venerable *National Intelligencer* in January, 1865, when the paper passed into new editorial hands.[67] If so, this must have made his cooperation all the more desirable in the eyes of Latham, his sponsor in the lobby. Latham, as we know from his letters, took care to gain the support of Thomas B. Florence, editor of Washington's leading Democratic newspaper.[68] It is evident that Secretary Seward and his friends were keenly aware of the importance of the press. Though we have been unable to establish their identity, at least two members of the lobby were themselves newsmen connected with the New York *Herald*.[69]

Among the lords of finance and power upon whom George O. Jones turned his back when he decided to expiate his past services as lobbyist by future services to the people was one who had been his fellow worker in the Seward lobby. Richard Schell was a Wall Street "insider," a bold and daring speculator. His financial exploits "furnished food for innumerable witticisms and

sarcastic reflections for more than a generation," and for unrestrained invective as well.[70] Eldest son in the large family of a
Dutchess County merchant, Richard Schell had the advantage of
little formal education but of much self-teaching. By temperament
optimistic and a born gambler, one lesson was beyond his ken: he
never learned to husband his winnings, and his career as Wall
Street broker was finally shattered by the panic of 1873. This left
him with liabilities exceeding a million dollars and dubious assets
of a comparatively small amount. Some creditors charged favorit-
ism and duplicity and succeeded in foiling his attempt to go
through bankruptcy.[71] This ungenerosity was said to have had
such a disheartening effect upon him that it hastened his death.

Schell himself was as generous and open-handed as he was
optimistic. He accepted his losses with perfect good humor and
was never known to have uttered an unseemly oath. Genial,
quick-witted, kind-hearted, delighting in good company and
festive occasions, he was welcome everywhere and always the
"life of his circle."[72] These social graces undoubtedly endeared
Schell to the Secretary, and more than a hundred letters in the
Seward Papers at the University of Rochester bear witness to the
intimacy of their friendship.

Although Schell reportedly was not overly scrupulous in turning to personal profit the opportunities afforded by personal
friendships, he had a genuine devotion to the Secretary of State.
His wide circle of friends was ever at Seward's service. They included Northern capitalists, Southern statesmen, national and
local Democratic leaders (Schell was a "Democrat of most inflexible character" and a prominent member of Tammany Hall),[73]
and European figures of political and financial eminence. In the
dreary days of November, 1861, he wrote, "I am a little tinctured
with Sewardism [I] want you to rise and when it costs nothing
[Schell was proposing that the Secretary send a New York
capitalist to visit France] you may as well make a friend that
might be of use to you hereafter, as this Rebellion is not to be the
End of all things. . . . You will all find the Sun and the Moon
will rise again."[74] On close terms with James Gordon Bennett, he
used his good offices with the crotchety editor to promote

Seward's interest.[75] Assuming a role of confidential adviser to the Secretary, he sent financial advice of political import and behind-the-scenes information in respect to Democratic politics and Southern peace maneuvers.[76]

In the last years of his life, Schell became an ardent Green-backer, but this did not convert him into a reformer. His prefer-ence for paper issues as opposed to a hard-money policy was of long standing. He scorned the egocentrism that led others to cry panaceas "from the top of a house," and he considered the outcry against Administrative corruption sheer nonsense. "Read Lecky's History of England in the Eighteenth Century," he advised. "You will find that there was more bribery and corruption in the British Parliament than we ever dreamed of. And it did only good to England in the long run."[77]

Such was the unforgettable cast of forgotten men whom the Secretary of State placed upon the stage of history at a momen-tous hour in the nation's development. The major actors—Bilbo, Latham, and Schell—undertook their roles out of a sense of warm and respectful friendship for the Secretary. Secretary Seward himself was chief director of their performance.

The earliest letter to throw light upon the activities of the lobby was written to Secretary Seward by Bilbo in late Novem-ber, or early December, 1864. He reported calling upon Thurlow Weed "as you directed," but Weed had replied " 'that he was no Abolitionist and that he would not have anything to do with it.' Of course I was much surprised," Bilbo continued, "but not less determined—I promised you the requisite votes, and neither energy time or money shall be wanting upon my part to attain our end—We will accomplish it I believe in spite of my Lord Cardinal."[78] Weed's refusal to help must have been both a blow and a challenge. Whether Seward's chief dispenser of patronage eventually relented and gave assistance cannot be determined with certainty. When the prospect of success darkened during the con-gressional debates, a member of the lobby asked Seward to send for Weed; but we know only that Weed was in Washington soon thereafter[79] and that some two months later the press was com-menting on the "strangest of Mr. Weed's inconsistencies and vagaries," namely, his shift from pre-election denunciations of the abolition policy of the government to recent assertions that the war was continued by and for slavery."[80] It seems unlikely, however, that Weed contributed his formidable influence to the cause. Writing in November, 1865, Bilbo expressed willingness to forgive Weed "for refusing to aid us in the passage of the Constitutional Amendment."[81]

On December 12, again from New York City, Bilbo reported success "in procuring the requisite number of Democratic votes to pass the measure so dear to your heart." He was leaving for Washington the next night with much news for the Secretary about movements hostile to the Administration policy.[82] From Willard's Hotel at the nation's Capital a week later, he sent written word that George O. Jones had returned from New York after seeing Democratic Governor Horatio Seymour and Dean Richmond, the powerful behind-the-scenes leader of the Albany Regency.[83] Richmond and Seymour had committed themselves not to advise Democrats in Congress to vote against the Amendment and had admitted that "no party North can maintain its political status that opposes it." Jones says, concluded Bilbo, "that the New York Democrats will suffice to carry it." Then a postscript: "Jones may tomorrow see you."[84] The same day from the same hotel, Jones sent Seward a note explaining that engagements made by Judge Nelson before Bilbo's return from Seward's home made it necessary that he and Nelson postpone their engagement to see the Secretary until ten o'clock the following morning.[85]

When the Amendment came before the House after the Christmas holidays, R. W. Latham was on hand in Washington. In two separate letters written January 7, he sent Seward an accounting of what must have been a very busy round of persuasive interviews. He had seen Senators S. C. Pomeroy of Kansas and John S. Carlile of Virginia, Representative Samuel S. Cox of Ohio, Colonel Berret, and T. B. Florence, editor of the Democratic *Constitutional Union*. He hoped that day also to go to Baltimore and "enlist some of the Democrats there." Senator Pomeroy had been "much pleased with your views and will do all he can to carry them out." This promise from the Radical Midwestern Republican appears out of place in the pursuit of Democratic votes, but perhaps had reference to some master strategy that Seward had evolved.[86] Senator Carlile had proved to be "not only your friend but an enthusiastic friend." Carlile, a Unionist who acted with the Democrats in the Senate, had absented himself from the voting on the Amendment when it was before the upper house; presumably this Southerner would carry weight with representatives of the border states and the Northern Democracy. Cox was an outstanding figure in the House, witty in debate and influential with his colleagues; he had talked with Lincoln and promised aid in passing the Thirteenth Amendment provided the Administration made an earnest effort to obtain peace with the South.[87] The Democratic leader, Latham reported, would call upon Seward, and so would Berret and Florence if they knew when it would be convenient for the Secretary. Latham was confident "that it can be passed"; he would be in to talk with Seward for a few moments in the morning.[88]

Two days later, taking care to mark his communication "Private," Latham wrote that "our friend Carlile has been completely bluffed off"; he "has not the courage." Editor Florence, however, would "do his best." Latham hoped shortly to have Emanuel B. Hart and Richard Schell in Washington. He still had "no doubt about passing it. Money will certainly do it, if patriotism fails."[89]

The next day, however, came a less encouraging report from Bilbo:[90]

The discussions in Congress, are not aiding us—the most strenuous efforts are made by the Leaders of the Democracy, to unite every member in the House against the Amendment. If your friend [Schell?] has arrived send him to Judge Nelson and let them confer. He will make a speech today if he deem it discreet. [Nelson made no speech.] They beset him on all sides because he is on the Democratic National Committee.[91] I can not do anything with Fernando Wood[92] nor do I much regret it. All our party should work today. We will leave at 12 o'clock for the House. Write if you have any suggestions to submit us.

At this juncture, as Bilbo accurately indicated, matters were not progressing well for friends of the Amendment. The course that discussion had taken in the House, the *Herald* correspondent reported, was "tending to consolidate the opposition."[93] The New York *Times* dispatch from Washington on January 11 told of fears that there was now "no hope" for the Amendment's passage.[94] In this crisis, the lobby was strengthened by the arrival of Hart and Schell and the close cooperation of John W. Forney —Secretary of the Senate, proprietor of the Philadelphia *Press* and the Washington *Chronicle*, and a key figure in Pennsylvania's prewar Democracy whose support of Lincoln had been richly acknowledged by Administration patronage. Forney had the reputation of a "manipulating and trading politician."[95] Called out of town that same day on important newspaper business, Forney telegraphed explanations to Hart and Seward, and on his return immediately sought a conference with the Secretary. Meanwhile Hart and Colonel Berret were "working with all their power."[96]

On January 12, Samuel S. Cox, with whom it is only reasonable to suppose that Latham and Seward had continued their contact, created a sensation in the House by arguing that the Amendment, while inexpedient, was unquestionably constitutional, thus pulling out from under the Democratic opposition its major argument.[97] It was during these critical days when "rumor was rife that three votes were lacking" that Cox made it a point to see party friends in his boardinghouse room in order to persuade them that it was necessary for the "upbuilding of the party . . . to drive this question [slavery] . . . from the political arena."[98] In the biography written jointly by a nephew and a good friend, it is noted with pride that Secretary Seward in a public speech of 1868 praised Cox as the man "to whom personally, more than any other member, is due the passage of the Constitutional Amendment in Congress abolishing African slavery."[99] This tribute was made despite the fact that, in the end, Cox voted against the Amendment.

By January 13, the *Herald*'s correspondent reported that friends of the measure were much encouraged and believed that a sufficient number of Democrats would change their votes to secure the necessary two-thirds. The following day, however, found Bilbo writing his friend Andrew Johnson, then military governor of Tennessee, that the vote had been postponed two weeks because "we need *two* votes more for the Bill, and three absentees." He urged Johnson to have the Tennessee convention at once emancipate the slaves and provide for the election of members to Congress, so that the congressional votes of Tennessee could "come to our assistance."[100] On a scrap of paper of the same date, Bilbo sent word to Seward that he was leaving for New York in the evening and desired to see him before he went.[101] Eleven days later, having meanwhile faced the ordeal of possible arrest and forceful return to Tennessee, Bilbo wrote from New York to thank Seward and the President for his release and to add "one word as to our 'Amendment Bill.' We have been very assiduous in our efforts, and now it is all safe. Governor Seymour said to George O. Jones that now he was perfectly indifferent as to its passage, and that he would not offer any opposition to it."[102]

Schell's activities in the Democratic metropolis centered upon the influential New York *World*. They were meant to be particularly persuasive, as the following frank letter makes abundantly clear:[103]

I have just had an interview with S L M Barlow one of the Proprietors of the New York World—he has promised to have an article written and show it to me in favour of the "Constitutional Amendment"—to be published in said paper which if done will pass the Bill—this is a matter that I cannot say will be untill [*sic*] it is done for here I have to depend on *others*—I have no doubt of his doing so—he has an object of doing me a favour for I have made him ten thousand dollars & paid him over the money today since I rtd from Washington which I think will give me controul [*sic*] over him —but shall know in two days as he told me he would submit to me the article tomorrow—

The reason of my not writing to you before I had a sure thing in the way of money making—and sent for him to come and see me let him and think I have got controul [*sic*] of him—

Richard Schell's "sure thing in the way of money making" was a gold speculation, a record of which is still preserved in the Barlow Papers along with Schell's note enclosing his check. A postscript reads: "Would like to see you a moment."[104]

The editorial position of the *World* was of key importance in the struggle for Democratic votes. In mid-December the paper had apparently absolved individual Democrats from any party obligation by conceding their right to think and act as they pleased on the subject of slavery,[105] but then its policy changed abruptly. In effect, the *World* directed Democratic congressmen to vote, but not to speak, against the Amendment. It defended its opposition on the ground that if Democrats held up the measure the result would be a "manifest advantage" to the South to return speedily to the union "*and defeat the Constitutional Amendment in the next Congress. It is the duty of the Democratic party to keep this door open.*"[106] In the midst of the House debate, the *World* had published the long, incisive editorial noted earlier, arguing that the Amendment was needless, inexpedient, and futile.[107] Even Bilbo's optimism was not proof against this hazard. Three days after writing that all was safe, he sent word that he had just returned from the editorial room of the *World*:[108]

The Editor [Manton Marble] told me that on Friday or Saturday he would write an article declaring it was no test of Democracy to vote "for" or "against" the "Amendment Bill" on Tuesday—rather indicating to its party that they had better vote for it. . . . Had you not better have the article copied in our Government Organ the Chronicle to ease some of the conscientious scruples of some Democrats. If you see Judge Nelson tell him this so that he can use it with Democrats.

Neither Bilbo nor Schell, however, succeeded in getting the *World* to publish the desired editorial. Barlow, on whom Schell had used such tempting "persuasion," was never convinced of the expediency of the Thirteenth Amendment. In a letter to Samuel S. Cox shortly after House approval of the measure, he stated that it had always seemed to him "an utter blocking of the wheels of peace and union" and an intrusion "upon questions which were intended to be left to the control of the States."[109] To August Belmont, the banker, Barlow predicted that the Amendment would not be ratified, and of this he was glad, "as the time may come, when some of the Southern States will see that it is for their true interests to return to the Union and by voting against the Amendment, kill the monstrosity of unconditional, immediate abolition without any provision for the maintenance of the un-happy objects of our misapplied philanthropy."[110]

By the time Secretary Seward received Bilbo's letter, the final vote in the House was fast approaching. The outlook for success had brightened,[111] but prospective victory might still turn to de-feat. The extremely influential New York *Herald,* which flaunted its political independence but was generally to be found in the Democratic camp and was always ready to give the party friendly admonition, ran a long editorial on January 28, urging passage and taking precaution to sweeten its advice by assuring Demo-crats that the Amendment was opposed by the Abolitionist Radi-cals![112] There is no reason to believe that the efforts of the lobby slackened, although there were no more reports to "Headquar-ters," except a postvictory account from Bilbo of his final week's activities. He had not returned to Washington preceding the pas-sage of the Amendment "because while there the Woods, Brooks, Voorhees and some other intense Democrats seemed to suspect my purposes." Instead he had enlisted the assistance of "every Democrat whom I knew or my friends knew who had any influ-ence with the members of Congress."

Bilbo himself had managed a two-hour interview alone with Seymour when the governor providentially arrived for a visit in New York City. Seymour told Bilbo that he had resolved not to write letters to congressmen nor to express any opinion on the Amendment nor to make it a party question, in short "that it was no test of Democratic loyalty to vote for or against the measure." Bilbo immediately communicated this information to Democratic friends in Congress. "It was Governor Seymour," he wrote, "that silenced the 'World' which paper at first tried to make it a party question to defeat it." The Tennessean regretted that the *World* "disappoints us in the Article of last Saturday which it promised me it would write giving the measure an indirect support"; but concluded, "Perhaps its silence achieved as much for its sup-port."[113] Except for a plea for peace on the basis of "leaving slavery *in status quo*" which appeared January 24, the *World* published no last-round editorials that might be considered counsel to vote against the Amendment.[114]

Shortly after noon on Tuesday, January 31, 1865, the House assembled for final debate and vote on the Amendment. James Ashley in charge of the measure, at once yielded to Democrat Archibald McAllister of Pennsylvania, who sent to the Clerk of the House for reading a brief statement explaining why he had decided to change his vote and support the Amendment. This brought applause from the Republican side of the Chamber. Regaining the floor, Ashley again yielded to a Pennsylvania Democrat, Alexander H. Coffroth, for a similar explanation. One more time Ashley yielded to a Democrat, Anson Herrick of New York, who had decided to reverse his action of June and vote for the Amendment. This was too much for the opposition; a most extraordinary proceeding, they objected, this parceling out of time. But Speaker Colfax upheld Ashley. Herrick graciously granted five minutes to an irate Pennsylvania Democrat who lashed out at his renegade colleagues. Then Herrick spoke at some length, arguing that the vote was no longer a party question, that each Democrat was free to act as he thought best for the restoration of the Union, and that unless the question was disposed of the Democrats would lose every election contest in New York State except those in New York City and Brooklyn. If the Amendment were passed, he continued, there was a chance the Southern states, relieved from the humiliation of making terms on slavery, would return and other states be moved to "yet save slavery from the doom which certainly awaits it in any other contingency." Then came the speeches of opposition, Martin Kalbfleisch of New York, the last speaker, was bitter to the end. He hoped that this glorious country would "not be doomed to become the land of a race of hybrids, and thus by degrees be blotted out of existence in accordance with the immutable laws of nature"; he condemned the Amendment as "the consummation of a policy which has led to the bloodiest war in history."

Three o'clock came, the hour set for voting. Ashley allowed the opposition to continue talking; Thaddeus Stevens and other Republicans crowded about him, angrily protesting. At 3:30 every Republican member of the House, without a single exception, was present on the floor; the Democrats were still hoping to stall the voting. Ashley moved on to the preliminary tests, a motion to table, another to order the main question. There was profound silence, the crowded galleries were tense and excited. Senators and members of the Supreme Court were watching from the floor. Both motions passed, but a two-thirds vote was lacking. Now it was time for final decision.

Behind the scenes that afternoon much had been happening. The opposition had received word that Southern commissioners were waiting to talk peace terms, as indeed they were waiting at General Grant's headquarters. These reports were seized upon in a last determined effort to defeat the Amendment; wavering Democrats were pressed not to jeopardize peace and reunion. Arriving at the House at 12:30 prepared to vote for the Amendment, Samuel S. Cox was informed of the news. Cox was doubtful, having received assurances, apparently from Secretary Seward, that the recent mission of Francis P. Blair, Sr., to Richmond had failed, and that no further negotiations were possible. He insisted that Ashley check the truth of the rumors. A reply came from the President's secretary, John Hay, denying knowledge of a waiting peace commission. The reports persisted. Ashley feared the Amendment lost unless Lincoln could authorize him to contradict the rumors. Then a carefully phrased note came from Lincoln himself, denying that peace commissioners were on their way to Washington. Lincoln, of course, was well informed concerning the waiting mission and had issued orders permitting the Southerners to proceed to Fortress Monroe. Indeed, the very day of the vote, January 31, 1865, he wrote an authorization directing Seward to treat with them, and the following day the Secretary left Washington to meet them. Cox read Lincoln's note, made further inquiries, and decided that the President was either "mistaken or ignorant" of what was happening at Army headquarters.

The Clerk was calling the roll. James E. English, Democrat of Connecticut: "Aye." "A burst of applause greets this unexpected result, and the interest becomes thrilling. The speaker's hammer falls heavily, and restores silence. Clerk—'John Ganson' Democrat of New York: 'Aye.' Applause again, repressed by the Speaker. Angry calls among the Democrats and great irritation of feeling."

And on went the roll, with Speaker Colfax calling repeatedly for order. The Speaker added his own "Aye," an almost unprecedented action from the Chair, and Democrats muttered angrily. Then came the announcement of passage and an outburst of enthusiasm. Republican members sprung to their feet, ignoring parliamentary rules by cheering and clapping. Men in the galleries waved their hats and called out; the ladies rose and waved handkerchiefs. All was excitement. Then a motion to adjourn "in honor of this immortal and sublime event," and again the cheering and demonstrations.[115]

When the news reached New York, George O. Jones wired Seward congratulations. "You deserve all credit for the Amendment." Then he added, "Now extend the olive branches to all who ever took pride in calling themselves Americans and if possible give us an ocean-bound republic."[116] Bilbo sent congratulations the same day, and they carried similar admonition and anticipation of a magnanimous policy toward the South. "If Peace Commissioners do visit Washington from the South, *do you be personally kind to them*." He counseled generosity in respect to amnesty and confiscation and even a few millions to the South in compensation for the loss of slave property.[117] It is worthy of note that these messages of Jones and Bilbo implied a verbal commitment from the Secretary of State that passage of the Amendment would be coupled with a policy of peace and reconciliation which Southerners might accept with relief and Northern Democrats with enthusiasm.

The last word from the lobby was yet to come. It arrived in the form of a letter from Richard Schell addressed to Secretary Seward's son and Assistant Secretary. The letter merits quotation in full:[118]

A Gentleman called today to have me give an acct of expenses to Washington.

Which amt to nothing at any time that I can be of any service to the Hon Sec of State or yourself I will do all I can but at my own expence [sic].

One of the members of Congress told me not to come on the floor the day the Vote was taken for I might be attacked—So I went to buying shilling Gold & made five thousand out of my visit besides my Expencess.

We played Poker on the way home and I took the Boys for one hundred fifty besides this is private So you see I had a good time—

The New York speculator had obviously enjoyed his venture in national politics!

The antislavery amendment was through Congress and on its way to the states for ratification. Would it have passed without the efforts of the Seward lobby? No answer to this question can be definitive, but the weight of evidence indicates that the lobby played a critically important role. As the *World* laconically observed the day after passage, "The affirmative vote of a few Democratic members and the absence from their places of others, secured its passage."[119] The measure passed with just two votes to spare; the count stood 119 for, 56 against, and 8 (all Democrats) absent.[120] In fact, the Amendment commanded support from fewer than two-thirds of the entire House membership. While it is true that Lincoln had exerted pressure independently of the lobby, particularly upon border-state members whose support was of great importance, and while other influences were undoubtedly at work to convince wavering Democrats, the number of New York Democrats to vote for the Amendment strongly suggests the influence of the Seward lobby, which centered its attention upon New York congressmen. Of the sixteen affirmative Democratic votes,[121] six came from New York men.[122] Pennsylvania took second honors, with three Democrats voting for the measure and one absenting himself from the roll call.[123]

The importance of the lobby in shaping newspaper comment and the weight of such editorial opinion are impossible to assess, but these factors certainly were not negligible. Although the *World* disappointed Bilbo and Schell, its silence was undoubtedly golden. Moreover, its early editorial seemingly freeing Democrats from any party obligation may well have owed something to Bilbo's early work among New York Democratic leaders. The *Herald* may have arrived at its support of the Amendment quite independently of the lobby, but the fact should not be ignored that at least two members of Bilbo's active staff were attached to that paper. Also, Seward may have set the stage for the *Herald*'s approval. The Seward manuscripts reveal that the Secretary had approached James Gordon Bennett through a trusted intermediary in October, flattering the erratic but susceptible editor by giving him a memorandum on the projected policies of the Administration.[124] The cooperative T. B. Florence edited the leading Democratic paper of the Capital. The *National Intelligencer*, the other Washington paper that might have carried weight with Democratic congressmen,[125] was at least neutral. Having reprinted the *World*'s damning editorial of January 9, it did not otherwise join in the attack upon the Amendment. It is possible, though it can not be definitely established, that Colonel Berret played an important role in obtaining the *Intelligencer*'s silent acquiescence.[126]

After Lincoln's death, in an effort to discredit Seward and Weed and to advance his own claims for political preferment at the hands of the new President, Montgomery Blair wrote Andrew Johnson a letter that indicates Blair had some vague knowledge of the Seward lobby. "I know," he stated, "that Mr. Seward made Lincoln believe that he had carried that amendment by corruption." This, Blair maintained, was false. The Amendment was carried through the influence of Dean Richmond, whose upstate or "County Democracy" he distinguished from the "Demoralized City Democracy" with which Thurlow Weed acted. The writer claimed to have had "some influence in persuading them to go the Amendment which they did exclusively for patriotic & party considerations." Only one man had been influenced by corruption, Anson Herrick, "whose vote was paid for by an appt & was not needed for we had a dozen more votes that were not cast for it but would have been cast if they had been needed."[127] Blair's contention that the Amendment had votes to spare does not square with contemporary accounts. Nor can Montgomery's belittling of Seward's influence carry weight. The Blair hostility to Seward was notorious. Seward and Stanton, Montgomery wrote frankly, "are indeed obnoxious to me & to every one & it will be a relief to me and will be to the country when they are dismissed from public employment."[128] Furthermore, it is clear that Blair had not been privy to the details of Seward's activities, for we know that the Secretary was acting independently of Weed and that Dean Richmond was among those leaders of the New York Democracy with whom the lobby had excellent contact. On the other hand, Blair's statement that Lincoln attributed success to Seward is credible and significant.

The Blair letter raises the question of corruption. There are a number of hints from contemporaries (but for the most part they are only hints) that bribery was used to gain votes. George W. Julian of Indiana, then a member of the House, later wrote obscurely of negotiations "the particulars of which never reached the public."[129] Lincoln's secretary, John Hay, was probably one of the sources for the intimation in the Nicolay and Hay biography of Lincoln that along with public and moral considerations there were "not unlikely influences of a more selfish nature."[130] In the House debate there were allusions to Presidential patronage, to arguments "outside of the legitimate subject-matter which is before us," to *"motives* moving Gentlemen" that were hidden from view, "if not impalpable they are invisible."[131] During the New York campaign the following fall, Senator Wilson of Massachusetts asserted that Democrats voted against the Amendment "unless they had their pay for it," a charge that was interpreted as an accusation against William Radford, representative from Yonkers.[132]

A direct accusation of attempted bribery came a number of years after the event from Samuel S. Cox. He told of a boarding-house incident in which his Radical Republican host, in anger at Cox's vote against the Amendment, had blurted out the information that it had lost him ten thousand dollars promised by "New York parties for influencing the writer's vote favorably to the amendment." Cox continued, "The writer discovered the party who raised the fund which was said to be ready and freely used for corrupting members. Can anything be conceived more monstrous than this attempt to amend the Constitution upon such a humane and glorious theme, by the aid of the lucre of office-holders?" He claimed to have made this charge "after the war in response to Mr. Dawes, and with much detail. It was never challenged. It is true."[133] Unfortunately, Cox's reference to the congressional debate is so vague that we have not been able to find his exchange with Mr. Dawes. Cox's version of the incident, however, although he claimed to have received verification in writing long afterward, is highly improbable. In the light of the reports of the lobby to Seward, it is difficult to believe that they would have been so inept as to have given a Radical Republican the assignment of influencing an outstanding Democratic leader of the House whose cooperation they were enjoying through personal contact.[134] That money and patronage were available to speed passage of the Amendment, however, is not merely credible; it is undoubtedly correct.

In their letters to Secretary Seward, it will be recalled that Bilbo, Latham, and Schell each referred to money—and only Bilbo's statement might with charity be interpreted as an allusion to any other use than bribery. Bilbo, however, in a letter to Andrew Johnson, clearly indicated that some form of bribery was used to persuade Democrats to vote for the Amendment or to absent themselves from the roll call. "As you may well conjecture," he wrote, "we have had to use . . . some 'knockdown' *material* arguments."[135] Future patronage and favors were implied in Bilbo's retrospective letter to Seward. He listed the names of most of the members of the lobby and reminded the Secretary of State that "the President and yourself must not forget" them.[136] The fact that Seward or his son sent a "Gentleman" for an account of Schell's "expenses to Washington" suggests not only that cash expenditures were expected but also that the Secretary's office was prepared to pick up the bill. That no accounting was made does not constitute proof that there were no expenses. On the other hand, it is clear that personal friendships and "patriotism," including all manner of political argument, constituted the lobby's first line of persuasion. In short, money was available for bribery; the records do not establish whether it was used for that purpose.

Information as to payment by patronage is only a little less obscure. Anson Herrick of New York, according to Blair, was paid by an appointment. This reference was undoubtedly to the

promise of an appointment as internal revenue assessor in New
York to Herrick's brother, a promise to which Judge Nelson was
a party.[137] Moses F. Odell, a lame-duck congressman from
Seward's home state—one of the two Democrats to vote for the
Amendment both in June and in January—was later made Navy
Agent in New York. George Yeaman, the Kentucky Democrat
with whom Lincoln's personal influence was decisive, became
Minister to Denmark in 1865. Judge Nelson, whom Bilbo reported "by far the most efficient" of the members of Congress
who had assisted him,[138] was offered, but declined, an appointment to a post abroad at the close of his congressional term in
March, 1865.[139] More than a year later, Nelson sought Seward's
aid in obtaining a Treasury Department office, citing among other
qualifications his vote for the Amendment.[140] Lincoln's tender
to James Gordon Bennett of the prestige post of Minister to
France in February is generally presented as a payment for the
editor's support of Lincoln prior to the November election,[141]
but Bennett's help in persuading Democrats to vote for the
Amendment may well have been the determining factor. Bennett's pre-election support was hardly of a character to justify
grand favors. After heaping reiterated scorn upon both Lincoln
and McClellan as failures and urging the Electoral College to
repudiate both and elect Grant, the *Herald* on November 7 and
8 condescended to admit that, while neither were first-class
candidates, it entertained "no fears of the ruin of this country"
with the defeat of either![142]

In evaluating the evidence of patronage, one should not consider a proffer of office after passage of the Amendment as proof
of bribery. Moreover, the technique of a respectable lobbyist,
such as George O. Jones, implied but did not promise favors to
come. The brazen purchase of votes offended Jones's sensitivities,
or so we are informed by the official stenographer of the New
York legislature. He added, however, that it was only fair to say
that a member who received no direct assurances from a lobbyist "got what he would have received had it been named in the
bond."[143] The motives of public men are seldom simple and
single; we trust that the historian, at least in this instance, may

be excused from a speculative weighing of the relative strength
of the diverse ingredients that motivated the Democratic vote for
the antislavery amendment.

For another query, the historian cannot shun a measure of
responsibility. What did it matter that the Amendment was passed
by the Thirty-eighth Congress instead of awaiting the action of
its favorably disposed successor, the Thirty-ninth? Waiving the
always possible occurrence of the unlikely, the historian can yet
say with assurance that such a postponement would have critically
altered the course of American post-Civil War history. Either
there would have been a special session of Congress on hand at the
time of Lincoln's assassination or shortly thereafter, or no constitutional amendment would have been on its way to the states until
the regular December session, months after Southern surrender.
Either alternative would have changed the course of Presidential
Reconstruction. It is inconceivable that with Congress in session,
President Johnson would have proceeded to set the conditions
for readmission of the Southern states without consultation and
compromise with congressional opinion. Had there been no special session, there would have been no antislavery amendment to
whose ratification the new President could commit the seceded
states as a condition of Executive support for reinstatement.

Furthermore, President Johnson fell heir to the plans for the
future implied in Seward's negotiations with the Democrats—
generous peace terms to the South, a swift and friendly welcome
of the returning states to full reinstatement in the Union, continued cooperation between Conservative Republicans and the
moderate elements of the Democracy. The long-range political
implications of the work of the Seward lobby will be examined
in connection with what we have termed the "Conservative Offensive." They were to prove a not insignificant element in the
confused pattern of national politics under President Johnson, for
they were part of a continuing effort to effect a major party reorganization.

2 THE CONSERVATIVE OFFENSIVE

Entangled in bitter conflict between President and Congress, Reconstruction policy failed "to bind up the nation's wounds." Until very recently, the consensus of modern scholarship has placed primary responsibility for this tragedy upon the shoulders of the Radical Republicans, although some historians, particularly in the early years of the century, attributed the debacle in part to defects of Johnson's personality and leadership.[1] The Radicals have been the subject of much hostile attention; often they have been presented in a role little short of diabolic.[2] In the interest of a more balanced historical appraisal, we wish here to focus attention upon the responsibility of their opponents, the Conservatives.

The Conservatives sought a realignment of political forces that would freeze out the Radicals and leave them politically impotent. Lincoln's policy of "Justice for all" had maintained a workable unity among the diverse elements that went into the making of the Republican party, but it had not lessened internecine warfare. With Lincoln's re-election in 1864, the Conservatives had reason to believe that they were in a position to destroy their party opponents. After his assassination and Andrew

Johnson's advent to the Presidency, success for a time seemed within their grasp; for President Johnson, after an initial flirtation with their opponents, himself assumed leadership of the Conservative movement. In the end, it was Johnson and the Conservatives who were isolated and beaten. Their wounds were not those of innocent bystanders; they had flung down the challenge. And in a stubborn pursuit of total political victory, President Johnson destroyed all possibility of a moderate, constructive reconstruction of the Union.[3]

In order to gain the support of War Democrats for the sustained civil and military effort needed to win the war with the South and in order to attract the votes needed to avoid political defeat by the still powerful and critical Democracy of the North, the Republican party in 1864 had assumed the "Union" label and had chosen Johnson, a life-long Democrat, as its vice-presidential candidate. Secretary of State William H. Seward later spoke of the 1864 victory of Lincoln and Johnson as the choice of the people who "were neither a republican party nor a democratic party, but avowedly and heroically a Union people."[4] Thus, by 1865 a new postwar party structure already had some foundation. Further, the November defeat had shaken the confidence of many who had clung to the Democracy. During the campaign, the Democratic party had been successfully stigmatized as the sympathizer, even the abettor, of treason. Might not the politically ambitious better face down this accusation, and also the party's pre–Civil War record of support for Southern slavery, under a new party label? Republicans looking to the future also faced hazards. Theirs had been a minority sectional party—how could it gain majority support in a reunited nation? The cement of the party had been opposition to slavery; with slavery dead, what would hold the party together? What issues should be substituted?

Plans for a reshaping of parties might have been harmless enough except for two things. Planners among the Conservatives were tempted by a vision of practically unchallenged political control, of a fusion in the name of national unity so embracing that effective opposition would be impossible for a generation or two. And they were determined to isolate the Radical Republicans along with the Copperhead Democrats as if the former had contributed as little as the latter to the national effort to preserve the Union—as if the antiracist convictions of the one were as irrelevant to the postwar nation as the proslavery sympathies of the other.

With the shape of things to come uncertain, party leaders were constrained to speak with circumspection. A reporter could be more bold, particularly when attached to one of the few papers of the day that was not a party organ. The Washington correspondent of the New York *Herald* wrote on February 10, 1865, "There are rumors as numerous as the frogs of Egypt of reorganization of new parties. The drift of events is in that direction." The occasional harangues and innuendo threats against the President by the Radicals, he noted, "have generally arisen from fear that they are soon to be considered outside of the administration party. They have seen the growing confidence of the conservative or moderate men of both parties in the President, with an apparent desire to cut off from them."[5] This statement, showing the Radicals as victims rather than aggressors in the political struggle, is of particular interest and carries a special weight, since the *Herald* was consistently hostile to the Radicals. The tone of the report was not one of sympathy but rather one of gloating at their discomfiture. The correspondent reported the exact nature of the developing realignment as yet uncertain and did not name names, with a few significant exceptions—Thurlow Weed, Secretary Seward, Dean Richmond and the Albany Regency. Clearly, a major impetus for the new political order came from the Conservative leaders of New York.

In New York the split between Radicals and Conservatives was embittered by memories of Horace Greeley's part in frustrating Seward's 1860 bid for the presidential nomination and by Weed's desperate effort to maintain his long dominance of party machinery and patronage, first Whig, then Republican. During the Civil War years, Weed's ascendancy was challenged with some notable successes by the opposing Greeley-Field-Opdyke-Bryant forces.[6] By mid-1862 there were rumors of Weed's maneuvering for cooperation with the Democrats at the expense of the Republican Radicals, and the rumors reappeared in 1863 and 1864.[7]

The harassment and uncertainty which Lincoln faced in the fight for re-election in 1864 afforded the Weed-Seward faction a golden opportunity. Seward supported his Chief with unqualified loyalty; if his own desire for the Presidency lingered, no political move was permitted to give it expression. The Radicals, on the other hand, carried the onus of a series of anti-Lincoln movements: the early Pomeroy Circular attacking Lincoln and promoting Chase, Seward's Radical rival in the Cabinet; Fremont's nomination by the Cleveland convention; the unsuccessful effort to postpone the regular (and Administration-controlled) Republican nominating convention set for Baltimore in June; the forcing of Montgomery Blair from the Cabinet despite Lincoln's personal confidence and wish to retain him; the Wade-Davis Manifesto with its intemperate blast at Lincoln's Reconstruction policies; the postnomination attempts to replace Lincoln with a "stronger" candidate, climaxed by the call for another convention in Cincinnati.[8] Radicals were not the only element in the Republican party to disparage the President and his political strength; not all Radical leaders were equally implicated in the anti-Lincoln moves, and in the end Radicals closed ranks to help carry Lincoln and the party to victory. Weed, however, exploited the situation to the utmost.

In the press, and in private correspondence meant for the President's eye, Weed attacked Chase. He pictured the Treasury under Chase as a malign political influence used to undermine the President, a center of supplies for the Rebels, a nest of fraud and speculation![9]

I care not how much of political neglect and injustice the friends of Mr. *Lincoln* in this state have been or may be subjected to if the welfare and safety of the Government and Union are assured. Individuals and Parties, in this connection, are as nothing. Our Country is the first, last, and only consideration. It is in this aspect of public affairs that I regard Mr. Chase's connection with the Administration as alike disastrous to the President and the Government. . . . He has, and can have, no motives in remaining in the Cabinet of a President of whom he speaks contemptuously, but to prolong a system of official rapacity which will bankrupt the Treasury, disgrace the Administration and destroy the Government. . . . I do not now say or see that Mr. *Lincoln's* reelection is certain under any circumstances but I do see and say that if he goes into the canvass with this millstone tied to him, we will inevitably sink.

A Treasury appointment in New York that aroused Weed's ire was actually the occasion for Secretary Chase's reluctant exit from the Cabinet. Throughout the campaign and beyond, Weed also carried on a private vendetta, in bold public view, with his local political enemies.[10] His accusations of fraud and plunder resulted in a sensational libel suit against him by ex-mayor Opdyke, lawyers' fees of eleven thousand dollars for the defense (paid through subscription by Weed's friends), and a hung jury— generally regarded as a Weed victory. The *Herald's* correspondent, a month later, characterized the suit as "simply part and parcel of the contest that is waging between the factions to secure the control in the new deal of parties."[11]

Meantime the Weed-Seward forces had labored strenuously and effectively for Mr. Lincoln.[12] The Seward Papers bear convincing witness to the Secretary's active concern both with major strategy and with the indispensable minutiae of the election campaign. Henry J. Raymond, who as the new chairman of the National Union Executive Committee held—at least nominally— top party command and responsibility, was a close political ally of Seward and Weed. He sought the Secretary's advice and his intercession at Washington to effect needed "cooperation." In early August, Raymond was appealing to Seward for assistance in getting Government contractors paid more in bonds and less in certificates subject to discount (this would be worth fifty thousand dollars to the campaign fund in New York City alone); in obtaining dismissals and political contributions in the Navy Yard, Customhouse, and Internal Revenue Service; in establishing a more generous allocation of permits to bring cotton from the rebel states.[13] Through his personal friend Richard Schell, the Democratic politico and New York speculator who was to figure

so prominently in the Seward lobby for the Thirteenth Amendment, the Secretary received confidential information on Democratic maneuvers. Weed, too, used his personal friendships with
opposition leaders to keep Seward well posted on political strategy.[14] Other informants wrote Seward, apparently at his invitation, from New York, New Jersey, Pennsylvania, and Ohio. The
Secretary's Auburn address in September, 1864, was itself a
major political contribution, widely hailed and distributed as a
campaign document.[15] Seward also undertook the delicate task of
neutralizing the hostility toward the Administration of the influential editor of the *Herald*, James Gordon Bennett.[16]

These evidences of Seward's hand in practical politics are all
the more notable because it was his practice to leave such matters
to Weed or to his son Frederick. The calculated image of himself
that the Secretary sought to draw for contemporaries and pos-
terity was that of the great statesman, aloof from the details of
political battle. He took care to keep from his correspondence
"matters unsuitable to a public record," such as mention of local
politics and patronage, and directed friends to make inquiries in
regard to such matters "other than by direct correspondence."[17]
"Heads of Administration," he once explained irritably when
under pressure from an importuning friend, "can't write freely
about appointments . . . as corner grocers or stockholders can.
Anything any one wants to know can be learned verbally from
me." He would depart from practice so far as to say that there
was no such vacancy as the one desired. "Show this to Mr. M.
Burn it and tell him that my patience is taxed enough by opponents. It ought to be spared by friends."[18] Seward's concern to
keep from the record his behind-the-scenes role in practical
politics underlines the importance of his activities in 1864 and
1865.

With New York in the uncertain column until the very end
of the 1864 campaign, and with the President eager for a decisive
vote of confidence, the skillful marshaling of support constituted
an important political asset for the Seward-Weed Conservatives.
Before the election, they obtained the most coveted Federal
patronage plums available in New York: the customs collector

of the port, the surveyor of the port, the postmaster of New York City.[19] Incoming letters to the Secretary after election, requesting a variety of Government offices, strongly suggest that Seward enjoyed wide influence in the general distribution of patronage. The Weed-Seward ascendancy was clearly demonstrated in February, when Lincoln sent to the Senate the nomination of Edwin D. Morgan, New York senator, as Secretary of the Treasury. Indeed, on the national level, Seward emerged as the dominant personality in the Cabinet. Blair and Chase were out, and the Secretary of State enjoyed a unique place in the confidence of the President. No wonder that a close friend could write of a pleasant visit with Seward at Washington early in December: "The talk of Sunday night was more like old times than any that has occurred for a long time—it explained many things about which many of your best friends have thought hardly of you during the last 3 or 4 years—I did not realize or appreciate before the difficulties & embarrassment which have encompassed you as well from Mr. Lincoln as from the nefarious crew that surrounded him in the offsett [*sic*] & monopolised his confidence and abused it."[20] The implication is clear; after the election victory, Seward felt that his ascendancy with the President was secure.

The Seward-Weed maneuvering on behalf of the Conservatives at the expense of the Radicals also drew strength from President Lincoln's desire to welcome back the Southern rebels with moderation and generosity. In his September address, Seward in effect spoke for the President when he gave assurances that returning Southerners would be received into the "common ark of our national security and happiness" in a manner that "becomes a great, magnanimous, and humane people to grant to brethren who have come back from their wanderings."[21] Already the Secretary had gone on record as approving a simple plan of reconstruction by which the vacant seats in both Houses of Congress should be declared ready for the return of the representatives of the seceding states.[22] Seward combined loyal support of the President with an effective personal appeal to Northern War Democrats and to Southerners themselves. His September speech, as one correspondent wrote, voiced sentiments that "I as well as many thousands of true Southern Union men will ever hold in grateful remembrance."[23]

In the Cabinet, the Secretary of State held the key role, next to that of the President, in the negotiations for peace;[24] it was Seward to whom Lincoln entrusted a share of responsibility for the promising but abortive conference with Southern leaders held at Hampton Roads, February 3, 1865. It will be recalled that both Bilbo and Jones, Seward's lieutenants in the lobby for the Thirteenth Amendment, expected him to assume leadership in making a generous peace with the South.[25] "Governor," Bilbo had written, "you are regarded by the public outside as the great Pacificator of the Administration. If you can staunch the multitudinous wounds of our afflicted country—if you can bind us once more in an indissoluble fraternity of affection and interest the transitory renown of being President would pale its ineffectual light before an achievement like this. For he who accomplishes this—his name will be ubiquity—his fame eternity."[26] There is reason to believe that the Secretary of State recognized the political advantage to be gained from his close association with the Executive clemency. The *Herald*'s correspondent reported that peace negotiations at Hampton Roads were linked to the movement for party reorganization, "and that Secretary Seward seized upon the movement to secure whatever *éclat* there might be connected with it, in hopes that if peace was the result he would be able to ride upon the wave of joy of a grateful people, and thus become the standard bearer of the great conservative party in 1868."[27]

There is little in Seward's own letters to throw light upon his political thinking. However approachable and informative he may have been in private conversation, the Secretary attempted to keep his letters free of political comment. He believed in discreet silence, not only as to patronage but as to grand strategy as well. The following from Seward's answers to friends make this intent unmistakable: "I cannot discuss in my private correspondence policies which divide the country into parties"; after some vague political comments, "I err in writing at all about them"; the effect upon "party organization" of the abolition of slavery and renewed loyalty in the South was "too low a question for you to consider or even for me to write upon"; "It would be foreign from my habits to discuss legislative questions or even popular ones in private correspondence"; "I abhor confidential or private letters of statesmen upon public questions."[28] And to the latter correspondent he added, "I try to make myself understood therefore always by public debates."

Seward's mastery of vague generalization in public address makes questionable his desire always "to make myself understood." But in view of the elusive character of his public and private pronouncements, Seward's speech of November 11, 1864, in response to a serenade celebrating the Administration victory at the polls is revealing. A careful reading confirms the hints and speculations found in other sources: the Secretary was looking forward to a grand alliance that would dominate the future political scene. All must be friends, he said, both Unionists and the Democrats who have been voting against them. Four years hence, he predicted, "we will be in perfect harmony, not only throughout all the free states, but throughout the whole Union. And I will tell you why I think it will be so." Then he proceeded to recount the disappearance of the Tories after the Revolution, and of the Federalists after the War of 1812, and the coming of an era of good feeling when all the people were Republicans. "It is my judgment that we will all come together again." There would soon be a constitutional amendment abolishing slavery, and with slavery removed, gone would be "the only element of discord among the American people." "I know that it will not be the fault of the administration if we do not have an era of peace and harmony, and go on, resuming our proud career among the nations, and advancing the interests of our country, of freedom, of self-government, and humanity."[29]

The abolition of slavery by constitutional amendment—here was a cause befitting the statesman of the "Higher Law," a course that could only strengthen the Secretary's hold upon Presidential gratitude, a milestone on the road to a new political order. Whatever the balance of motives that gave it birth, Seward's lobby for the Thirteenth Amendment unmistakably gave impetus to a realignment of political forces. W. N. Bilbo, the hard-working Southern member of the lobby, wrote Seward the day after passage of the Amendment: "Governor, you have by this measure allied to you all the conservative Democrats of the Nation. This is true, and the President and yourself can rely upon them in any great Conservative object."[30]

Significantly, the other two leaders of the lobby had earlier anticipated a national political reorganization. In December, 1861, Richard Schell advised Seward's son to "make yourself friends with some of our Party. In the Revolution going on the probability is we shall all be together."[31] The previous February, Latham, as an "old friend, and a faithful friend," had implored Seward "to take the lead in, and be the head of, the great national union party, which is sure to be the great power and ruling influence in this Land, if the Country holds together."[32]

The House debate on the Thirteenth Amendment also bore witness, though cautiously, to the expectation of new political strategy and patterns. When this amendment is an accomplished fact, Yeaman of Kentucky had prophesied, there will be an end to "the other dangerous schemes [i.e., of the Radicals] that are now associated with it in the public mind."[33] "Upon the consummation of this measure," said New York's Democratic Herrick in urging adoption, "a new organization of parties will be inevitable."[34] "We are told," scornfully commented a member of the Democratic opposition, that if we adopt this amendment, "all conservatives can act together against this radical party and defeat the purposes by which they really seek to revolutionize this government."[35] And one of his like-minded colleagues, significantly a Democrat from New York, bitterly repudiated advice to the Democracy "from men who have spent their lives in misrepresenting the Democratic party and in vilifying its leaders. These men have become very suddenly solicitous for the welfare of the Democracy, . . . I am suspicious of this new-born zeal." Too much importance, he warned, had been given to "this new school of Democratic advisers."[36] All signs point to Seward as the current head of "this new school."

Suggestions of impending political realignment linked with passage of the Amendment also appeared in the press. In an editorial written in mid-January, James Gordon Bennett anticipated that before the year's close there would be an end of slavery and "a reconstruction of States and parties upon different principles than those of Northern abolitionists and Southern fire-eaters."[37] When the measure passed the House, Bennett commented, "We can look forward now to a reconstruction of the Union, of our political parties, and of Northern and Southern society upon a harmonious footing."[38] A few days earlier, in words reminiscent of Seward's November address, the *National Intelligencer*[39] characterized the contemporary political scene as "An Era of Good Feeling." It thought the Administration would not be "unmindful of the elements upon which this generous and patriotic support is based," that the President "thinks comparatively little of mere party." Should he "in a party sense" go into retirement, "the machinery which usually appertains to party would be found without much motive power to propel it." *The Intelligencer* stood ready to defend the President from hateful intrigues among those claiming the special title of his political friends.[40]

The February 10 dispatch of the *Herald*'s Washington correspondent made all this explicit in a retrospective report. In evaluating this column, it should be recalled that at least two *Herald* men were active members of the Seward lobby; it is not unlikely that the Washington correspondent was one of them.[41]

Long before the constitutional amendment passed the House there were rumors afloat that the moment that question was disposed of there would be important developments in reference to the formation of a new party, composed of the conservative elements of both of the old parties, leaving the extreme men of each out by themselves to seek an alliance or quarrel, just as they might deem best. . . . This movement, although it was almost exclusively a secret one, had more to do with the passage of the amendment to the constitution than is generally supposed. It was one of the strong powers that secured its passage.

In plain words, Seward in pursuing Democratic votes for the Amendment had let it be understood that there would follow a generous policy of peace and reconstruction, and that there would be a secure political berth for moderate Democrats in a new Conservative coalition.

As soon as the Amendment was passed, the *Herald* correspondent continued, there was pressure upon the President to reorganize the Cabinet so that it would leave out entirely the radical element of the Republican party and secure the support of conservative men of all parties. On several occasions it looked as though the movement would carry everything before it, but "some trivial matter has at each time prevented it, and for the time being, seemed to have defeated the whole thing." The reporter was uncertain what turn the whole question would take. But he held as certain that the President was inclined to a conservative course, that the Democrats were willing to enter a new conservative party if given Administration encouragement, and that whatever the issues and whoever the guiding minds "new party lines will have to be drawn."[42]

Had Lincoln lived through his second term of office, the Radicals might never haved faced the danger of political ostracism. It is true that the Seward-Weed faction during Lincoln's last months in office was enjoying more influence than at any time prior to the November, 1864, elections; it is also true that Lincoln desired to pursue a moderate and magnanimous policy toward the South. But despite these signs of a "conservative" Presidential course, there were others indicating that Lincoln had not abandoned his policy of "Justice for all." If patronage appointments were weighted in favor of the Conservatives, that group did not have the field to itself, especially in respect to positions of major importance.[43] No Presidential decision was more distasteful to the Conservatives than Lincoln's appointment of Samuel P. Chase to the Chief Justiceship on December 6, 1864. Nor did the Conservatives gain control of the Cabinet. Lincoln confirmed the interim appointment of William Dennison, a Radical, as Postmaster General and named James Harlan, also a Radical, Secretary of the Interior. These selections were balanced by that of Hugh McCulloch, a Conservative, to head the Treasury after Senator Morgan had declined the post and that of James Speed, then considered a Conservative, as Attorney General. In fact, both the

Speed and Harlan appointments were more personal than political choices.

While Lincoln's intent to "bind up the nation's wounds" was clear enough, the exact nature of his peacetime Reconstruction plans and strategy was still under consideration and undecided. A fragmentary bit of evidence is suggestive of Lincoln's probable attitude toward a reorganization of parties. Writing to President Johnson in June, 1865, John Hogan, a Democratic representative-elect from Missouri and a personal friend of Lincoln, offered to sustain Johnson under a new party label. He told of a conversation the previous winter with Lincoln in which the President had suggested that Hogan retain his political affiliation "so as if possible to bring the Democratic members into such union with his Conservative friends, as might insure an ample majority of the House to carry out his conciliatory purposes."[44] The distinction between support as a Democrat and support as member of a new party may not have appeared important to Hogan. It suggests, however, that Lincoln while laying a basis for Democratic support of his Reconstruction policy was not contemplating the formation of a new Conservative party. Also relevant to conjectures regarding the course Lincoln might have taken was his loyal support during the 1864 campaign of Radical Republicans seeking renomination and election to Congress. When opposing party factions threatened George W. Julian of Indiana and William D. Kelly of Pennsylvania, both outstanding Radicals in the House, Lincoln intervened on their behalf. He also brought pressure upon Secretary Seward to disavow the opposition of his New York political friends to the nomination and election of Roscoe Conkling, whom Seward's allies were reputed to have defeated for re-election in 1862.[45]

In retrospect, Secretary of the Navy Gideon Welles wrote that Lincoln "continued to be on friendly and intimate terms with certain prominent and leading minds that were for extreme and radical measures, such as Lovejoy and Sumner. . . . He often consulted them on important measures and had at all times their support and confidence."[46] A fact often obscured is that Lincoln's nomination for the Presidency in 1860 was based upon assurances to the extreme antislavery faction that Lincoln possessed—together with his "constitutional conservatism"—"that radicalism which a keen insight into the meaning of the anti-slavery conflict is sure to give."[47] Declared the Chicago *Tribune* editorially, "In all the fundamentals of Republicanism he is radical."[48] Also worthy of note is the private judgment of no less a political sophisticate than the Democratic leader, S. L. M. Barlow. To him Lincoln seemed "insane on the subject of slavery."[49] Barlow believed Lincoln's re-election in 1864 to be an endorsement of every "fallacy & monstrosity, which the folly of fanaticism of the Radicals may invent, including miscegenation, negro equality, territorial organization and subjugation."[50] He later wrote:[51]

No unprejudiced man can deny that every appointment, every letter, every act of Mr. Lincoln for four years, has looked in the direction of slavery and the negro in some form. . . . The wailing of a dozen New England women, "slab-sided, who believe in God" has always been more powerful with him than the united voice of the great democratic party . . . which might at any time in the past, as now, be brought over in solid phalanx to the support of the President if he would "ignore slavery."

The Radicals had been troublesome for Lincoln throughout the war; but he had lived with them, made concessions to them, and, more importantly, understood and valued them. In their antislavery position, the Radicals had been ahead of public sentiment, ahead of Lincoln; but they had helped set the stage within the party and throughout the North for the achievement that, next to preservation of the Union, Lincoln prized most—the death of the institution of human slavery. It is not likely that Lincoln would have willingly scuttled the Radicals; nor is it likely that Lincoln, with his great understanding of men and of issues, would ever have driven them into a position from which there was no exit except by open and unrelenting conflict with the Executive.

This unhappy development—open warfare between Radicals and the Executive—was due primarily to President Johnson, but Seward shared responsibility. Had Seward stood opposed to a realignment of parties and remained loyal to the old Republican amalgam rather than helping to forward the idea of political

reorganization, the whole course of Reconstruction would have
been vastly different from the tragic sequence of events that is
now recorded history.

After Lincoln's assassination and the attempt upon his own life,
Seward emerged with heightened prestige as the nation's foremost
statesman, the spokesman of the martyred President, the man
who could stem the tide of angry vindictiveness toward the South
that surged across the nation.[52] There were rumors of his retirement, but they were forcefully denied on behalf of both the
Secretary and the President. Johnson let it be known that he regarded the preservation of the stricken Secretary's life "as second
to that of no man in the nation," and that he awaited impatiently
the time when he could have "the benefit of Mr. Seward's counsel."[53]

The relationship that developed between the new President and
the Secretary was undoubtedly based upon both political and
personal considerations. Among the latter was the critically important support that had been given Johnson by the Seward-
Weed forces in the contest for the vice-presidential nomination.
Probably even more endearing to the Tennessean was the fact
that Seward and Weed had refrained from joining in the criticism after the humiliating episode of his drunken inaugural address. In fact, the Vice President's critics had also aimed their
barbs against Seward and Weed as the culprit's sponsors. Lewis D.
Campbell, a personal friend and political adviser, could assure the
new President that "Seward had been his devoted friend through
good report and through evil report."[54] Johnson was not a man
to forget such loyalty, particularly when it coincided with political expediency. And to have dumped Seward overboard would
most certainly have been inexpedient. For one thing, it would
have freed Seward and his friends to make an open bid for the
Presidency in 1868. For another, had the President repudiated the
Secretary of State, he would have antagonized the whole Whig
wing of the Republican party and many others beside. Seward
was, and remained, Johnson's most important link with the party
that had elected him; so long as the President had Seward's support he could brush off accusations of "Tylerizing" the party.

Had Seward ever repudiated Johnson, the political consequences would have been momentous.

During the early months of the new Administration, the Secretary was weighted down by his physical injuries, by anxiety for his son's life, and by grief at the loss of his beloved wife; but his influence on affairs of state was not long absent. Less than three weeks after Lincoln's funeral the President and Cabinet met with Seward at his home, and ten days later the Secretary was at his office.[55] Neither did he lose touch with local politics. Thurlow Weed was writing Seward of patronage problems by May 11, and soon thereafter was conferring with his chief in Washington.[56] Although far from being the sole architect of Administration policy, as was sometimes charged, or the unchallenged dispenser of Administration patronage, Seward had undoubted influence with President Johnson throughout his term of office. Gideon Welles, no friend of Seward, bore witness to this by the complaints and criticisms he entrusted to his diary, and by his later references to the close relationship between the President and the Secretary of State.[57]

Despite the Secretary's characteristic silence as to political objectives, there is no reason to doubt that the Seward-Weed forces continued to seek leadership in a broadly based Conservative movement. The new coalition would center about a generous policy toward the South and support for President Johnson. The New York *Times,* their recognized organ (Raymond told Weed to " 'go in and have things as you like' ")[58] left a friendly door open to the Democrats. The Democratic party, it argued gently in May, 1865, could not survive public remembrance of its 1864 platform; it would go the way of the old Federalist party. Individual Democrats should recognize this "and prepare themselves for some other political organization, the better for their own credit and for the good of the country."[59] The paper hailed a giant public meeting for endorsement of the President held at Cooper Institute in June as an indication that public opinion was overriding all divisions of party and "rallies to the support of ANDREW JOHNSON."[60] The resolutions presented and endorsed at the rally included a sharp attack upon the perpetuation of parties, now that the principles and issues that had formerly divided them were "substantially settled and decided." Parties without principles were decried as mere mediums for corruption and intrigue, "wholly pernicious in their influences and effects."[61] Surveying the political scene in May, 1865, the New York *Herald* saw the "New York Seward clique" as systematically at work to obtain the inside track of a new organization of parties.[62] In June it confidently foresaw a union of "the war democracy, the Richmond Regency, the Seward-Weed faction and the independent portion of the free soil democratic element" in a party to support President Johnson's administration, and confidently predicted that the organization would be "irresistible."[63] In July, its Albany correspondent reported that the state Democracy was moving to "back up Seward and Weed with a power that promises impregnable strength to them and permanent ruin to the radical interest." Weed and Seward were maneuvering to "place the abolition radicals in a situation which must result for them in a far more miserable *fiasco* than their Fremont failure in opposition to Lincoln."[64]

Weed and Seward were quietly building wide contacts and friendly support in the South, especially among former Whigs. Indeed, their vision of the new Conservative party may have been very much like the one that Woodward has shown to have guided the conciliators in the compromise of 1877 in bringing together Southern Democrats (mostly former Whigs) and Hayes' Republicans.[65] Southerners wrote to the Secretary of State to give firsthand accounts of political and social conditions, to ask help in untangling personal postwar problems, to seek his influence in gaining office, and to obtain interviews for fellow Southerners. To these overtures Seward replied graciously and helpfully.[66]

Weed was alert to the sensitivities of Southerners. When he read reports of the handcuffing of Jefferson Davis at Fortress Monroe, he dashed off letters to Seward and to Secretary of War Stanton, beseeching the latter to take action. "It is impossible that such a dreadful blunder can have been committed."[67] Seward promptly replied that he had spoken to Stanton.[68] By September, Weed was writing to ask whether Stephens of Georgia could not be pardoned. "Loyal Georgians say that he is disposed and can do good and the public judgment is against his longer imprisonment."[69] He was also raising money for a Virginia newspaper, the Richmond *Republic*.[70] The New York *Times* maintained a friendly and sympathetic attitude toward the South. By June it was counseling patience, pointing out that Southerners had been sincere in their attitudes that led to rebellion and that it would be unwise to break their spirit or crush their self-respect.[71]

The position of influence that Seward and Weed enjoyed, however, was not unchallenged. In their letters one senses a nervous uncertainty lest political opponents gain ascendancy with the President. Writing in August to James W. Webb, an intimate friend and old political associate, who apparently was seeking a change in diplomatic post, Seward explained that his own illness together with that of the President had led to delays and even to lack of communication on such matters. More importantly, he feared that this condition would continue. "There is a preference for new men from new states and political operations which you will be able to imagine although I err in writing at all about them. . . . I have endeavored to abstain from writing anything that would embarrass me if it should become known yet I fear that I have written too much."[72] And some weeks later in an unusual burst of anger precipitated by a letter from Webb that Seward had returned to Webb's son, the Secretary wrote:

If you knew what has occurred here how it has affected the government and how it has affected myself physically mentally morally only half as well as you assume to do you would not think that anyone much less you have a right to reprove or upbraid me.

He added that despite all Webb's unwise effort, he would not be drawn into writing about matters unsuitable to a public record.[73]

About the same time, Seward's New York supporters were worried lest Abram Wakeman, Seward's friend and political ally, be removed as surveyor of the port of New York, the most important patronage post then held by the Seward-Weed forces. Rumors reached the press that Wakeman was soon to be replaced by a War Democrat.[74] Seward forwarded to the President a letter which made clear both Wakeman's loyalty to Johnson and that his removal would inflict a personal wound upon the Secretary.[75] Wakeman remained as surveyor of the port, but Seward's action suggests that his friends' apprehensions were not without cause. Letters from Secretary of Treasury McCulloch confirm the fact that a new appointment to the office was under consideration.[76] Whether or not alarm was justified in respect to Wakeman, there is no question but that political opponents of the Secretary were wooing the President and had his confidence.

3

THE BLAIRS AND THE DEMOCRACY

JOHNSON'S ELEVATION TO THE PRESIDENCY HAD PRECIPITATED A MUCH more dangerous and persistent challenge to Seward's leadership than the often noted but short-lived encouragement it gave to Radical leaders. Loyal Democrats, shocked by the assassination, reacted first from impulse, then with calculation, by a tender of support to his successor. The day after Lincoln's death, S. L. M. Barlow, the *World*'s influential part-owner, was writing in private that "for myself I feel that there can no longer be an opposition to the Government—The very existence of the Country seems to be at stake."[1] Within a week, Barlow was intriguing to obtain a reconstruction of the President's Cabinet that would "secure the united support of the whole democracy North & South." His counsel, meant for the President's eye, was sweetened by the prediction that "with ordinary prudence, Mr. Johnson, if he is ambitious of public ———* may build up a party that will be irresistible in 1868."[2] By June, Barlow was writing in confidence, "We cannot *now* expect an abandonment of the Republican party, its organization or its principal men—all this will follow in

* Illegible word.

good time."[3] Seward and Stanton were the "principal men" marked for "abandonment."

Johnson's succession to the Presidency had fired Democrats with a vision of political rejuvenation and predominance. One of their own, an old Democrat never turned Republican, was now President. He was publicly stating that his future course of action would be determined "by those principles which governed me heretofore"; he was emphasizing the integrity of the states and giving assurance of his opposition to centralization of power.[4] President Johnson's proclamation of amnesty and his order for the re-establishment of state government in North Carolina, both dated May 29, 1865, indicated a conciliatory policy toward the South that Democrats North and South might conscientiously and advantageously support. Some of the Democratic hopefuls were men who formed part of the amalgam that was the Republican party, some were War Democrats who had acted with the Union party in 1864—in both these groups there existed explosive resentment against old-Whig influence; others still carried the party label of the Democracy. These rival claimants for Presidential preference, it should be noted, were overwhelmingly of Conservative rather than Radical bent. The danger was that the anticipated great Conservative party of the future would be a thinly disguised resurrection of the Democracy.

In the first months of his administration, Johnson received a stream of letters from Democrats, showering praise and pledging support. Within a week, a committee of New York War Democrats were writing to ask greater recognition in appointments and party machinery, and to express their confidence that under Johnson's leadership "a regenerated liberty-loving and redeemed Democracy, with you as their chosen chieftain, will control the destinies of the Republic for years to come."[5] A few days later George Bancroft, historian and prominent Democrat, sent word that the new President's speeches were winning friends everywhere—"I hope we may rally to your side the best part of the old democracy."[6] A War Democrat of Philadelphia, writing on behalf of a number of associates, appealed to Johnson for their political protection. They did not want to lose their identity and

be subject to the discipline of the old Whig and Republican leaders, nor did they want to be driven to acting with their old party
that had been "polluted by lawless sympathy with traitors."[7] A
Harrisburg politician, a delegate to the approaching state Democratic convention, wrote of plans to commit the "Great Conservative Democratic party of Pennsylvania" to Johnson's administration.[8] John Hogan, Missouri Democratic member-elect to
Congress, pledged support in the next Congress and reported that
"in all this region the old Democratic masses hope much from
your position, and whether old party names are maintained or not
I think they will rally to your standard."[9] George W. Morgan,
prominent Democratic leader of Ohio, reported that in the next
Congress the President would "find your firmest supporters in
the democratic party, provided your policy of 'restoration' be
continued. A strong conservative element is growing up in the
republican ranks, which must soon place the democracy again
in the ascendant."[10] Republican Senator James Dixon of Connecticut reported that Johnson was receiving warm support
among Democrats, and that an "era of good feeling" seemed at
hand.[11] The old and honored Jacksonian, Duff Green, sent
counsel and a reminder that he was a good friend, ever ready to
serve Johnson.[12]

A number of important New York Democrats visited the new
President or sent friendly letters. Davis S. Seymour, lawyer of
Troy, talked with Johnson in May and then returned home to
work for an endorsement of the President by the Democratic
party at its September state convention.[13] An interview with the
President in July by John Cochrane gave rise to newspaper
speculation that the Democracy was to be brought to support the
Administration through the intercession of leaders of the War
Democrats.[14] Daniel S. Dickinson, prominent War Democrat who
had received appointment as U.S. District Attorney from Lincoln
shortly before his death, wrote at length of New York politics,
the reorganization of parties, and of Johnson's political future.[15]
He sent a letter from the former editor of the Albany *Argus*,
Edwin Croswell;[16] the *Argus* was the leading upstate Democratic
paper. One of the New York Democrats who had voted in the

House for the Thirteenth Amendment, John Steele of Kingston, wrote Johnson on his return from a visit to Washington to thank the President for a reappointment of a local postmaster, made at Steele's request. He pledged his personal support and his influence with leading men of the party. As for the officeholders in his congressional district, presumably Republicans, Steele promised that he would make no effort "to have any one of them removed so long as they discharge the duties of their office faithfully and are true to their President and his administration and Policy."[17]

Steele's letter suggests both the friendliness of Johnson's response to Democratic overtures and his desire not to antagonize Republicans. The new President was in an enviable and unprecedented position of power. From all directions came the expectation of party reorganization, with a powerful new coalition finding its center and leadership in Johnson himself. To be certain, this power position was not consolidated in the summer of 1865; Johnson did not yet have the official party endorsement of the Northern Democracy—for this he would be expected to give hostage for future actions. Moreover, so experienced a political figure as the Tennessean must have realized that party reorganization, even under the most favorable conditions, would be a delicate operation. None the less, with support from both Democratic and Republican politicos, and overwhelming public approval, Johnson seemed the master of his own and the nation's political future. That he would share the power and future destiny more largely with his Democratic supporters than with his Republican adherents was the hope of moderate Democrats, the fear of Republican Conservatives. To use the *Herald's* phrase, there were "so many irons in this fire, that some of them must get spoiled by too much heat."[18]

Of Seward's rivals for Presidential support, the Blairs presented the greatest immediate danger. Prominent in the Democratic wing of the Republican party, the family maintained important contact with the opposition Democracy. Indeed, prior to the election of 1864, Montgomery Blair had attempted, through his friend Barlow, to keep General McClellan out of the political opposition and to obtain the support of regular Democrats for Lincoln as head of a Union party.[19] Like Seward, Blair looked to a reorganization of parties.[20] Also, in striking parallel to Seward's action, he had urged upon his Democratic friends support of the Thirteenth Amendment as a way of putting an end to the slavery controversy and of opening an avenue to a magnanimous settlement with the South. This would, according to Montgomery, "slaughter the malignants of the confiscating disfranchising party," strand "the whole abolition crew," "utterly demolish the indignants [so] that all fears of bad usage will disappear at the South," and together with the "destruction of the radicals" bring a reconstruction of parties.[21] The Blairs were in an even better position than was the Secretary of State to solicit future political support from the South. "No man on earth is more thoroughly a southern man than I am," Montgomery had written, "my kindred all dwell there and they are a most numerous and most clannish family of the South— I am studying their real interests in all I do—I want to save their lives. . . . I want to prevent the confiscation of their vast real property & secure to them that most inestimable right—the right to share in the Govt of this great republic."[22]

After the passage of the Amendment, Montgomery sought to draw a political dividing line between the "ultra-abolitionists," on the one hand, and the South with its Northern friends, on the other. In the latter category, he would include both Lincoln and the Northern Democracy. The issue, as he saw it, was to be "Negro Equality" in Reconstruction.[23] Barlow, to whom Blair had appealed for support, was still unreconciled to abolition by Federal action. He wrote Montgomery that a union of the "Conservative elements of both parties" could be had only if President Lincoln would ignore slavery and be prepared to restore the Union without its destruction.[24] In that event, it would be possible to build up a great national party in opposition to the Radicals that would draw "many adherents in the present Republican party" and "control the entire South, so far as it is ever brought back to us."[25] Neither Lincoln nor Blair, however, was prepared to compromise on the extinction of slavery by constitutional amendment.

With Lincoln's death, the Blairs quickly embraced the concept of a Johnson party—one that would accept the new President as its head but be under the firm control of former and present Democrats. The family had won a place of personal esteem and influence with Johnson after his unhappy inaugural as Vice President. Together with his, and their, good friend Preston King, former senator from New York, the Vice President had been whisked off to the Blairs's home at Silver Spring for refuge and recovery. Soon after Johnson's succession to the Presidency, the press and contemporary politicos were agreed in recognizing the influence with the new President of this powerful, ambitious, and arrogant family. Early in May, the *Herald* commented that "the Blair family are looking up again in the world; that they have 'great expectations'—Old Blair and all the Blairs—of 'Andy Johnson.' "[26] Leaders of the Northern Democracy looked to the Blairs to restrain Johnson's "ultra proclivities" toward severity against Southerners and the South.[27] These public and private expectations had solid foundation; the Johnson Papers bear unmistakable testimony to the privileged position of the Blair family with the new President.

Before Lincoln's remains were laid to rest, the Blairs were sending on to Johnson a pledge of support from the independent Philadelphia *Public Ledger* provided that Johnson would carry out the conciliatory policy of Mr. Lincoln. The *Ledger*'s editor expressed the hope that the Blairs would keep the President "out of the hands of the radicals for if they should control him there will be trouble ahead."[28] His assumption that the Blairs would oppose the Radicals had firm foundation; the Radicals had forced Montgomery Blair from Lincoln's Cabinet—to them, he was the leading Republican exponent of an intolerable attitude: namely, that "This is a white man's country." The antagonism was reciprocated in full measure. The Blairs wished to "smother the Radicals," and they stoutly maintained that the Negro could never be the equal of the white man socially or politically. Negroes were, and must remain, a caste apart; the only possibility of full citizenship and equality for the Negro, according to the Blairs, lay in his removal to some territory set apart for his exclusive use.[29] According to Montgomery, a war with Maximilian's Mexico, should it come, would carry the advantage of obtaining "a home for our negroes . . . where we can send some 100,000 black soldiers to take possession permanently & send their families to join them thus opening the way to the separation of the races & disposing them on the soils adapted to their special natures."[30] His father, of like mind, viewed "colonization & segregation as the means of saving the colored race."[31]

Montgomery was soon forewarding warnings to the new President that Supreme Court Justice Chase, formerly the outstanding Radical in Lincoln's official family, was making political hay in Florida and that Johnson should take steps to counter his influence.[32] He also relayed political reports and advice from Kentucky, telling of opposition to the surrender of any state regulatory power over the emancipated Negro and counseling the removal of martial law.[33] Old Frank Blair, through his son, cautioned the President in respect to Stanton's attitude toward General Sherman. The reference was to the Secretary of War's open opposition to the political commitments Sherman had made in accepting General Johnston's capitulation. This, according to Blair, was creating a "bar" to the Democracy's inclination to join the Administration, a "stumbling block" to Johnson. The remedy suggested was the appointment of Frank Blair, Jr., as Secretary of War.[34] In August the patriarch sent Johnson a twenty-page letter of observations and advice ranging from race relations to the formation of a new Cabinet. He saw a new combination of parties in process and assured Johnson that the Democrats would support him.[35]

Of major political importance was Montgomery's role in interceding for the President with Northern Democratic leaders, particularly those of New York State. He forwarded to Johnson what amounted to the terms upon which they would support the President and at the same time urged the Northern Democracy to give Johnson their unqualified and immediate support. To use his own expression, Montgomery attempted "to bring about an *entente cordiale* between him [Johnson] and his natural supporters."[36] In this effort, S. L. M. Barlow was Blair's chief contact with New York's Democratic leaders. He also sought to influence

Dean Richmond, the Albany boss of the party, more directly through Representative Samuel S. Cox, key Democrat in Congress.[37]

In his shocked reaction to the news of the assassination, Barlow had at once written to Montgomery Blair offering to be of service to Johnson through the New York press.[38] Montgomery promptly replied that he would "make known to the new President your sentiments," adding that "the Democracy if they are true to their own principles must sustain Andrew Johnson."[39] There followed during the spring and summer a steady correspondence between the two men, supplemented by at least two visits from Montgomery, one in early May and the other in early June.[40] Barlow conferred with Democratic leaders and participated in conferences held to determine policy in respect to the Administration. These he reported in his letters to Montgomery. Until late July, the regular Democrats, though interested, drew back before any action that might be considered a definite commitment.

The major issue of principle that made them hesitate was the Administration's continued use of arbitrary arrests, military courts, and the suspension of *habeas corpus*. They insisted upon "a return to laws and constitutions" and an end to "the meddling impertinence of Provost Marshals."[41] The military trial, conviction, and hanging of Booth's associates in June and early July deeply troubled Barlow and his friends. They made no case for those convicted, but believed the method used unconstitutional and the precedent set a dangerous one. The most consistently principled opposition of which we have evidence in the Barlow correspondence came from his intimate friend Judge William D. Shipman of Connecticut. Shipman's criticism of military courts was scathing. Unlike more charitable or more politic Democrats, he was unwilling to absolve the President from major responsibility and to strike only at Stanton and Holt. "I am afraid that J. *loves* to play the tyrant. If this is his game, I prefer a radical in his place, provided only the radical is sound on personal liberty."[42] As late as mid-August, Judge Shipman believed that Johnson was "either destitute of principle or he is a weak instrument wielded by unscrupulous hands." If the Radicals would publicly avow support for personal liberty and the supremacy of civil over military power, he was ready to work with them, "even to the support of their negro suffrage scheme." He saw Johnson as building political power "to secure a second lease of office" by courting Southern support in opposing Negro suffrage and Northern Republican approbation by using military courts and military commanders in the South.[43]

Montgomery sent vague reassurances: Johnson was being "stiff on the punishment of traitors" only *for the present*," as a preliminary to a break with the Radicals; after a conference with the President, he wrote that there was "a growing feeling against Military Tribunals." He emphasized those aspects of Administration policy pleasing to Democratic ears. In private conversation Johnson had committed himself against interference with suffrage in the South, "further than to exclude traitors from voting"; he had accepted "the Democratic principle in the fundamental question of Reconstruction."[44] This meant the restoration of the Southern states to their old places in Congress and constituted "the transcendant interest of the Democratic party . . . without that Representation we shall not have a responsible Executive Govt—With it we shall have a faithful Execution of the law & the constitution."[45]

Gradually Barlow's doubts and indignation over the Administration's use of military power subsided; these activities became mere "pricks," against which it was "useless to kick . . . no matter how much we may dislike the action of the Pres't or of Holt & Stanton."[46] Judge Shipman clung to his apprehensions somewhat longer. The President's words might be satisfactory but "words amount to nothing unless verified by deeds," and Johnson's "official acts are purely revolutionary."[47] Even in early September, Shipman remained skeptical. To him the political situation looked dubious, and only one thing seemed certain, "and that is, *somebody* is to be sold—Who, & at what price I am not able to guess."[48] Even the good Judge, however, shortly weakened in his opposition and succumbed to the assurances of words. He was encouraged by Johnson's friendly response to a delegation of Southerners on September 11. The President had assured them that he was "of the Southern people, and I love them and will do all in my power to restore them."[49] Meantime, Shipman had digested a long incisive letter from Barlow arguing for the strategy of Democratic support of the President and affirming his personal belief in Johnson's promises. The Judge had also heard the news that the New York Democracy, in convention assembled, had strongly endorsed the President.

In their negotiations with Johnson prior to endorsement, Democratic leaders had not been concerned with principle alone. From the beginning they were insistent that Seward and Stanton compromised the President in the eyes of the party and that both should be eliminated from the Cabinet. Their presence in the Administration was interpreted as support for a policy based upon military authority, but national policy was not the only issue. The Democracy were prepared to support a political reorganization that would "bring them a large portion of the moderate men" from the Union-Republican camp, but only if they could "be entirely freed from the worst part of the Republican party, viz: their leaders here." To negotiation and argument they added a not too subtle threat. If Johnson sought such allies as Seward, Weed, and Raymond, he would be "overwhelmed."[50] In a letter that the Blairs laid before the President, Barlow warned: "If the democratic party, which combined with that of the South will be overwhelming, in its strength, ceases to be an administration party, the President alone will be the cause."[51]

With a sharp eye for the fulcrum of political power, Boss Richmond refused to make any commitment to the Administration so long as Johnson was uncommitted on "the main question of the Seward control." In his view the Democracy held the ace card: Johnson could not hope "to retain the support of the late Republican party, as a unit"; he would "be forced to ask the aid of the Democracy."[52] Richmond and a number of his political associates intended to give that aid upon their own terms. Apparently they would consider abandoning the old Democratic party and supporting Johnson as presidential candidate in 1868, but only if these maneuvers were guaranteed to bring them the substance of political power.

Montgomery Blair's reassurances were not limited to matters of principle but included as well the hard realities of political power and patronage. If the Democratic leaders would support the President, they "should soon have not only a Democratic policy but democratic politicians to execute it."[53] In a subsequent letter he stated categorically, "I know that Johnson will give them [the progressive territorial Democracy] the Govt if they will take it."[54] Montgomery made use of the gentle threat. Dean Richmond was merely playing into Weed's hand. It was unwise for Democrats to postpone support of Johnson simply because "for the time the President deems it expedient to keep them about him." Only as "the Democratic party rallies to Johnson & he can dispense with the support of the Radicals just in that degree he will dispense with them in office." The President could not be driven; he would take his own course and come out right in the end. Johnson was certain to carry with him a large part of the Democratic party; and if their leaders hesitated now and waited until he had turned out his Cabinet, "there may be mischief done."[55] New York's Democratic leaders, however, could not be convinced by assurances and arguments from the Blairs alone. As secessionists from the old Democracy, and a family strong in its own ambitions, the Blairs were undoubtedly viewed with some misgivings.

Suddenly, on July 24, Barlow capitulated. He sent word to Montgomery "that the whole party is today a Johnson party: that the South just as rapidly as his reconstruction plans are carried out, will be a Johnson party." His Democratic friends were even willing to put up with the present Cabinet so long as Mr. Johnson's general Reconstruction policy remained sound. The *World*'s owner anticipated surprise "at so great a change in my views." He attributed his conversion to "Dick" Taylor, Major General in the Confederate army, son of Zachary Taylor and brother-in-law of Jefferson Davis. Taylor had been in New York and was on his way to Washington to see the President. Barlow described him as a statesman—farseeing, able, a Union man, "and more than all . . . a Johnson man. He says the Southern people are universally pleased with the Johnson course. . . . He says Mr.

Johnson must be supported, at the North, no matter what he may
do, that we think wrong, or injudicious; as otherwise he will
never get right, and . . . that it must be earnest and active and
unqualified [support] from the outset." Barlow ended his letter
with the hopeful prediction that the Seward-Weed forces would
be well whipped in the coming Republican state convention. He
added plaintively that this could not be certain "so long as Weed
claims, with seeming truth, to be the immediate representative of
the controlling power in the cabinet."⁵⁶ Barlow's hostility to
Weed was still bitter and uncompromising. He confided to Montgomery, who thought the confidence intended for the President,
that Weed had been willing to trade with the Democracy for a
month after Lincoln and Johnson's nomination, then backed down
after the adoption of the Chicago peace platform. "Then, we lost
him and shall never find him again, with our consent."⁵⁷

The capitulation of the New York Democracy was neither so
abrupt nor so unconditional as Barlow's letter seemed to attest.
News reports of mid-July indicated that leaders of the party
were hesitant to act and wished reassurances.⁵⁸ Barlow's paper,
the *World*, continued to qualify its confidence in the President.
In late July it asserted that Democratic principles under the
Democracy's banner would triumph "either with him [Johnson]
or over him."⁵⁹ A few days later an editorial sharply criticized
the Administration for nullifying the results of the city elections
in Richmond, Virginia, and for continuing "this wretched business of administering local affairs of the South by the federal
government."⁶⁰ A week later the *World* predicted that the state
Democracy in its coming convention would endorse the President, but "no farther than he agrees with them"; whether they
would continue to support him after the restoration of the
Southern states was left to the future.⁶¹

In this politically uncertain atmosphere, Thomas G. Pratt,
former Democratic governor of Maryland and wartime supporter
of the Confederacy, supplemented the efforts of Montgomery
Blair and General Taylor as intermediary. In mid-August, Pratt
had "a very satisfactory talk" with the President and sent a full
report to Barlow, a fact of which he duly informed the President.

The interview as reported by Pratt was most certainly "satisfactory"; indeed, it was quite extraordinary. The President had declared that he would "go for the admission of the Southern States, they to decide for themselves in regard to negroe [sic] suffrage—He will restore the Habeas Corpus to ea state having an organized Govt & consequently abolish the military trials & arrests." When Pratt pressed for the removal of Seward and Stanton, Johnson "said that *this shld* be done." In answer to Pratt's complaint that "Thousands of persons had taken the oath of allegiance under his proclamation who were still treated as Rebels & that this tended to keep up excitement," the President "said that all persons who had taken this oath, shld. be considered loyal unless by subsequent conduct their disloyalty was evinced." Pratt "told him that however far he might go with the Radicals, that there was no chance of his getting their support. He [Johnson] said he was fully aware of it, & that he would get rid of them as fast as he could." In addition to all this, the President indicated that a public and official announcement of principles would be shortly forthcoming.[62]

Barlow was delighted with Governor Pratt's report. If the President "adopts the course proposed he can without difficulty secure the constant, earnest and effective support of the Democratic party, North and South." Still, he hedged, "By any other policy he will find himself without a party, in three months." The New York state Democratic convention was fast approaching, and Barlow thought it imperative to "make our people believe what you believe"; in that case, "there would be no trouble in securing an endorsement of the President." He had urged Richmond to see the President for confirmation, but the Albany boss had insisted that Barlow and Tilden make the visit and report to him. "If the Prest will remodel his cabinet, conform generally to our ideas of policy and they are his, as well as ours, I will do all in my power to support him as I know the whole party will."[63]

Pratt asked permission to place Barlow's letter before the President, a request to which Barlow consented in a letter meant for the President's eye. "So far as I am concerned," he wrote, "and I have no doubt with Richmond also, your statement of the position of matters, which you ascertain directly from the President, in person, will be entirely satisfactory and conclusive." He continued, "So far as I know, and I do not speak without reasonable knowledge, the United Northern Democracy will cheerfully support Mr. Johnson, and this too, without attempting to control him, even by a suggestion, as to offices, in his cabinet or elsewhere. . . . The most that anyone would think of doing would be to suggest those who *should not* be appointed." Barlow warned Pratt to use the utmost discretion: "you will understand that the fact that there has been any correspondence on this subject, in which Mr. Richmond's name is mentioned, should not be made known to anyone but the Pres't—or some other equally discreet person."[64] Governor Pratt sent both of Barlow's letters on to the President. "I believe they will do good," he wrote, "but I still hope you will see him, & get from him the reiteration of the views he expressed to me."[65]

What the Northern Democracy desired of the President in return for its official endorsement had been spelled out at great length by Jeremiah Black, prominent Pennsylvanian who had served in Buchanan's Cabinet as Attorney General and Secretary of State. Black had been informed by the former chairman of the National Central Committee of the Democratic party, after a "long and satisfactory interview," that the President was outspoken on the subject of states' rights and "old fashioned democracy." The Democratic politico had hopes of Johnson's return to "the true fold" and had urged Black to visit or at least write the President.[66] In a July letter to Montgomery Blair, which his father took to the White House, Black bluntly stated that the Democracy of Pennsylvania wanted to make up "a perfect reconciliation" with President Johnson, provided he would adopt measures they could "conscientiously" approve. In that case they would sustain him against the opposition he would provoke among "the Abolitionists."

The desired assurances were explicitly stated and numbered as seven "fundamental points of our faith." The President should hold to the following positions: that the states had not gone, and could not go, out of the Union; that the states stood where they had stood before their individual members engaged in rebellion; that the South must be governed by the Constitution and laws, not military force; that there must be trial by jury, *habeas corpus*, free press, and free speech; that no act of Congress or the Executive could determine suffrage within a state; that the army be reduced to protect the country from insolvency and the South from Negro domination; and finally, the recognition that "this is a government framed by the white race for themselves . . . and we will not agree to hand it over to the negroes." Black added that he did not believe the President could be "bullied by the Abolitionists into measures opposite to those which his past records show him to be sincerely attached to . . . but it becomes more and more important everyday that we should know it." The Democratic state convention was fast approaching, and Johnson was "more interested than we are. He can not be indifferent to the opinion of such a state as this—We are I firmly believe in a clear majority."[67] Johnson's response is not known; there is evidence, however, that Black saw the President in the company of Montgomery Blair and that Johnson assured them that he would not abandon the Reconstruction policy he had initiated.[68] The Pennsylvania Democratic state convention in August did give the President approval and support, but qualified their endorsement. It was conditioned upon "the belief that he will execute the law . . . in all parts of the country . . . not allow the military to interfere in state elections . . . suffer no person to be murdered by military commission." Montgomery Blair complained to Black that "too many qualifications" were made.[69]

The leaders of the New York Democracy were more tactful, and their terms were less exacting and explicit. Johnson gave them assurances, though the records do not indicate the extent of his commitment. The understanding between the President and state leaders initiated by Blair, Taylor, and Pratt, and promoted by Barlow's and Johnson's friend Russell Houston of Kentucky, was confirmed personally by Samuel J. Tilden. A few days before the Democratic state convention, at Barlow's request and as the representative of the New York Democracy, Tilden went to Washington to see the President. Richmond and Barlow did not accompany him because they felt that their visit would be widely commented upon and might embarrass the President.[70] These astute politicians recognized that the Union-Republican President would hazard his prestige and influence among Republican voters if he openly negotiated with the opposition. However, Barlow assured Tilden that the President "expects to see you," made arrangements to insure Tilden an early reception, and furnished him with a letter to be read to the President. On one subject only, Barlow indicated, was it necessary "to be entirely free from ambiguity," namely, "freedom from military power," North and South.[71] There is no record of the Tilden interview, but we know from Barlow's references to it in his personal letters that the meeting lasted for two hours and that the "Prest promises all that we could ask," especially on the subject of military power.[72] Tilden "returned satisfied," and the result of his report was the formulation of resolutions, duly passed by the convention, strongly supporting the President. The substance of the resolutions as they were finally passed was drawn in the *World* office, a fact Barlow took care to make known to the President and his intimates. They were then put into final shape in Albany by Manton Marble, the *World*'s editor, Tilden, and Cassidy of the *Argus*.[73]

Though negotiations were kept secret, rumors reached the press. Shortly before the opening of the state convention, but prior to Tilden's trip to Washington, the Albany correspondent of the Democratic *Sunday Mercury* sent word of a report circulating among politicians that the President had given assurances to several very prominent Democrats that he would, as soon as possible, restore to the Southern states their constitutional rights, remove the Federal troops, and rid his Cabinet of Seward and Stanton. "If half of what we hear is true," the reporter commented, "certain Democratic leaders occupy relations with the President entirely too intimate to suit the party that elected him." He looked for a hearty endorsement of the President despite the hostility of ex-governor Horatio Seymour and his friends, for Dean Richmond was firmly in control of the party machinery.[74] The New York Democratic convention did, indeed, give the

President "a hearty endorsement," unblemished by any of the qualifications embodied in the Pennsylvania party platform.

This development, added to the evidence in the private papers of Johnson, Tilden, and Barlow, leaves no doubt that the President was actively and deliberately negotiating with the Northern Democracy. His commitments to them, his interest in their support, and their pressure to realize the principles that were "his, as well as ours" would affect the President's policy toward the South. They would also influence his attitude toward the Radicals: from a party that had reluctantly accepted the Thirteenth Amendment came no counsels of forbearance or concession toward those who had championed emancipation and were vitally concerned with the freedman's future status as a free man. Quite the contrary. Barlow had explained to the doubting Judge Shipman that opposition to Johnson on the part of the Democratic organization would only "compel him so to change his present plans as to secure unanimity on the part of the Radicals."[75]

In backing Johnson, the New York Democratic leaders believed that they had much to gain and nothing to lose. They were in no degree overlooking the "absolute necessity of taking good care of our own rights." This could best be done by getting the Southern representatives back in Congress, then "we not the Pres't., will . . . have an absolute majority in both branches of Congress, and he will then be under the control of our organization, or powerless outside of it." If the President did not keep his promises, "in six months we shall have the whip hand."[76]

The anti-Seward animus of the Blairs and their New York Democratic friends tremendously complicated the political scene. They were determined to destroy Seward's influence and sooner or later force him from the Cabinet. Montgomery used every conceivable means of undermining the Secretary, overlooking no opportunity to set the President against him. For example, in transmitting one of Barlow's letters, he had commented invidiously, "I have no apprehensions that either Seward or Stanton or anybody else would rule you, and in time I am sure others will see it as I do."[77]

When private persuasion failed, Montgomery made public

attacks upon the Secretary of State hoping to arouse enough public pressure to force him out of office. Montgomery openly accused Seward of responsibility for the Civil War by paralyzing action and deceiving the President in pre-Sumter days. In his handling of the Mexican situation, the Secretary of State was denounced as subordinating American interests to Napoleon's policy, of "treachery to the Monroe Doctrine." Blair insinuated that Seward's motive was an unprincipled desire to foster personal political fortunes by posing as the champion of peace and thereby gain the support of bondholders, who "prefer to run up their stock by submission to France rather than . . . preserve the free institutions of their country . . . by patriotic sacrifices."[78] He asked Barlow to get his diatribe published in the *Herald* and in the *Tribune* and to enlist the support of the New York Democracy in making an issue of the Monroe Doctrine. In doing all this, Montgomery assured Barlow, he knew that he was not hurting Johnson's feelings.[79] Although arguing that a bold policy would prevent bloodshed, he was quite ready to hazard outright war over Mexico. Montgomery's stand was in keeping with his father's attempt the previous January to bring peace between North and South by proposing to Jefferson Davis a united offensive against the French in Mexico.

Montgomery's performance was both a bid for support of the Blair family as champions of the Monroe Doctrine and a vicious, demagogic attack upon the Secretary of State. Seward's friends were outraged.[80] The Secretary himself took the view that "the Blair thing" was not worth an official or authorized answer.[81] However, even before Montgomery's public blast, Seward was well aware that the Blairs were trying to make a political platform of "decided and minatory action toward France."[82] It is more reasonable to interpret Seward's official silence as political strategy rather than as complacent security; the Blairs were dangerous enemies. And just ahead loomed a major test of strength, the New York state election of 1865.

4 THE NEW YORK BATTLE

In New York's apparently insignificant off-year election for lesser state offices, much was at stake. Seward and Weed faced bitter battle with the Blair-Democratic alliance, one in which defeat would jeopardize Seward's influence not only in the state but in the nation's counsels as well. Even more momentous consequences rested upon the outcome, perhaps the very course of national action in respect to the South. "Everything depends on yr vote this fall," wrote Montgomery Blair to Barlow. "If it is carried by the Democrats I think there will be no contest about the admission of the South to seats in the Houses of Congress. If not we may have a most serious struggle between the Executive & Congress."[1] Barlow himself predicted that "upon our success here, the success of the Prest. policy will in great degree turn."[2]

The fall campaign was preceded by startling developments on the New York patronage front. In mid-August Simeon Draper, the collector of the customs, was replaced by Preston King, Johnson's personal friend and confidant, a Republican of Democratic antecedents and a man possessed of an unusual faculty "for concentrating, combining and organizing men in party measures and action."[3] There was a long-standing friendship between King and the Blairs; Weed, on the other hand, had deserted him in 1863, when, with Greeley's support, King had sought renomination as senator. The *World* saw King's appointment as an attempt to harmonize Republican factions and conciliate the Democrats. This was all very well as a temporary arrangement, but the *World* warned the President that "any such no-party namby-pambyism" would not do as a permanent policy, that the hostile elements were irreconcilable.[4]

A few days later the Democrat Moses F. Odell, one of the New Yorkers who had voted for the Thirteenth Amendment, was appointed naval officer.[5] Politicians considered Odell "a strong democratic politician," who would "make his appointments from that side."[6] The *Herald* hailed these changes as an indication of the President's determination to make a clean sweep of "Chase, Jacobin and disunion radical agitators," and the news columns of the *World* agreed that the Radicals were to be "decapitated."[7] At first, the *Herald* interpreted the moves as making possible a revival of the Democracy "which will control its [New York's] action for half a century."[8] Soon, however, it recognized that there was no certainty as to which political faction would benefit from the patronage changes, that the President's intent was to build a new "Andy Johnson Party," and that in feeding this new amalgam by "serving out the Custom House soup" Thurlow Weed stood at Preston King's elbow.[9]

Though Simeon Draper had been a close associate of Weed and Seward, his removal from the all-important collector's post was not unwelcome to them; indeed, it may have been engineered by Weed. Draper had maintained good relations with the opposition Radical faction of the Republicans, and seems to have sided with Governor Fenton when he turned upon the Weed-Seward interests early in 1865.[10] Weed was shrewd enough to recognize that in building for the inclusive party of the future, a cooperative former Democrat in the state's key patronage post could be of immense service. A postelection letter from Weed stated that King's appointment "accomplished all I promised. Without it this state would have been demoralised and lost. Now it is fixed with the President and for his Policy."[11] Despite the implication in this letter, it is unlikely that Weed had suggested King's appointment, though it is true that he had earlier established a good political relationship with King.[12] There is no doubt, however, that Weed was intimate with the new collector and helped guide him in an effort to build a broad pro-Johnson Union political machine.

Some limitations upon King's exercise of the patronage power may have been directed by the President. In the ensuing campaign the Democrats, though angered by King's close bonds with Weed and the Republicans, publicly maintained that Johnson had given instructions that the Federal patronage should not be used to defeat the Democratic ticket, that the President's position was one of neutrality.[13] The *Herald* later reported as a fact that King had been prohibited from making any removals of note until after the fall elections.[14] Whatever in fact may have been Johnson's policy, Democratic leaders in private made bitter complaint during the campaign that "the whole power of the adm'n through the Custom House and Post Office is against us" and "in the hands of Weed playing for Seward." They were particularly affronted by assessments levied against officeholders for the support of their opponents.[15] They were not appeased by the explanation that if such assessments had been made, it was without the President's knowledge.[16]

The political struggle for power between Johnson's friends made neutrality on the part of the collector a near impossibility. Just after the elections, King jumped into the cold waters of New York harbor from a Hoboken ferry. He had a past record of mental instability, but the strain of being in a position which was likened to that of "the famous donkey between the bundles of hay"[17] probably contributed to his untimely end. Just before the suicide, Weed had written that King allowed the small things of the Customhouse to worry him, and that he was imagining ruin and disgrace.[18] After King's death, the Democratic press insinuated that he had committed suicide because of conscientious scruples and remorse in yielding to Weed's pressure for political appointments, a charge which Republicans considered "thoroughly fiendish."[19] The demands of New York politics in 1865 called for finesse and fortitude; they might have driven mad most any man in the collector's post.

Before either party had gathered in convention, Horace Greeley smelled treachery. The state Union-Republican committee, by a shift of one vote, had defeated the Radicals who desired an early convention and set the date of meeting two weeks after that of the Democrats. Greeley in effect charged that Weed was acting in collusion with the Democrats and intended to jettison his own party.[20] It is possible that Weed contemplated a consolidation with the Democrats if union could be had on terms favorable to the Republican Conservatives. Barlow's *World*, however, had served warning that the Democratic party had no intention of accepting the New York *Times'* contention that it was a dying organization. As compared with the Republicans, the Democrats were "united on all rising issues of the future," their state-rights view was the "pivotal question of the epoch," and the margin of their defeat in 1864 promised victory for the future.[21] Certain elements of the Democracy may have been ready for union on their own terms; but the Weed-Seward men were certainly not prepared to accept a subordinate role in the party of the future. A possible explanation of Weed's preconvention maneuver is that he meant to use the expected Democratic approval of Johnson's policies as a weapon with which to wrest control of the Union convention from Greeley's friends; once the Democrats had endorsed the President's popular Southern policy, Radicals would have to accept the Conservative program or face the likelihood of party defeat at the polls.

Although anticipating Democratic support for the President, the Seward-Weed forces were hardly prepared for the dramatic action of the Democratic convention, which met at Albany September 6 and 7. Eliminating every trace of hesitation or criticism, it had adopted as the party platform the pledge of support for Johnson drafted by Marble, Tilden, and Cassidy. The chairman of the resolutions committee explained that the purpose was to give President Johnson such a hearty endorsement as "to make him *the great leader* of the people and *of the Democratic party*," and to reject "Vallandighamism," "Jerry Black Buchananism," and "Camden and Amboy Rip Van Winkelism"—a reference to the Ohio, Pennsylvania, and New Jersey Democratic platforms.[22] To head their ticket as candidate for secretary of state, the convention chose Henry W. Slocum, a Union general who had been a Republican in good standing since prewar days. For judge of the Court of Appeals, the Democracy named another old Republican, Martin Grover; and for comptroller they selected their opponent's own incumbent, Lucius Robinson, a thoroughgoing Radical who had deserted the Unionists in 1864 because he distrusted Lincoln on the slavery issue. The Democracy clearly was determined to "get back its men" from the opposition ranks.[23] The *World* heralded the convention's action as marking an end of questions that had divided parties in the past and as an open invitation to all who agreed with the Democracy on present issues, chief of which was the President's policy toward the South.[24] The *Herald* thought the New York Republicans now had no choice but "to fall in line with the reconstructed democracy and their comprehensive ticket."[25]

The first reaction of Raymond's New York *Times*, speaking for the Republican Conservatives, was to view the whole proceedings as a "surrender of the Democratic party" which Unionists could accept with pleasure.[26] The *Times*, rejoined the *World*, is at its wit's end; it "is perfectly silly" to speak of Democratic surrender. If the Republicans approve the Democratic candidates and platform, let them vote the ticket; then it will be apparent which party has surrendered![27] The *Times*' enthusiasm quickly abated; an apprehensive editorial termed the Democratic action a bold and treacherous "*coup d'état*," a characterization that delighted the *World*. Now, exulted the Democratic organ, Republicans are beginning to see what the Democratic "surrender" really amounts to! The Republicans might choose to disguise their defeat by endorsing the Democratic candidates and claiming victory as their own, but such a claim would be a preposterous and transparent fraud.[28] The *World* could rejoice. The Weed Unionists might not choose to surrender, but their design to erect a broad pro-Johnson party had been anticipated by the opposition. They now faced the possibility of desertion by the War Democrats as well as the probability of battle with their Radical protagonists for control of the state Union party. Republicans conceded privately that they would be defeated in the fall voting.[29] Montgomery Blair rejoiced at the prospective "overthrow of Seward & Weed as political powers. Between two fires one from Greeley & the other from the Democratic press we have these rogues in a tight place."[30]

Thurlow Weed, the seasoned political generalissimo, was equal to the challenge. His masterly skill was mobilized to corral sympathetic delegates to the forthcoming Union convention;[31] the *Times* argued persuasively for unity of the party in the face of danger.[32] When the Union convention met at Syracuse, Weed was securely in control, a goodly array of War Democrats were conspicuously present, and Radical hostility yielded grudgingly to the forms of harmony.[33] The Unionists endorsed the President, and Weed fashioned a state ticket "in man fashion, with doors open to all true friends of the administration."[34] The slate was headed by an ex-Democrat and general, Francis C. Barlow; no Republican on the Democratic ticket was given endorsement. "We are alright in the state," Weed triumphantly reported to the Secretary of State, "and only need to be left alone"—that is, to be free from Presidential displacement of Union officeholders.[35] Weed hastened to Washington but returned without seeing the President. Still, he was in good spirits and confidently predicted success. "A very few extreme Radicals may bolt," he wrote Seward on his return to New York, "but we can spare them." He seemed even to have found some comfort in the camp of the enemy; Dean Richmond had paid him a visit. "We do not differ much in our view of the course things will take."[36]

For all Weed's assurance, the uncertainties of battle lay ahead, and the hostility of Barlow and Blair was implacable. The state offices to be won or lost were almost irrelevant. Each party sought the favorable verdict of the people in order to gain "the inside track" with the President and to establish itself as the controlling nucleus for what the *Herald* called "the Ruling National Party for the Next Fifty Years."[37] The revival of the Democratic party through a New York victory was a prospect frightening to

Republican insiders. Even in the last weeks of the campaign, Assistant Secretary of the Treasury William E. Chandler wrote from Washington of his anxiety. Better "lice and locusts" than a Democratic victory; if only the Union ticket could carry the state, "all lingering doubt as to the policy of certain parties here will vanish."[38] The President, apparently, was watching the race from the judges' stand.

As Johnson's position became apparent to Barlow, the tone of his personal letters took on a sharp edge. "If he [Johnson] desires our defeat as I suppose he does," he wrote to General Richard Taylor, "he *may* accomplish it—If we win we owe him nothing and will pay it!"[39] Barlow received no satisfaction when he complained that the President "if he wants us to win . . . must call off his dogs [the reference was to the campaign activities of Stanton, District Attorney Dickinson, and General H. J. Kilpatrick] and do it effectively and publicly, through Genl Grant or the War Dept., and at once."[40] Taylor tried to get some definite answers from the President but reported, "I am of the opinion that there is no intention of giving such answer."[41] In writing to Judge Shipman, Barlow tried to maintain a calm perspective. The Judge had needled his friend by suggesting that it would be a huge joke "if you should all be sold by the President—To go on *such* a shearing expedition and come home shorn down to the skin would be a practical joke of the roughest kind."[42] Barlow explained:[43]

Johnson is trying to ride two horses and he probably means to join the party which finally keeps uppermost—If we win he will gladly join us. If we fail he will avoid a break with the Republicans and submit to the leadership of Seward & Stanton, distasteful as it really is to him—I look upon him as a consummate politician, and as possessing many of the most important elements of a statesman.

His course toward the South has been continually wise. . . . No matter what his political course may be in the future, we shall have secured for the people of the South the practical blessings of peace. . . .

If he finally becomes Radical and compels us to oppose him I shall be sincerely sorry, but I shall feel that *he*, not we, has been shorn in this pursuit of wool—But apart from this, we had no other course.

To have opposed him in any of the Northern States at this election, would have been madness as a mere question of party policy. We should have been beaten terribly and the prestige of such a success of our opponents would have injured us three years hence. Now we are free. If the Prest. does as he ought, we can make him the head of the great Northern & Southern party which is bound to win the next fight and if he joins our adversaries we can beat him.

The contest for the votes of the uncommitted was vigorously pressed by the *World* on behalf of the Democrats and the *Times* on behalf of the Unionists. They made it quite clear that the issues, as they saw them, were of major national importance. Their arguments revealed publicly, though perhaps unintentionally, the general political confusion and the partisan bids for power that had developed in the summer of 1865 about Johnson's program of restoration. Both sides championed the President and spoke in his name, but their views of his wishes and intentions were contradictory. Both claimed disinterested concern for the nation's welfare, but each showed a keen eye for party advantage. Both freely predicted the course of congressional policy, but saw it headed in quite different directions.

The *World* did battle with a confidence equal to Weed's own. At first taking credit for forcing the Republicans to endorse the President, it soon began an attack upon the Syracuse platform as "a cloud of cajoling words," an "intolerable straddling," and a refusal to approve Johnson's plan of immediate restoration. Weed had succeeded only in spreading over the Republicans a "thin conservative varnish." He could not control the Republican party; he did not have the confidence of its majority. Acquiescence in his conservatism was a fraud, a temporary expedient. Republicans would not follow Weed for long. The real issue in the canvass was between the President and the Radicals. The President recognized that the recently insurgent states were now states in the Union, entitled to recognition when Congress convened; the Radicals did not, and would refuse to seat Southern representatives elected under the President's plan. They would destroy the rights of the states and hold the South under military rule. Even Republicans who professed to sustain the President's policy dissembled: "Why *should* they approve a policy which is certain, if successful, to bring their political opponents into power?" Republicans who truly supported the President should rally for the peace of the Union and cooperate with the Democracy: "We appeal from conventions, from party organs, from politicians. . . . Men of the North, the nation calls upon you today not less loudly than it called in April, 1861." The *World* welcomed back into the fold Democrats who in their dislike for slavery had joined with old Whigs to form the Republican party, and spurred others to follow their example now that slavery was dead. The people could not elect members to Congress that fall, but they could express their opinion "in respect to President Johnson and his state-rights, anti-negro suffrage plan of restoring the Union," could express it so decidedly that Congress would not dare disregard their wishes. Indeed, the result of the New York election "determines the fate of President Johnson's plan for an immediate restoration of the Union." A victory of the party that elected him would imperil this "first and great measure of his administration."[44]

The Democracy pictured itself as the party of the Union. The *World* reported a revolution in public opinion; Northern sentiment wanted no more of the old sectional antipathies now that the Southern people had nobly submitted to the decision of war. The only hazard to a beneficent consummation of the Union in affection as well as form lay in that sectional party of the North "founded on hatred of the South" and "so long the curse of the country." But it had "nearly run its mischievous career."[45]

For the Democracy, the *World* claimed the President as their very own, "a Democrat, following Democratic principles." Readers were assured that he would cast his lot with those who supported him on the issues of the day. Midway in the campaign, John Van Buren, Democratic candidate for state attorney general and a leading party strategist, proposed the immediate nomination of Andrew Johnson as Democratic candidate for the next presidential election. This question, trumpeted the *World*, is the "fork in the road"; the real supporters of the President were those who would nominate him for re-election, the sham supporters those who would not. "The 'party of the President' must necessarily be the conservative Democratic party of the Union," for the opposition was disintegrating. The Republican *Evening Post* was already "squirming out of the Republican ranks," and Greeley in the *Tribune* was proclaiming his preference to act as a minority in opposition rather than sacrifice his Radical principles. The "Weed-Raymond club" was behaving like a "jealous, petulant child," insisting "that the executive shall have no friends unless they be enrolled in the little joint-stock company of which Seward is president." But, concluded the *World*, "Mr. Johnson has no idea of making the number of his friends in this state so 'conveniently small.'" Its editorial columns heaped ridicule upon the New York *Times'* claim that the President was interested in the success of the Union party in the state. "President Johnson would be a very intelligent politician, would he not, to desire the success here and now of the party which opposes his policy, or even of the Weed rump, called and confessed to be the Judas rump, which can't control a party, help him in Congress, or strengthen him in the country." The President, the *World* asserted, shared the "wide-spread conviction that the Republican party is out of harmony with the condition of the country," that it "now exists only to keep the South out of the Union."[46]

Democratic campaigners used the specter of Negro suffrage as a major campaign weapon. They tried to make it the foremost "living issue" of the contest. Their opponents, they argued, did not intend to permit the return of any Southern state until it allowed all Negroes to vote. The Syracuse convention had adopted with deliberate intent a "platform with a negro in it." The Republican party was the party of Negro suffrage, of Chase and Sumner and Wendell Phillips, however much a "dozen or so Republicans" might try to hide the design. Montgomery Blair, speaking at a Democratic rally in New York City, developed the Negro suffrage theme at some length. The "fate of races" was at stake. If Negro suffrage were imposed upon the South, the Negro and "poor white" would be demoralized, the old aristocracy driven out, Northern capitalists would dominate, and amalgamation of the races would be the order of the day. "It is for this end we are to have negro equality, negro suffrage, negro freedmen's associations, negro troops to take full possession of the country; while the right of the white race in the constitution, in the soil, in all the improvements of property to which their civilization has given birth is to be surrendered."[47]

As this quotation suggests, Democratic campaigners tried to tar their opponents with a broad brush, and did not hesitate to exploit anti-Negro feeling. Their arguments were generally built upon the premise that the opposition stood for an immediate grant of the ballot to all Southern Negroes imposed by the Federal Government in violation of the constitutional right of the states to govern their own internal affairs. But recognizing the prejudices of their supporters, spokesmen for the Democracy did not conceal their opposition to the unquestionably constitutional right of Northern states to extend the ballot to Northern Negroes by state action. The Democracy also voiced its equal distaste for suggestions that the Negroes of the South be permitted a limited suffrage based upon military service or the ability to read and write. The defeat of a state constitutional amendment extending suffrage to Negroes in Connecticut, where literacy tests were required of all voters, was welcomed as a party victory for the Democrats. The *World* pointed to Johnson's record as military governor of Tennessee as an indication that the President, like the Democracy, opposed the extension of suffrage to the Negro even by state action.[48]

The New York *Times*, whose editor, Henry J. Raymond, was both an ally of Weed and Seward and chairman of the Union Executive Committee, parried the *World*'s blows and landed some of its own. The one aim of the Union party, the *Times* confidently asserted, was to hold the state firmly in support of the national Administration; it was united in that resolve. Democrats were inventing tales of conflict within the Union ranks because they were dismayed by the harmony that had prevailed at the Syracuse convention. There was not the slightest ground for the expectation of any material disagreement between the President and the Union party in Congress. The party had no intention of destroying states rights; it would uphold the true

rights of the states but also the constitutionality of the war powers. Negro suffrage was not at issue in the campaign; politically
bankrupted by the late rebellion, the Democracy was straining to
make it an issue—they could not yet surrender the Negro as
political capital.

The whole suffrage question was a complicated one, the
Times explained. There was no difficulty in deciding that color
ought not of itself to exclude from the franchise, but how could
such a decision be made practically operative in the South where
not one white man in forty would agree? If either the President
or Congress forced Negro suffrage upon the South, the states
once restored would act as they pleased. Contrary to the *World's*
insinuations, the Republican paper asserted that the President was
not opposed to Negro suffrage as such. He had taken no stand
except to disclaim any right himself to impose such a condition;
he was leaving the question to the deliberations of Congress.
There were differences of opinion among party members on this
matter, and there were questions other than suffrage that would
be considered by Congress before receiving back the South; but
differences would be discussed in a fair spirit and decisions would
receive universal acquiescence. The *Times* itself agreed with the
President that suffrage was a matter for the states to determine.
Northern opinion might approve of Negro suffrage per se, and
be pleased if Southerners would admit intelligent and deserving
freedmen to the franchise; but Northern opinion was not in favor
of attempting to establish it by the Federal Government. There
was no basis at all for saying that Negro suffrage as a condition
for the readmission of the Southern states was one of the essential
principles of the Union party. Democrats were trying to create
a "first class bugbear."[49]

As for the Democracy's own support of the President, Raymond and Weed challenged its sincerity. They pointed out that
the Democratic party opposed what Andrew Johnson stood for:
his denunciation of treason, his support of the Thirteenth Amendment, his encouragement to Negroes, his admonition that the
South elect as congressmen only men who could take the required
ironclad oath. Had the New York Democracy been sincerely

determined to uphold the President's policies, they would have offered to support the Union party on condition that it nominate a ticket and adopt a platform pledged to the President or at least have offered to meet with the Unionists and together select the candidates and frame the platform. But no, the Democracy had sought to destroy the Union party, to drive Union men away from the President, to create mutual suspicions, and get the President under their sole and exclusive control. Could any conclusion be drawn except that the Democrats were after power and office? If the Democracy were sincere, they could stand the test of party defeat at the election; only then, should they remain true to the President, would their professions be worthy of confidence. Meanwhile, every man who believed what the Democrats pretended to believe, should vote the Union ticket.

The *Times* made a long and careful analysis to demonstrate that the Democratic theory of Reconstruction and the Presidential one were in sharp conflict:

Their theory is that the close of the war of itself revives the relations of the rebel States to the Union. . . . On the other hand, President Johnson's principle is that the abeyance of constitutional rights does not pass away with the mere close of the war. . . . The Democratic party considers that the Southern States have a right to restoration, immediate and unconditional. President Johnson, on the other hand, deems it to be both his right and his duty to impose conditions.

The position of the Northern Democracy was encouraging the Southerners to talk of their constitutional rights and withhold assent to the President's conditions. Defeat of the Democratic party in the North would show the South that it must accept in good faith the logical consequences of the war. Here lay the road to speedy restoration.

To the *Times*, the *World*'s claim that Johnson covertly supported the Democrats and would turn his back upon the party that had elected him was sheer effrontery. Nothing Johnson had said or done gave the slightest foundation for such "outrageous misrepresentation." There had been no changes in his Cabinet.

The only Democrat he had appointed to office was a personal friend; not a Copperhead nor an adherent of the Democratic organization had received an appointment. How could the President be going over to the Democrats when he insisted that the Southern states declare their ordinances of secession null and void, prohibit slavery in their constitutions, and ratify the Thirteenth Amendment? And did the *World* suppose that President Johnson had forgotten the invective it had formerly directed against him, the charge that he was a demagogue, low-lived in manners and morals, a public figure comparable to Nero and Caligula!

Beyond the denials and the countercharges, the *Times* relied most heavily upon a call to voters to support the party that had saved the Union, to repudiate the party that had nourished disloyalty. The overriding question was whether any party could "safely play the game of faction in a National crisis." The Democracy should be spurned on the basis of its war record and its Chicago peace platform. "A fate should be visited upon the political organization which lent itself to Copperheadism that shall serve as a warning for a thousand years." The loyal people of the North should fix the lesson that "no political organization can befriend treason with impunity." The Democratic party should be dealt "blow after blow" until it should become "utterly defunct."[50]

The Radical's chief organ, the New York *Tribune*, took little part in the early weeks of the campaign. The public exchange of recriminations between Greeley and Weed together with Weed's triumph at Syracuse robbed the *Tribune*'s editor of any enthusiasm for the cause. The cautious wording of the platform in respect to Negro rights, and developments in the South under Johnson's program of restoration were further discouragements to Greeley. At one point he appeared ready to call upon Radicals to repudiate the Conservative platform and to demand Negro suffrage.[51] However, he rallied to the support of the ticket with a strong appeal addressed to those intending to stay away from the polls in protest against the Syracuse platform and Johnson's course. His readers were told to stand firmly by the Union party even though it might not be all that they wished. To break down the party would "throw the Government wholly into the hands of our Democratic politicians, with whom negro-hate and negro degradation form their most profitable stock in trade."[52] The *Tribune* faltered in its confidence in the President, but did not renounce its faith in his good intentions. Its editor was immensely reassured when Johnson let it be known that were he in Tennessee he would support a limited, gradual enfranchisement of the Negro.[53] The close of the campaign found Greeley attacking the opposition candidates and calling for a resounding defeat of the Democracy.[54] The *Times* made no comment on Greeley's threatened bolt or on his return, but its editorial policy was consistently conciliatory and respectful toward those of the party who favored a program more vigorous than its own on behalf of the freedmen. This reflected both Raymond's own reasonableness and the fact that a widespread deflection of Radical sympathizers would have jeopardized the Conservatives' bid for power.

The national significance of the New York contest was also indicated by the personal attention it received from both Montgomery Blair and Secretary Seward. Blair campaigned vigorously for the Democracy, speaking in Manhattan, Brooklyn, Rochester, and Auburn. Though he began by affirming that he did not speak "as a party man," he made clear his support of the Democracy in their drive to unite under Johnson's leadership Democrats who supported the war and Republicans who were opposed to compelling Southern states "to resign their constitutional rights and receive dictation from the North."[55] Seward's role was more restrained, in keeping with his custom and his official station. Before his townsmen of Auburn on October 20, he delivered an address that was a paean of praise for Andrew Johnson and his plan of restoration. The latter, he asserted, had "distinctly offered itself to the last Administration" and was "the only plan which then or ever afterward could be adopted." Duty required "absolute and uncompromising fidelity" to that policy from all, "whosoever and whatsoever party they may be."[56] His appeal reads as though it were addressed as much to the confidence of the President as to that of his fellow New Yorkers. Barlow's friend Judge Shipman scornfully referred to it as Seward's "Uriah Heap speech."[57] Senator Henry Wilson of Massachusetts and Representative William D. Kelley of Pennsylvania were brought into New York for active assistance in the canvass, probably to reassure Radical sympathizers. And Secretary of War Stanton, at the time closely linked to Seward, used a visit to New York City, made ostensibly for relaxation, to work behind the scenes quietly but effectively for Weed's ticket.[58]

Seward's private papers hold unmistakable evidence of the Secretary's keen concern for success in the New York contest. Less than a week before the election, he received through Weed a check from two New York friends amounting to thirty-five hundred dollars to be used to insure an Administration victory. In transmitting their contribution and letter, Weed explained that he had told them "how important we regarded the approaching election in this state."[59] On the night of the election returns, Weed sent Seward three successive telegrams to report the reality and extent of victory.[60] A few days later, a Seward worker wrote with enthusiasm of the election's rebuke to Radicals and Democrats. It was a verdict "which must satisfy President Johnson that he is in no wise reduced to a reliance upon the *World* and the *Argus* for efficient support."[61]

The victory for Weed and Seward was a decisive one, a majority of over 27,000 votes as compared with one of less than 7,000 for Lincoln in 1864. Although the elections were reported as quiet and arousing little interest, the number of voters was better than 78 per cent of those who had cast their ballots in the presidential campaign, a very good showing indeed for a minor off-year election in which there seemed little choice between the two parties in platform or candidates.[62] Significantly, the *Times* greeted the news of the Union triumph by wishing Mr. Montgomery Blair a "return to the bosom of the Blair family a wiser if not a better man."[63] And preserved in the Seward Papers is a yellowed clipping of a lengthy doggerel, "Respectfully dedicated to Montgomery." Its ending reads as follows:

Montgomery changes his coat once more,
Rejoins the party he'd hated before.
Democracy's heart to him at once warms,
And it bids him welcome with open arms,
And thus receives with becoming mummery
The convert Blair whose name's Montgomery.

Then to the stump Montgomery flies
And calls on the copperheads to arise;
Some thought they had heard the blare of a trumpet
When Montgomery B. began to stump it;
But it proved to be only a penny affair
Faintly blown through by b–l–air.
But it rallied the copps in New York state,
And over in Jersey they grew elate;
For they hoped to kill the party radical,
And for this they fancied Montgomery had a call,
    But the votes were counted
    And they amounted
To such an insignificant sum
    That each Democrat, he
    Said Montgomery B.
Would have served them better by staying to hum;
So now when a copperhead wants to find,
An orator suited to his mind,
    To speak without notes
    And to drum for votes
He says if he wants to get a good drummer, he
Wont call on the Blair that's christened Montgomery.

In battling the Democracy and wooing voters from the ranks
of the Radicals, the Seward forces did not forget their ultimate
objective, a grand national Conservative party under their
hegemony. The door was left open for Democrats who fought
them in this campaign to join them in the next. Raymond would
not restrict the great work of restoring the Union "to Republicans or any other party class."[64] If the Union party were foolish
enough to divide in the future and refuse the Administration
support, then "it will inevitably give rise to new political organizations and combinations."[65] Should the seed sown by the Democracy at Albany take firm root, despite the lack of harvest
this election, the next election would show "the full advantage

of being on the right side."[66] "Whether the Union party is to be perpetuated in its present form or not, it is enough for it that its name will stand forever honored. . . . If ever the time comes for the Union party to die, let it die."[67] After the election, the *Times* consoled its opponents with the thought that their position was in some respects better than had they pursued a different course; they had professed to be loyal and patriotic, and if they had the wisdom to remain so, they would have laid "the foundation for more substantial claims upon the country hereafter."[68] But the *Times* told the Democracy to accept the verdict of the people and to recognize that their party organization was doomed. Democrats should join with the great Union organization sustaining the President, and gradually find an honorable place in the new parties that a new order of things would generate.[69]

Barlow's *World* showed little inclination to accept the *Times'* invitation. It professed to have obtained its objective in foiling the designs of the Radicals to prevent a return of the Southern states except with Negro suffrage. The Democracy had coerced the Republicans at Syracuse; now it would "practice the same kind of coercion on the Republican Congress." If Republicans chose to go before the people in the congressional elections as opponents of the President, Democratic victory would be easy. If they should consent to the President's program, the Democrats would still be the victors. The Southern states would return to the political arena and the Democratic party would be on the "high road to permanent success." It would dominate in the coming reorganization of parties.[70]

In private Barlow expressed much the same views. He professed to have no regrets for the course pursued and "few for the result of the election"; the Democrats had forced Republican support for Johnson's policy, and their own proper attitude had placed the Democratic party in a position where it could maintain itself in the future. He did not try, however, to disguise the general resentment of Democratic leaders at the President's lack of support; and he indicated no willingness whatsoever to be reconciled with Seward and Weed. "When he [the President] succeeds in building up a Johnson party in the North without us, through Seward

& Weed, the millennium will be close at hand."[71] Barlow attempted to draw a line between future support of the President's policy and support for Johnson personally. All save success for the Reconstruction plan, he asserted, was unimportant "except perhaps to himself, if he is ambitious of remaining at the head of a great party."[72] Although Barlow would have liked Taylor, whose mediation had played so important a role in bringing Democratic leaders to Johnson's support, to stop in Washington for a talk with the President, he recognized that Johnson had "no occasion for his services" and that a visit would be "embarrassing to both."[73]

Montgomery Blair saw the Republican victory as a result of party prestige gained by success in the war effort, their support of Johnson, and the fact that the new question of restoration was not yet "fully ground into the public mind." He expected the Sumnerites soon to carry the party organization for Negro suffrage and rejection of the Southern members-elect to Congress, thus creating a distinct issue that would bring advantage to the Democracy. Montgomery advised that Marble, the *World*'s editor, "keep the even tenor of his way, make no point with the Administration whilst the President adheres to his policy of referring suffrage to the States . . . & we are as sure of triumph as the sun rises."[74]

The *World* still had high hopes for the defection of old Democrats from the Union-Republican ranks and their reunion with the Democratic party. The Republican *Evening Post*, which represented the former group, was then criticizing its own party for a tendency toward dangerous centralization of power and predicting that out of the prevailing political confusion and ferment would emerge a new Democratic party with "fresh young blood and hope in its veins."[75] The *World* quoted the editorial at length, praised the views of the *Post*, and commented that there was no need for haste. Events would accomplish the reunion of Democrats without "engineering by small politicians." Until the time was ripe, the prodigal brethren might as well stay in the Republican party as "a sort of missionaries."[76]

Seward, Raymond, and Weed had blunted the drive of the Blairs and the Democracy to obtain ascendancy with the President, but the Democracy had not capitulated. The two forces would unite with the President against the Radicals in 1866, but theirs would be an uneasy and contentious alliance.

5 THE MAN WITH TWO COATTAILS

Those decisive moves of the Conservatives against the Radicals which invited open warfare, were directed by Andrew Johnson. Even before the break with Congress his actions were no mere reflex to pressures from the Weed-Seward or Blair-Democratic forces. He weighed the opinions and reports of others, particularly of those more singly attached to his person; and he made up his own mind.

No voice spoke more loudly and persistently to Johnson of his virtues, his power, and his political future than that of James Gordon Bennett's New York *Herald*. During the summer and fall of 1865, in both its editorials and in its news columns, the paper extolled the new President personally, approved his every political move, assured him that he was "master of the situation." He was the "right man in the right place"; he had few vices, clear convictions, the highest intellectual power, moral and physical courage; he was comparable to Abraham Lincoln and Andrew Jackson—in short he was a "great man."[1] Andrew Johnson could do no wrong. When other papers faltered in their support, the *Herald* liked to boast, it alone held steadfastly to the President.[2] The *Herald*'s uncompromising approval of what the President did, and of what the *Herald* thought the President was about to do, involved its editorial columns in turnings and twistings and evasions, but its editor could correctly assert that "We have kept up with Andy Johnson thus far, and shall never let him get ahead of us upon the right road."³

The *Herald* saw Johnson as the leader in the "revolution of parties," the unchallengeable head of an emerging Conservative party that would control the nation for the next fifty or a hundred years. He would "keep his own conscience and his own counsel; give advice instead of taking it, and make a start from a new standpoint."⁴ With scorn and delight, Bennett informed all political factions that they were impotent without the president. Fortunately, he consoled them, Andy Johnson had two coattails; the Republicans could cling to one, the Democrats to the other. All the South was for him, the Middle states too; he could count upon the whole loyal people—"except the Chase-Sumner faction who don't belong to the people." Let the politicians, the "wirepullers," the cliques beware of opposing his policies; they would be courting disaster. And they—particularly the Democrats—should not be so presumptuous as to call upon Johnson to join them. "He is the mountain—Mohamet must go to the Mountain."⁵ Before the November elections in New York, Bennett counseled the contestants, "The Northern party which adopts him now as its candidate for the succession will be the party of the future."⁶ After the election, the *Herald* reminded Republicans that they owed success to their support of Johnson. Should they falter in adherence to his policy, their power would be superseded by that of a new party; the "masses" would uphold the President.⁷

Such unstinting praise and support from one of the most widely read newspapers of the country would please any President. Johnson was grateful. Two days after the *Herald* called for his immediate nomination as presidential candidate for 1868, Johnson wrote James Gordon Bennett a long letter marked "Private." He thanked Bennett for the "able and disinterested manner" in which he had defended Administration policy. He hoped to prove that Bennett's "timely help and confidence" had not been misplaced. He wrote in general terms of his policy, his determination to abide by the law and the Constitution and to restore the Union. He assured Bennett that he would not be deterred by "taunts or jeers," or "over-awed by pretended or real friends, or bullied by swaggering or presuming enemies." Johnson identified himself with the people. They had always sustained him in public life, and he would stand by them. In their name, "in the people's cause, I need and ask your aid. . . . There is no man in America, who can exercise more power in fixing the Government upon a firm and enduring foundation than you can—with such aid the task will be made easy."[8]

There is additional evidence to suggest that Johnson maintained confidential relations with Bennett, and that he considered carefully the editor's advice and views. In reply to Johnson's letter, Bennett sent his son with a brief note stating that whatever was said to the son "will be the same as what is said to me."[9] A member of the *Herald* staff, first Henry Wikoff and then W. B. Phillips, acted more regularly as intimate liaison between editor and President. At a later date, the *Herald*'s Washington correspondent was chosen at Johnson's request, and was given more intimate access to the President and his Cabinet than any other member of the Washington press.[10] Wikoff and Phillips reported Bennett's views, sent copies of *Herald* editorials, and consulted with the President about others to come. Phillips wrote, "If you think proper, as I said to you when I had the honor of an interview, to suggest any views of your wishes through your son or otherwise I shall be happy to attend to them."[11] Before public announcement of one of the most critical decisions in Johnson's career, the veto of the Freedman's Bureau Bill, a telegram went from the White House to James Gordon Bennett, Jr., notifying the *Herald* of the President's decision.[12]

In view of the relationship between the *Herald* and the President, the "disinterested" nature of Bennett's support and views merits careful examination. The *Herald*'s self-characterization, that it was "independent of everybody and everything" and set forth its views "with perfect frankness and impartiality" has often been accepted uncritically by students of this period.[13] The paper was an independent one, in the sense that unlike most of its contemporaries it was the organ of no political party or faction. It not infrequently appeared capricious in its editorial twistings and turnings; and it was undeniably outstanding in its news coverage. But the *Herald* was not objective or impartial, nor was it fair in presenting views with which it disagreed. Though noted for its sensitivity to public opinion, its ability to shift with the prevailing winds, it often miscalculated or distorted. Bennett's cynicism, his sense of *Realpolitik*, made for a lively and informative paper; it also crippled his ability to detect or understand motives other than those of garnering the loaves and the fishes.

Bennett had decided political opinions and prejudices, which were reflected in the *Herald*'s editorials and often in its news columns. His attitude toward Johnson, whom he championed, was no more objective than had been his attitude toward Lincoln, whom he had for the most part criticized and deprecated. Toward Seward, he was restrained, but his dislike of the Secretary was obvious. Bennett thought Seward had presidential ambitions, which he gladly predicted would be fruitless. For what he termed the "Blair-Seward War . . . for Control of President Johnson's Policy," the editor had a pat solution—cast both aside for "new and honest men." He was quick to accuse Seward and his closest political associates of treachery toward the President, though he did not press the charge.[14] Independent of party and bitter toward the Copperheads, still Bennett was at heart with the Democrats. Of all the local politicos, Dean Richmond of the Albany Regency came nearest to being the *Herald*'s fair-haired boy. Bennett's columns made known his desire to see the Democrats victorious in the New York elections of 1865 and predominant in the new "Andy Johnson party" of the future.[15] One cannot read page after page of *Herald* editorials without sensing that its editor wanted to be a political power. This hypothesis is consistent with the reports to Lincoln that what Bennett most desired was attention and recognition. It also squares with the editor's flat assertion that the paper had the power not only to judge public opinion, but also to "influence and direct it."[16] In the midst of the New York pre-election struggle, Bennett boasted that "the only *political magnates* that are left with heads upon their shoulders are

Andy Johnson, John B. Haskin, Dean Richmond and the NEW YORK HERALD."[17] In respect to Andrew Johnson and his political future, Bennett was not at all "disinterested."

Bennett's attitude toward the Radicals was one of intense hostility; his references to them were invariably intemperate, either vindictive or disparaging. They were "nigger worshippers" or "niggerheads," "Jacobins," "political thugs," "fussy and impracticable" Abolitionists, "demagogues" who proposed to abolish the Pope, the Jews, religion generally, and distinction of dress between the sexes.[18] Bennett's characterization had contradictions: the Radicals were impractical idealists, but they were also men who "look upon the negro, not as a man, but as a mere voting machine."[19] Whether idealists or realists, they were linked with Southern fire-eaters and Northern copperheads as "Rebels," and Bennett hopefully predicted that they would be "buried so deep in the grave of public opinion that they will never have a resurrection."[20] Bennett helped to build up the myth, already popular among Southern sympathizers, that responsibility for the Civil War lay with the opponents of slavery, and he added the charge that the "negro worshippers" were conspiring to foment race strife and even the dissolution of the Union in order to divert an indignant public from holding them accountable for the spent blood and treasure. The Bostonians who supported suffrage for the Negro, including the Board of Trade, were Jacobins and traitors, inciting to insurrection. The President should arrest them and incarcerate them in Fortress Monroe alongside Jefferson Davis; or better still, their leaders should be strung up on the same tree with a half-dozen leading Southern rebels. This being impractical, Bennett counseled seriously that the Radicals be "completely expelled from our National party organization."[21]

A *Herald* editorial of July 7, 1865, reached a vicious low that fully revealed Bennett's venom and distortion. Headlined "The Abolitionists and their New Crusade," it struck out at Abolitionists past and present. Looking at the past, it ridiculed the idea that Lovejoy had been a martyr, and spoke instead of his "worthlessness." Before the organization of the "negro party," the Abolitionists—according to Bennett—had been Fourierites, attempting to bring the millennium but instituting societies that were "mere brothels." Not content with the end of slavery, like Jacobins "their taste of blood has but sharpened their appetite for more." They were now working for "universal negro suffrage, universal free love and amalgamation of races. Such at least is the inevitable tendency of their new crusade."[22]

As the quotations indicate, Bennett's hostility was indiscriminate. Although generally identifying the "negro worshippers" with the demand for immediate universal Negro suffrage, a characterization of the Radicals' position which was too sweeping to be accurate, the *Herald*'s net of vituperation was so broad as to endanger any friend of the Negro. Among its victims was the Freedmen's Bureau. Serious students of the Bureau have all found much more to commend than to criticize in its work. In the first days of its organization, the *Herald* itself viewed the Bureau's problems sympathetically and commended its chief, General O. O. Howard, as able, practical, and conscientious.[23] By August, however, it was attacking the Bureau's policy as one of arbitrarily acting on the principle that the white man had no rights the Negro need respect.[24] In mid-September Bennett opened up with gross ridicule and exaggeration. There were millions of helpless women and girls; if there were no bureau to take care of their rights, how absurd to maintain one for "broad-shouldered, gigantic Sambos, well developed, greasy wenches, and pickaninnies indescribable and innumerable." Why couldn't the "gigantic nigger" fight his own way in the world as well as "these faint-hearted and feeble ones"? General Howard was managing "the bureau for the support of big, fat buck niggers with great piety and success," but what benevolence was there in his pious and charitable heart for the nation's four million poor women? Not that Bennett was serious in his concern for the women. Why *not* ridicule a Woman's Bureau, he asserted; "no one considers the Freedmen's Bureau either a piece of Quixotism or a joke—of course not."[25] With characteristic inconsistency, the *Herald* had kindly words for the Freedmen's Bureau the following January; but a few weeks later, when the bill to renew the Bureau was before Congress, its editorial columns returned to the attack. The bill was denounced as wild and wicked legislation designed to demoralize the Negro; the Bureau was characterized as a gigantic and preposterous government poorhouse.[26]

The *Herald*'s recklessness was not merely one of words; it affected the substance of Bennett's advice to the President. Implicitly and explicitly his editorial pages urged no compromise with congressional opposition to the President's Southern policies. If Congress should reject the Southern representatives elected under procedures set by the President, its action would be revolutionary. The President would then have full authority to exercise all powers vested in him in times of insurrection "to put an end to their revolutionary work."[27] A conflict between Executive and Congress would be unfortunate, would embarrass national finances and paralyze industry, but "would not necessarily be the worst of evils. The country would be kept disturbed another year or so; but the people would settle the difficulty at the next elections," and a new Conservative party would grow up and sink present factions.[28] The President had fulfilled his role as Republican; he was free to "stand upon his own platform and build up his own party."[29] Harmony between the two branches of government was desirable, but "it is clear that it is the legislative branch that should harmonize with the executive."[30] Johnson should not alter his course; he held the trump cards, such as the New York Customhouse, and these would be effective against the "present republican party" whose cardinal principles were "the five loaves and two fishes."[31] The President should pay "no more attention to their antics than General Grant to an army firing popguns."[32] Congressional abuse was a compliment; Johnson should be bold.[33]

This was extraordinary and dangerous counsel. The *Herald* was prodding Johnson, a man who had inherited rather than won the presidential office, to ignore the majority opinion of the nation's elected legislative body. He was urged to do so, not on an issue of limited scope, but in a broad area of decision arising out of four years of bloody warfare and one clearly critical to the nation's social and political development for years to come. The exact degree of responsibility that rests upon the *Herald* for Johnson's fateful decision to declare war on his congressional opponents cannot be assessed; the historian has no precision scale in which to weigh such matters.[34] But for the tragic consequences of that warfare, the *Herald* can not escape indictment.

The assurances that Bennett publicly gave the President of his power to shape the future and emerge as its dominant political personality were apparently confirmed by the praise and predictions that reached Johnson in private letters. His correspondents likened him to Washington and Jackson; he was "the greatest man living."[35] Johnson's prospects of restoring the Union were bright, wrote Senator Dixon of Connecticut early in May, and "a grateful people will reward you with renewed honors."[36] Even Supreme Court Justice Chase in those early days was writing Johnson of his desire for a presidential success so illustrious that "the people will be as little willing to spare Andrew Johnson from their service as to spare Andrew Jackson."[37] Duff Green prophesied that the good opinion of the country would be "indicated by the election of 1868."[38] Others wrote, too, with hope or assurance that popular acclaim would continue Johnson in the Presidency.[39] Who should be the standard bearer of the new party so truly democratic, so catholic, so comprehensive that every true patriot could adhere to it, asked New York's influential Daniel S. Dickinson. He gave the answer: "He must be before the people now, & well & widely known, & enjoy the popular confidence. In *your own person*, you have these essential requisites, & fine success in your administration will give you the future as you have the present. . . . If you have future ambitions, as it is right & proper you should have . . . present success will secure future triumph."[40]

Was it possible that Andrew Johnson was without the ambition it was "right and proper" he should have? Any occupant of the White House, even one of great humility and little ambition, would have been stirred to hope. Andrew Johnson was not a humble man, nor one of small ambition. He had raised himself from the obscurity of an illiterate tailor by a fierce ambition; and he had done battle behind a shield of self-confidence, hard tempered to protect him from the slights of those who considered themselves his superiors. He was, indeed, a man incapable of self-effacement. In the bitter contest of 1866, Johnson's "I," "me," and "my" opened him to ridicule; they were no new phenomena. In his uninhibited inaugural speech as Vice President, Johnson had used the personal pronoun "I" no less than twenty-seven times![41] Lincoln in his classic address upon the same occasion had used the pronoun but once, and that parenthetically.

Johnson's sympathetic biographer, R. W. Winston, believed that Johnson had visions of succeeding himself, "but this was not his operating motive."[42] The knowledgeable Washington correspondent of the Springfield *Republican* wrote in October, 1865, "Andy Johnson is a shrewd politician, and I have little doubt means to be the next president."[43] Johnson disclaimed any ambition except to be an instrument in restoring the Union,[44] but such a disavowal is in the innocent, accepted pattern of political verbiage. Gideon Welles, cynical observer of the political scene but true friend of the President, believed at the time that Johnson clung until the bitter end to the expectation of presidential nomination in 1868.[45] In a draft manuscript of recollections concerning President Johnson, Welles later wrote: "It was a mistake, a fatal error on his part that he ever thought of prolonging his term and being a candidate for the presidency in 1868. I know not from any record or expression from himself that he entertained an idea of being nominated, but I can in no other way account for errors and acts which I lamented and sought to prevent."[46]

According to his confidential private secretary, President Johnson in 1868 also seemed "anxious for the nomination," more concerned about it than he had been about the results of the impeachment proceedings. When word of Seymour's nomination reached the White House, the President "said little but I could see that he felt the disappointment."[47] The same source recorded Johnson's earlier derogatory view of potential rivals, notably of General Grant and Secretary of Treasury McCulloch. In the President's eyes, Grant was "controlled by prejudice and passion," incapable of "understanding in respect to government," an inept general, "a mere figurehead who, by fortuitous circumstances had won a reputation far above his real deserts."[48] Johnson had thought well of Secretary McCulloch; but when he had reason to consider the Secretary an aspirant for the Presidency, Johnson remarked that "there was a man out West who could do infinitely better as Secretary of the Treasury than the present incumbent."[49] On the other hand, the President expressed himself as willing to help Secretary of State Seward "in seeking a nomination for the Presidency," but at the same time made it clear that "the old man" had "lost all strength in his own state," and was "rather a dead carcass."[50] In other words, the only candidacy other than his own which Johnson could regard with equanimity was a hopeless one.

The spark of ambition for presidential office was kindled in Johnson before fate thrust him into that high office. As Tennessee's senator, according to the recent work of a careful Johnson scholar, he was an eagerly ambitious man with an eye on the Presidency.[51] In 1860 he had been a favorite-son candidate for the Democratic nomination, and his political lieutenants for a time were not without hope. Again, during the war, there had been a movement to promote Johnson as presidential timber.[52] Certainly there was no good reason for Johnson to have shed presidential ambitions upon his accession to the office of Chief Executive, and there was much to rekindle them. Lincoln, a statesman of unusual humility, admitted to a desire for a second term; a like ambition on the part of his successor was not only "right and proper" but to contemporaries a self-evident reality of political life. Indeed, the surprising fact is that historians have so generally disregarded Johnson's ambition in seeking to understand his stubborn and uncompromising course. To weigh the goal of re-election in interpreting Johnson's course is not to make of it the one "operative motive," not to view Johnson as the victim of unprincipled ambition. Human motives are too complex and interrelated, the political situation in 1865 and 1866 was far too confused and uncertain to make the historic Andrew Johnson a mere seeker of power. But a recognition of his ambition explains much that can otherwise be accounted for only on the premise of a stubborn disposition and an inflexible adherence to a limited states'-rights view of the Constitution.

Johnson's record does not warrant the interpretation of inflexibility and of scrupulous regard for states' rights which has been
offered to explain his policy as President. As state legislator he had
shown an ability to accommodate when he reversed an opposition
to internal improvements after it had brought political defeat.[53] No
change of attitude and policy was ever more startling than Johnson's transformation from an advocate of vengeance—[54] his opposition to Lincoln's amnesty, his assertion that treason must be
made odious, traitors punished and their property confiscated—
to the embodiment of Executive clemency. To one position, it
is true, he held with unqualified consistency. In Johnson's view,
no state of the Union by secession could lose its character as a
state and be reduced to mere territory or conquered land; but
this view of the Constitution was theoretical warrant for his
own status as loyal senator from Tennessee, Vice President, and
finally President. In practice, Johnson's constitutional and states'
rights scruples were not unyielding. As a senator he had found
nothing without warrant in the Constitution in Lincoln's call for
volunteers without congressional consent.[55] As military governor
of Tennessee he had displayed no tender regard for the rights of
the state and the people thereof. On the contrary, he had welcomed rigged and unrepresentative political conventions that upheld his objectives. He had sanctioned, perhaps initiated, an extraordinary election oath that disqualified not only state citizens who
had been rebel sympathizers but in addition loyal men who supported the Democrat's McClellan against the Union ticket. He
had brushed aside consideration of state constitutionality. "Suppose you do violate law," he counseled, "if by so doing you restore the law and the constitution, your conscience will approve
your course, and all the people will say, amen!"[56] Johnson may
have been stubborn and principled, but these characteristics were
not so unqualified as to alone explain his conduct as President.
The political temper of 1865 and Johnson's own ambition were
important elements in determining the course of Presidential
policy toward Reconstruction. In retrospect Johnson may appear
to have defied inexorable forces of political power, but at the
time he seemed to be riding a mighty wave of the future.

Johnson made no obvious, open bid for re-election; to have done so in the first year of his presidency would have been politically inept, premature, and unnecessary. The policy of generosity toward the vanquished and restoration of national unity became so intimately linked with his person that public approval of the policy and public support for Johnson's personal future were inexorably intertwined. There was, it is true, some effort notably on the part of Secretary Seward to represent Johnson's policies as simply Lincoln's policies extended into action. This view has colored historical assessments, but it does not represent the dominant note struck by Johnson or sounded by his contemporaries. The Democratic New York *World* with persistence and pleasure pointed to "the absurdity of the claim that Mr. Lincoln's rottenborough system . . . is the same as Mr. Johnson's plan of restoration."[57] Johnson frequently invoked, and so did his admirers, the authority of the Constitution, the example of Washington and of Jackson, but seldom the name of Abraham Lincoln. The "great principles of our government . . . enunciated by me," Johnson asserted in an address typical of his response to public commendation of his Restoration policy, "comprehend and embrace the principles upon which the government rests, and upon which, to be successful, it must be administered. . . . Taking all my antecedents, going back to my advent into political life, and continuing down to the present time . . . they have been my constant and unerring guide."[58]

A disavowal in February, 1866, of any ambition beyond the restoration of the Union, "for my mission will then have been fulfilled," and the affirmation of a readiness then to retire—"if there be any envious and jealous of honor and position, I shall be prepared to make them as polite a bow as I know how"[59] could not disentagle Johnson's own future from that of his policy. Perhaps as a transient impulse they were meant to do so, but even that is doubtful. General William T. Sherman, after the confidence of such a disavowal made in private, sent the President on February 11, 1866, an "earnest wish" that he would not only succeed in restoring the Union "but that by a renewal of the term of office you may perpetuate the peace that you have done so much already to secure.[60] When Bennett's *Herald*, in a surprising shift of editorial policy a fortnight after Johnson's public renunciation of presidential ambition, came forth with fair words for General Grant as a presidential possibility, W. B. Phillips, the paper's editorial writer and liaison with the President, was obviously embarrassed and sent Johnson an extended explanation. Bennett's decision had been made with the idea that it was "the true way to aid you in the work of restoration and bringing peace to the country." It would "take the wind out of the sails of the politicians," would "allay hostility and rivalry to you." Phillips continued, "Mr. Bennett has a very high opinion of General Grant. . . . He has not, however, a less exalted opinion of you. . . . He would be as ready, and, perhaps, more ready to go for you as a candidate for the next term, when the proper time shall arrive."[61] A few days later a Southern supporter of the President revealed even more explicitly the friendly disbelief in Johnson's prospective abdication; indeed, he interpreted Johnson's recent public disavowals of further ambition as leaving the door open for a presidential nomination in 1868. "I trust that nothing will impel you to express a purpose, on any occasion, to decline a reelection. Your enemies will try to provoke you to make such a declaration. I trust you will be guarded against it. The ground taken by you in one or two of your late speeches, is the true position."[62]

That Johnson accepted the prevalent assumption of a realignment of parties, and also the *Herald*'s prediction that he was the man with "two coattails" around whose leadership the triumphant party of the future would coalesce, seems certain without a reasonable doubt. That he did so is consistent with contemporary opinion and with his own actions and his words. When in a private interview of October, 1865, later made public with the President's sanction, he was faced with the charge of "going over" to the Democrats, Johnson laughingly replied that the Democratic party had found its position untenable and "is coming to ours; if it has come up to our position, I am glad of it."[63] A few days earlier he had been reported, less authoritatively, as having told the Democratic leader Dean Richmond that he considered himself pledged to no party, that only those who approved of his present policy would be regarded as his friends.[64] In analyzing the political situation shortly thereafter, Barlow wrote General McClellan, who was in Europe, that "Johnson is insane enough to suppose that he can build up a personal party in the South as well as in the North, which shall embrace the conservative elements of all the old factions and that thus he can rid himself of the necessity of an alliance with the democratic party proper."[65]

Some months later, just before he threw down the gauntlet of challenge to the Radicals by his first veto message, Johnson declared that those who accepted his principles would find themselves "surely coming together . . . while those who disclaim them, who are willing to repudiate them, and set them at naught, will be found disintegrating and travelling in a divergent direction. . . . I care not by what name the party administering the Government may be denominated—the Union party, the Republican party, the Democratic party, or whatnot."[66] During the preliminaries of the 1866 campaign Johnson admonished his followers: "Let parties sink into insignificance. If a party must be maintained let it be based on the great principles of the constitution."[67] Even after his hope of an independent candidacy had been cruelly dashed and the only avenue of vindication and ambition lay through nomination by the regular Democratic convention, Johnson scorned supplication and held to the conviction that the Democratic party should seek him. "Why should they not take me up?" he remarked plaintively to his private secretary. "They profess to accept my measures. . . . I am asked why don't I join the Democratic party! Why don't they join me?"[68]

President Johnson took care to create a public image of himself as one who could "afford to do right," who thought only of the Union, and one who rested secure in the approbation of the great masses of the people. There are, however, a number of indications that his own political fortunes were not left entirely to chance. In the early days of his presidency, Johnson summoned to Washington as one of his most intimate political advisers the man who had initiated a Johnson-for-President movement in 1861,

Lewis D. Campbell. Campbell was a hard-drinking Ohio politician, whom one of Johnson's staunchest Ohio supporters privately characterized as a "low fellow" and a "scamp."[69] The Ohioan was considered by fellow politicians to be a man of "*extraordinary tact* in the management of political matters."[70] The letters of advice which Campbell sent on his return home did not explicitly refer to the presidential campaign ahead, but they spoke first of his "indescribable interest in your success" and then of his paper's having raised the Johnson banner for President as early as 1861.[71] In writing the President's son-in-law, Campbell sent an oblique warning meant for the President's eye: the friends of Chief Justice Chase (a recognized aspirant for the Presidency) were "impregnating the popular mind with prejudices against Johnson." At the same time he expressed a conviction that the Union party was "going under" and that the only hope lay in organizing "a party *on the basis of the President's patriotic policy*". The President should take the initiative and cut himself off from his enemies. Of particular interest is the argument that he stated as follows: "If he [Johnson] has the remotest idea that he will ever be accepted as a *leader* among these radicals (even if he could adopt their vagaries) he should at once be relieved of such a delusion."[72] Campbell not only gave advice, directly and indirectly, he also kept an active hand in Ohio politics and acted as consultant on Ohio patronage appointments.[73]

Of all the emissaries President Johnson sent to the South, perhaps the one he trusted most was Harvey M. Watterson, fellow Tennessee politico, life-long Democrat, and Unionist. From June through October, 1865, Watterson sent back a series of dispatches on conditions in the South. As with Lewis Campbell, so with Watterson there are intimations of a sharp eye and a helping hand for Johnson's political future. From North Carolina he wrote that many had sought his acquaintance because he hailed from the President's own state. "In every instance you formed a large share of the conversation. Of course I am at home on that subject, and rest assured that I have done it ample justice. You know, and I know, what you have done for the Southern people since your inauguration, and I never fail to detail all that—act by act. . . .

I say to these people, suppose Chase, or Sumner or even Hannibal Hamlin were president." In one paragraph he gave assurances of the growing confidence of the people in Andrew Johnson and in the next predicted that "you are to have a war with the friends of Chase, who is evidently a candidate for the next Presidency."[74] From Alabama, Watterson wrote that the Southern press now had nothing but compliments for President Johnson, and that "an undivided South and every conservative man in the North, will ere long be rallying around and sustaining the National Administration.[75] From Mississippi, he sent word that "Long life to him [President Johnson], is the fervent prayer of all."[76] From Georgia came the assurance that the South would stand by Johnson, "it was just as certain as that God made Moses. I need not tell you that I have done all I could to strengthen and give consistency to this confidence."[77] On his return to Washington, Watterson was appealed to as "an intelligent & reliable source" and as "the personal and political friend of Prest. Johnson" for advice on the senatorial election in the Georgia legislature in order that nothing inexpedient would be done that might "bring down on the President an *immediate* attack by the Thad Stevens faction."[78]

Harvey Watterson's son, the "Marse Henry" of later fame whose journalistic skill had effectively served the Confederate cause, was engaged in a successful newspaper venture at Nashville. In December, 1865, he wrote the President: "On arriving in Nashville after I left you, I began work in earnest and have labored ceaselessly ever since. How far my work may have proved of value in a political point of view, I am of course unprepared to decide. . . . I wish to repeat what I said to you at Washington, that my object is to support your policy and to strengthen your hands. I wish to join, so far as one of such poor capacity can do, in the construction of that National Administration party, on which reposes the sole hope of the country. . . . I have nothing to ask of you but your confidence and counsel. I don't need any patronage; and am already indebted more than I can repay, for your kindness to me and mine."[79] According to his biographer, young Watterson was ready to support Johnson as the leader of a third party had the movement crystallized.[80]

A number of letters in addition to Henry Watterson's indicate that President Johnson kept a vigilant eye on the political situation in Tennessee. In September he received word that plans were about complete for an Administration newspaper in west Tennessee.[81] He also had an encouraging report from the friendly Union general and Kentucky congressman, L. H. Rousseau, who had hurried to Nashville after seeing Johnson in Washington. Rousseau had spoken with most of the leading men of Tennessee and found them "heartily and cordially for your policy and your Self"; he was about to depart on a similar mission to sound out leaders in Illinois and Indiana.[82] About the same time, Johnson's friend and fellow wartime Tennessee official, Edward H. East, was consulting him on the advisability of encouraging public pro-Administration meetings, a delicate question that continued to be a matter of careful concern to Tennessee friends.[83] While young Watterson was busily getting his paper underway, still another Nashville editor with an "ambition to be useful" was reporting success and asking the President's son to suggest a partner for the enterprise and a good Washington correspondent.[84] Meantime an interesting series of letters reveal that Johnson at the instance of Tennessee friends had taken action to have the Government-operated railroads of the state turned back to private interests, and was receiving in return more than perfunctory thanks. Railroad men were reported as "doing all in their power to sustain your administration" and as having given assurances that they would employ no man on their roads unless he fully sustained the Administration. The new directors of the Nashville and Chattanooga had been selected either from a list approved by the President or from men known to be Johnson's "personal and political friends." At their stockholders' meeting, resolutions were adopted not only thanking the President for return of the roads, but also commending his general policy and extending to him a "firm cordial and hearty support." Similar resolutions followed at the annual stockholders' meeting of the East Tennessee and Virginia Railroad Company.[85]

The evidence of Johnson's intention to build up a third party that would carry him back into the Presidency in 1868 is largely circumstantial, but nonetheless conclusive. In the midst of the New York campaign of 1865, Barlow had sent a complaint and a warning meant to reach the President through the Kentuckian, Russell Houston, who had played an important role along with Montgomery Blair, Governor Platt, and General Taylor in securing the support of New York Democratic leaders for Johnson. "Mr. Johnson had it in his power to make our success certain— He has chosen to oppose us, certainly not from any doubt as to our principles, or our honesty of intention, toward him, but really, I suppose because he fears, in case he allies himself with us, and we are defeated, he will be practically without a party in Congress." But defeat of the Democracy, according to Barlow, would find the Republican party hopelessly divided with its main strength in the hands of the opponents of Seward, Johnson's "persistent and unappeasable" enemies. "Does he suppose that the Democratic party will be reconstructed to take in Seward & Stanton? If so he will soon be undeceived." With slavery dead, the Democracy could make an alliance with the Radicals because they were sound on questions of civil liberty, but "we cannot unite with Mr. Seward on any question. Nor will there be a party in any one of the Southern States during Mr. Johnson's life, that will be led by Seward and his allies—Again, when Seward gets the control of any party of *real* power, no matter when or how, it will be a Seward party, not a Johnson party. . . . Possibly if we had understood the President's views our actions would have beer different."[86]

Houston's reply from Washington gave Barlow little satisfaction and clearly indicated that the President agreed not with the Democrat's prognosis that he would be politically stranded but rather with James Gordon Bennett's forecast of a triumphant Andy Johnson party. The Kentuckian wrote: "As I have said to you before, in very earnest, if not very strong terms, Mr. Johnson is eminently a national man—is struggling to make his administration national. . . . I will trust him without a shadow of misgiving or doubt. Adhering to the Resolutions of your late Con-

vention at Albany, you cannot form an alliance with any mere
sectional party. Those are national resolutions . . . be patient.
. . . Carry out your resolutions & we will have, in a very short
time, a great National Party, embracing three fourths of the
American people. . . . That is my party & you must be of this
great family."[87]

6 THE PROBLEM OF PATRONAGE

JOHNSON'S USE OF THE IMMENSE PATRONAGE AVAILABLE TO HIM AS President merits close examination. In the eyes of political sophisticates it constituted the "loaves and fishes" of practical politics, and in its disposition they sought the clues to his larger intentions. Many letters to the President urged speedy and sweeping use of the patronage power and attributed the strength of the Radicals to his failure to dislodge opponents from office. These contemporary admonitions have misled historians into the conclusion that Johnson committed a grave and obvious error of practical politics by failing to wield promptly and drastically his power of removal and appointment.[1] Were this view correct, it would suggest that Johnson was unmindful of his chances in 1868, for no resource at the disposal of a Chief Executive has been a more effective or more recognized means of obtaining renomination.

There is no reason to believe that Johnson was restrained by any sense of delicacy about removing men from office for their political opinions or activities. According to James Ford Rhodes, Johnson "decapitated" some 1283 postmasters plus numerous customhouse and internal revenue officials in order to replace them with his own adherents during the campaign of 1866.[2] Judging from the incomplete appointments records of his presidency, this action was concentrated in the three months preceding the November congressional elections; and those who criticize Johnson's earlier restraint see in August a marked, if fatally belated, change of policy.[3] Published lists show that between December, 1866, and the following April 20, the Senate either rejected or failed to confirm 1039 nominations. Some of these represented a second choice for a rejected candidate, which would lessen the number of offices involved, but they do not, of course, include nominations which the Senate confirmed.[4] Whatever the exact number of removals, it was considerable enough to indicate that Johnson regarded patronage as a legitimate political weapon. And after the pro-Johnson Philadelphia Convention of August the President publicly stated his determination to give office only to men who sustained its principles; when clamor followed removals, he justified them by "that good old doctrine of rotation in office."[5]

The President's tardiness in making sweeping removals has obscured two interesting facts: namely, that he *did* make important use of his appointing powers before August, 1866; and that his restraint in making removals was a calculated political strategy attributable, at least in part, to the influence of Seward and Weed.[6] It cannot be construed as a want of concern to garner all possible support for his policies or for himself. That the strategy was a "mistake" is questionable; that it contributed materially to his defeat is even more doubtful. The congressional victory of 1866 was so sweeping that the role of place holders, Radical or Conservative, clearly could not have been decisive.

For the President to have adopted earlier than he did a policy of large-scale turnover in officeholders might well have lessened rather than improved his political strength. Before the sharp break with Congress initiated by his veto messages of February and March and climaxed by the call issued June 26 for a convention of his followers in mid-August, removals threatened to antagonize men who might otherwise remain loyal to the President. The appointment of new men, moreover, was beset by hazards on all sides. Who was friend and who was foe posed a question, the answer to which was necessarily obscured by the very lack of definition of the issues at stake. In mid-July a Michigan Johnson man advised that for the best interests of the President no more Federal appointments should be made in the state until after the Philadelphia Convention, when "we can see 'who is who.' "[7]

Uncertainty was confounded by the welter of animosity, suspicion and incrimination between parties and factions of parties. Democrats saw the vast majority of Republicans as enemies of the President's policies; Conservative Republicans viewed the bulk of their party as friendly to the President and potential battalions in his army. Strong Union men, whether of Whig or Democratic antecedents, bristled at the prospect of favors to "Copperheads"; Democrats who had reviled Lincoln labeled themselves the truest, most reliable friends of President Johnson. Since the Republicans were in office, and the Democrats out of office, change was almost impossible without either seeming to cast the coalition of the future in a predominantly Democratic mold or giving the appearance of ingratitude toward the now loyal Democracy. Even after the meeting of the Philadelphia Convention, patronage remained a dangerous weapon for him who wielded it. An anti-Radical Iowa Republican late in August appealed through Montgomery Blair to the "political good sense of the Head of Administration" not to let the contest over the restoration of the Union degenerate into a scramble for office. "Now it would be folly prior to the election to oust the well-behaved republican appointees. Fill one hungry aspirant's mouth, and the six others disappointed in the *boone broche* grow cold and disaffected. Wait, the ousted may also become open working enemies, where now they are half-disposed friends."[8]

Incoming letters to Thurlow Weed, who played a key though not unchallenged role in the disposition of New York patronage, abound in evidence of the difficulty in determining whether changes in particular offices would benefit the Administration. They also disclose the political damage that followed certain removals.[9] Just before the election, Weed wrote Seward apprehensively: "I do not know how we shall come out of the election. . . . We are weakened by removals and appointments of Postmasters. The changes at Little Falls and Oswego will cost many hundred votes."[10] Many patronage problems received the direct attention of the President, and his files also reflect their hazards. Complaints reached him that men were being discharged who were his friends; in some cases prudence or "justice" required reinstatements.[11] In one instance, the President wrote a personal letter of apology to an ousted official.[12] Not willing to trust the usual channels of patronage information, the President initiated private direct reports to advise him, in the words of one such informer, "of your friends in office and your enemies."[13] One of Johnson's agents was the colorful Dan Rice, famous circus clown, who combined politics with both his performances and his off-duty leisure. "Persons who hold office under the government I devote particular attention to," he reported; "from the nature of my calling I have a splendid opportunity to discover who are worthy and who unworthy of government patronage."[14]

The gravest danger, perhaps, was that appointments would seem to confirm the damaging suspicion that the President's party of the future would turn out to be the old wolf of the "Peace" Democracy hiding under the patriotic hood of Johnson's wartime record, or the deadly charge that the President himself was following Tyler's example in deserting the party that had elected him. As late as April, 1866, one observer could find the key to Johnson's political appointments only in "his frantic fear of being what he calls 'Tylerised.' "[15] Early in August a Philadelphia War Democrat was delighted that the work of removing officeholders had begun, but warned that "there is a Scylla as well as a Charybdis in the path." The reported appointment of a man identified with the sympathizers in the rebellion "cannot help, but will certainly injure your cause." He hoped that the rumor was erroneous and that a more judicious selection would be made from the War Democrats.[16] Though appointment of men with Union military records was the most attractive policy open to the President,[17] even that might appear injudicious in the case of a well-known Democrat. Some Democrats with an eye to ultimate rather than immediate advantage counseled against any Democratic appointments. From a Massachusetts man came the message: "What I mean by your friends touching the distribution of offices, is, conservative Republicans, not democrats—of which I am one—*they* will sustain you in any event."[18] George W. Morgan, Democratic candidate for the Ohio governorship in 1865, wrote that "the democracy have no favors to ask in the way of offices, but they do respectfully, but earnestly hope that your enemies . . . may be removed, and that conservative republicans may be appointed to fill their places."[19]

To find acceptable Republican Conservatives was often no easy task. The chairman of the Democratic State Central Committee of Kentucky asked that appointments be held up on the ground that the Democratic party in the state was the only political organization from which the President could hope for any support.[20] One New Hampshire Democrat who had returned from an encouraging patronage talk with the President in Washington wrote within a few weeks to complain of recent appointments going to men he considered Radicals. This was repelling the Democratic party, which would sustain the President's measures but would be "obliged to look only to its own organization for its future success." There was no support in the state for the Administration, he stoutly maintained, "outside the Democratic Party."[21] As this letter suggests, many Democrats were not content with the long view but expected recognition forthwith, and some scarcely veiled a threat that without it the Democracy would abandon the President.

Where the availability of Conservative Republicans was greater than in New Hampshire or Kentucky, formidable hazards to their appointment had to be recognized. Though loyal to the President when named for office, they might not remain so. The danger lay not only in their developing attitudes that might differ from those of the President, but also in their attachment to rival candidates for the 1868 nomination. "Don't appoint a General Grant man," a New Yorker cautioned Johnson in reference to the influential post of naval officer. "No, no. All Johnson men, or all radicals; but do not appoint any *from our side* who are for anybody but you: when the time comes should you *then* decline a canvass, it *will be time enough* to appoint men who are looking towards other men than yourself for President."[22]

Johnson's failure to make swift and sweeping use of the patronage does not mean that his power of appointments was a negligible factor during his first fifteen months in office. At his disposal were vacancies that occurred in the normal course of events, all Federal offices in the seven Southern states without loyal governments at the time of Lincoln's death, and even state and local offices there to which appointments were made by his provisional governors. Another aspect of his power is suggested by an exchange of letters between New York's Senator Morgan and an apprehensive California postmaster who had been appointed in July, 1865, but whose name had not yet been sent to the Senate for confirmation by March, 1866. "I will state," wrote Morgan, "that there are a great number of Post Master and other Federal Officers, whose appointments were made during the past summer and autumn, still awaiting the action of the President: and it is impossible to give any decided opinion, as to when they will be again considered by him."[23] Since without such Presidential action the appointees would be out of office after Congress adjourned, the delay made them in effect hostages for political fidelity. A few judicious removals, or even rumor of removal, could also serve as insurance against disloyalty. Action taken on one key office set off major repercussions. A removal made in San Francisco in November, 1865, was reported to have filled other officeholders critical of the Administration's Reconstruction policy with consternation and alarm. "It was an exhibition of power and nerve which appalled them."[24] S. L. M. Barlow, the influential New York Democrat, wrote in December that it was unnecessary to turn out any large number of officeholders. One or two prominent appointments if well made would insure the control not only of New York but of a half-dozen other states as well.[25]

The President, however, did not everywhere limit removals to a selected few. In Pennsylvania, before the end of April, 1866, he set "radical heads flying in all directions."[26] He may have intended to make the state an unmistakable example to others, or he may have meant the Pennsylvania removals as the beginning of a general patronage offensive. If the latter, he was probably persuaded to defer it either in view of the hazards already mentioned or because such an overt attempt to punish men for sustaining the views of Congress endangered Senate confirmation and stirred up a threat in Congress to cripple his patronage power by legislation.

In November, 1865, Montgomery Blair offered an interesting explanation for some of the appointments he did not approve—in particular that of General Kilpatrick, who had campaigned in New York for the Republicans, to a diplomatic post in Chile. He wrote Barlow: "These appointments tho disagreeable to me & such as I never wd adopt is yet intended to enable him to divide the Rep party & to insure our success. It is more effectual he thinks than my plan wd be. No one can tell which plan is best nor is it material. I think either will succeed. Mine has the advantage of being more direct."[27]

Perhaps the most important Federal patronage posts in the 1860's were those in the Customshouse of New York City. Here in mid-August, 1865, Johnson removed both the naval officer and the collector, gave the Democrat Odell the former office and his close personal friend Preston King the collectorship. These moves, as we have seen, were considered of major political significance in connection with New York's November election.[28] After King's suicide Johnson faced an important and difficult appointment decision, one he did not finally make until the following April. A wealth of private correspondence discloses the pressures and problems involved in this appointment, and their resolution illuminates Johnson's method and aim in handling the patronage.

The War Democrats, those who like Johnson had supported Lincoln in 1864, early began pressing for a man of their own. General John A. Dix and General John Cochrane, both of whom had supported the pro-Johnson Democratic movement in New York, were their leading candidates. War Democrats were not agreed on one candidate, but they were of one mind in opposing any Weed-Seward man and in urging delay until false friends could be separated from true. The appointment would be the signal to determine the future complexion of politics; it could be the bridge over which to bring the Democratic masses to a loyal support of the President. The most important consideration, they argued, was to beware of men long in politics and to find a man uncommitted to others who would *without any doubt whatever, support you and your policy* in 1868." Their motto was: "Grind your *own axe* upon *your own* grindstone." For aid they turned to Montgomery Blair, to James Gordon Bennett, and in their anti-Weed animus even wished to conciliate Horace Greeley.[29]

Other Democrats of greater political regularity and closer to the center of party power in the state also offered advice and candidates. Apparently overtures were not initiated until the third week in December. By this time the resentment of New York leaders over Johnson's failure to aid them in the November election had been buried under their satisfaction with his December message to Congress. After reading that state paper, Barlow had sent an enthusiastic letter to James Hughes, a political confidant and a Washington attorney who handled business matters and lobbying for Barlow. The letter had declared the President "in the front ranks of statesmen" and had predicted that if he pressed the announced policy "without being driven from his course by the Congressional Caucus, he will not only win, but will place himself above the partizanship of all sections, now seeking power through the ordinary acts of mere politicians."[30] Without asking permission, Hughes immediately sent Barlow's letter on to the President.[31] Barlow was not displeased, though he made it clear that he also wished Johnson to know that the one obstacle to a union of Conservatives powerful enough to give the President control of Congress was his adherence to Stanton and Seward.[32] Barlow thought the Republican party was on the verge of disintegration and held that moderate Republicans would join the Democrats in support of the President. He expected that "Seward and Stanton will seek to influence the new party as they have the Republican party in the past, and I am utterly opposed to any alliance with them and to the formation of any new party in which they are to become the permanent leaders."[33]

Writing for Dean Richmond as well as himself, and including the assurance that the state party was committed to the President's plan of reconstruction, Barlow in a letter of December 21 asked Hughes to talk with Johnson about the New York collectorship. He wanted the President to know "that if he wants any suggestions from Mr. Richmond . . . he can have them." If the President found it necessary to appoint a Republican or a Democrat under Weed's control, "we prefer to have nothing to do with the selection. If he is able to appoint a democrat, then we can readily suggest names to him." Barlow did not wait to name the man who would receive the most complete endorsement from his political associates. He was Sanford E. Church, a regular McClellan Democrat with a good record of supporting the war effort. "In one month he would have the state of New York in his hand against the combined force of Weed, Greeley and all the rest."[34] The next day Barlow wrote to recommend his friend Judge Shipman of Connecticut, as perhaps more available than Church since he was not so prominent a Democrat, having been out of active politics for some years. If the President could "screw his courage up to the mark . . . and appoint a full blooded war democrat, then Church is the man, but if he is afraid of this as being too bold, then Shipman will in reality do just as well."[35] Apparently Barlow obtained Dean Richmond's approval for his suggestion of Shipman, though Church was the Albany boss's first choice.

At Hughes' suggestion, Barlow sent Church an urgent letter early in January urging the candidate to make a special trip to consult with the Washington attorney. Church readily agreed to do so.[36] Barlow's preference, however, was for his friend the Judge; but the overridingly important consideration was that the appointee should be a good Democrat. If the President were ready to go even further with the Democracy than would be the case if he appointed Church, the *World*'s owner and his associates would be pleased to have John Van Buren, the prominent Democratic leader and vigorous campaigner of 1865, who had proposed the immediate nomination of Johnson as the Democratic presidential candidate for 1868. They had hope, however, of getting Van Buren into the Cabinet and another man of their liking in the collectorship.[37]

Barlow was soon writing Montgomery Blair to enlist his influence with the President. "We are all very much exercised about the Collectorship of the Port. Mr. Johnson has it in his power by one bold, wise, move to crush the Radical Congress. . . . But to make this move effective, the President must select a prominent member of our organization, one who had the confidence of Richmond,——,* Tilden and others of that class. If he does not, he will gain nothing from our side and will in the end find that he has no party. He needs a politician who can control our whole strength and at the same time draw from the ranks of the Republicans."[38] Montgomery was of a like opinion that the new collector should be a regular Democrat from the Democratic organization.[39] Throughout the negotiations he held himself "bound to act in concert with you [Barlow] & your clan in New York."[40] Within a few days Montgomery had a long interview with the President, presenting the Democratic position and buttressing it with his usual incisive arguments. He told Johnson that the latter could not succeed "except by recognizing the Democratic party as his party," that he could "get nothing from the Republican party but Mr. Raymond's very qualified support." Montgomery reported that his speech seemed to strike[41] the President, "& he will I have little doubt act on the views I expressed to him."[42] John Van Buren also saw the President about this time, and felt hopeful. Barlow had sent a long letter meant to guide him in the interview; it attacked all candidates for the office save the Democracy's own and ended on the note that the President had it in his "power to build up a great party."[43]

Names other than those of Church, Shipman, and Van Buren were offered by the New York Democracy, but they were men firmly committed to the party. John B. Haskin, who claimed as his own the pro-Johnson platform of the 1865 Democratic convention, thought it would be "poetic justice" and "a proper rebuke to the treachery of Republican leaders" if the appointment went to General Henry W. Slocum, who had headed the Democrats' fall ticket.[44] Slocum was acceptable to Barlow.[45] Haskin, Barlow and Tilden all counseled the President with a great flour-

* Name illegible.

ish of solicitude that he must appoint his own man, one (to use Haskin's words) "bound to *you* by 'hooks of steel.' "⁴⁶ They wanted, of course, a man "who will not be predetermined to help within the republican machine."⁴⁷ Apparently they saw no inconsistency in urging Johnson to chose as his "own man" someone firmly bound to their own interests. But then, they believed that the "future Johnson party will be the democratic party with accretions from all ranks at the North, and in the South" and that Johnson was "about to become our leader."⁴⁸ Even so, there was a note of conscious hypocrisy in their pleadings. "We are now trying to turn Cuckoo and lay our eggs in the Republican nest, with Johnson," Barlow wrote a close friend at the end of January, "and I think we shall succeed."⁴⁹

After Johnson's first veto, the Democrats had high hopes of a break between the President and his party, with an accompanying reorganization of the Cabinet. Their strategy then shifted from pressure for an immediate appointment to pressure for delay in selecting the collector. "His best friends here," wrote Tilden to Montgomery Blair, "are of the opinion that the President will best consult his own interests, the success of the policy upon which he has staked his own reputation and the hopes of the country, by deferring all *action for the present in this important case.* . . . It is decidedly expedient for the President to let men, cliques & parties develop themselves somewhat before he places a great power in hands from which he may wish, but feel embarrassed, in recalling it. . . . His disinterested and real friends here will be content to wait, to advise what is best for his interests, without seeking to check him into surrendering the great power of this office to themselves."⁵⁰

Until the very end, the Barlow-Blair faction maintained an adamant opposition to any reconciliation with Seward and Weed. In the very last days of the appointment uncertainty, Montgomery was still vigorously attacking Seward in public and in private. A draft letter to the President, which before sending Blair softened in words but not in sentiment, read as follows: "I intend to adhere to my opposition to Mr. Seward, who I really believe is more dangerous to our principles than Thad Stevens and Charles Sumner both together."[51]

Like the War Democrats and the regulars of the Democratic organization, the Weed-Seward interests, which included E. D. Morgan the businessman, former war governor and current senator from New York, and also Henry J. Raymond, the *Times*' editor now acting as leader of the Johnson Republicans in the House, had a lively concern in the collectorship appointment. As compared with the pressure from their opponents, their own counsel to the President appears relatively conciliatory. Their favorite candidate was H. H. Van Dyck, assistant treasurer in New York and a Republican of Democratic antecedents. Secretary of Treasury Hugh McCulloch opposed this suggestion on the ground that Van Dyck was too good a man to be spared from the Treasury post. Seward readily acquiesced in the elimination, Morgan did so more reluctantly, and Weed had a dozen alternate names to suggest. Moreover, Weed wrote Morgan that no one was "more concerned than the President this thing should be right—and what is right for him is right for us."[52]

That McCulloch's opposition was prompted alone by his concern for the Treasury service appears doubtful. His candidate was J. F. Bailey, a confidential agent of the Department. Bailey had the support of Parke Godwin of the New York *Evening Post*, a moderate Republican paper of Democratic lineage that clung both to the ideal of limited Federal power and to that of justice for the Negro. Godwin, like so many others, anticipated the disintegration of old parties and the emergence of new ones and advised the President to gather around him as officials able young men "not identified in any manner with the old factions or cliques" who would do justice to all and help mold the political future.[53] On the question of Bailey, the Weed forces, if not entirely adamant, certainly were not accommodating. Raymond believed the appointment would not be regarded as defensible by either the political or commercial interests involved, though "his *promises* on political matters are all that could be desired."[54] Senator Morgan was more emphatic: Bailey was unknown to the merchants and to the party; "it will not do."[55] Weed feared the appointment, considering Bailey "a Massachusetts man brought here by Chase, and can never be anything else."[56] The Chase allegation probably had foundation in fact, for one of Bailey's endorsers was John J. Cisco, the former Treasury official whom Weed had attacked and Chase had defended at the cost, as it turned out, of his place in Lincoln's Cabinet. Barlow, who was equally opposed to Bailey, considered him "simply Chase's tool."[57]

During the earlier phase of the struggle over the collectorship, Thurlow Weed would have willingly settled for a War Democrat. Henry G. Stebbins, a former Democratic member of Congress who had served briefly in the Union army, was on Weed's approved list; and he also had Democratic support,[58] though not that of Barlow, who called him a "mere *nominal* democrat." Barlow feared that Johnson would assume that Stebbins "represents the party," when in fact he was the "merest puppet in the hands of Pierrepont & Stanton & Blatchford & Seward"; and Barlow had taken steps to so inform the President.[59] A strong letter for Stebbins had arrived from J. W. Forney of the Philadelphia *Press* and Washington *Chronicle* early in January, when the relations between the editor and the President were still cordial. Forney had commended Stebbins as an able, honest, intensely national man with an organizing mind that "would make you a party or fight your battle, single handed."[60] After the break that followed Johnson's first veto, Forney's recommendation must have become a serious liability to Stebbins.

The political confusion among Union-Republicans and the delight among stalwart Democrats that followed upon the veto message and Johnson's intemperate February 22 speech attacking Sumner, Stevens, and Wendell Phillips as traitors, stiffened Thurlow Weed's attitude toward the New York appointment. Even before the break with Congress, a news report had gone out from Washington that the appointment of a Democrat would indicate that the President had gone over to the opposition.[61] After the veto such a choice would certainly be construed as evidence that Johnson was deserting the party which had placed him in office. At the end of February, Weed wrote Seward that it had become imperative "that a *Republican* be appointed Collector. *That* will confound the enemy."[62] And two weeks later his almost illegible scrawl reiterated the message to the Secretary. "Now it [the collectorship] is of vital importance. Two months ago I should have preferred to have seen it given to a War Democrat, like Col Stebbins, or Judge (A. J.) Johnson. *Now* it is essential—very essential—that some such man as Leavenworth, Littlejohn, Bowen or Harvey should be appointed." The same day Weed sent an almost identical report to Senator Morgan, adding, "*Now* it ought to be a man of Whig antecedents." Weed was consulting with "leading Democrats (not Copperhead) who are preparing the way for political reconstruction" and sent assurance that the "Loyal Democrats want to come to us."[63] Weed's "Loyal Democrats" could not have included Barlow or Manton Marble. Hearing that Leavenworth, "a friend of Weed and Seward," was about to be appointed, due to "Morgan's lately acquired influence," Marble urged Montgomery Blair to oppose the appointment as "an insuperable obstacle in the way of forming a Johnson party." Any such decision, according to Marble, would be a ruinous blunder in view of "the number of votes in the Electoral College cast by Ny."[64]

On March 16, there was a long consultation between Weed and Dean Richmond, leader of the upstate Democracy. If Weed's report was accurate, the Albany boss must have been acting independently of Barlow and Marble. According to Weed, the conference resulted in agreement upon a plan of political operation for the state and upon De Witt C. Littlejohn, a Weed Republican and former speaker of the Legislature, as the best choice "in the aspect we are viewing things."[65] Some time later Raymond sent Weed an account of a two-hour conference with the President. "We are out of the woods about Collector," he wrote. "The Prest. has been made to feel the absolute necessity of *at once* quieting the fears and strengthening the faith of the Union party." Raymond thought the appointment would be announced the following day and would go to either Bowen or Littlejohn or Depew.[66] In reply Weed expressed his hope that the choice would be Bowen or Littlejohn; he still thought of Stebbins, the War Democrat, as a possibility.[67]

By this time Senator Morgan was leaning toward Chauncey M. Depew, former New York secretary of state whom the Democrats, unhappily, held in bitter memory as the perpetrator of what they termed a "census fraud." Morgan was apprehensive about confirmation in the Senate if either of the other two candidates Raymond mentioned were chosen. Weed was willing to accept Depew, but distrusted him. Depew "has so far, kept along with both wings of our Party. I do not know him well enough to say that he *can* be a divided man." In this letter Weed spoke of the "Adversary" as vindictive and adroit, but predicted that the "People" would "be right" once they were satisfied that those who charge the President with deserting Union principles and Union men were in truth slanderers.[68]

The Weed camp, however, had to contend with the strong influence of Senator James Dixon of Connecticut, one of Johnson's three pillars of strength among Republicans in the Senate. Dixon had been supporting Judge Henry E. Davies of the New York Court of Appeals, a man of high repute but of uncertain past loyalty to the Republican party, and one generally tagged as an anti-Weed candidate. No less an authority than Secretary Seward believed in late January that Johnson preferred Davies over all others, and Weed had written the Secretary that Davies, "as you know, is a nuisance. Pray, if possible, avert such a calamity."[69] Barlow, too, emphatically opposed Davies, whom he considered "an obsequious ass" with "no friend or influence anywhere."[70]

Senator Dixon kept pressing the Davies appointment, and by March Secretary McCulloch had abandoned Bailey and embraced Davies' cause. Montgomery Blair believed that the New York judge would be appointed, although he himself thought Dixon had erred in not going for an "out and out Democrat."[71] Senator Morgan countered by inspiring and sending to the President a letter from Van Dyck, who bowed out of the picture as a candidate but took the occasion to do a polished hatchet job on Judge Davies. The Judge was bracketed with "your facile, softly-spoken, gently-pressing, individuals, who promise everything even before they are asked," and are " 'be all things to all men,' not in the Christian hope of 'saving some,' " but in the expectation of benefits for themselves.[72] Morgan thought he had scotched Davies, but three weeks after the President had read Van Dyck's letter the Judge still appeared to be Johnson's favorite candidate. R. M. Blatchford, banker intimate of Weed and Seward, wrote the Secretary on hearing from Washington that either Davies would yet obtain the coveted appointment or it would go to a Democrat after the Senate had adjourned. Davies had just seen Blatchford to tell him that his appointment waited only upon Seward's consent and had made "all kinds of promises of devotion to you and Weed, etc. Is it not best to take such promises and go in for him? I would be willing to be on his Sureties and thus help to keep him straight."[73] There is nothing to indicate that Seward withdrew his opposition. Just a few days before final decision was announced, Senator Dixon intensified his pressure upon the President and arranged "another interview" between Johnson and Davies. Senator James Henry Lane of Kansas, who had just deserted fellow Republicans to support the President's second veto, also made a last-minute appeal for Judge Davies.[74]

The Weed-Seward forces, as well as Dixon, had the President's ear, but it is not likely that they enjoyed his full confidence. The pleas that had reached him for delay in selecting a collector had largely been motivated by a desire to block an appointment favorable to the Weed interests. The insinuations and charges of disloyalty made against Seward and his allies appeared to have some foundation in Raymond's acquiescence at the opening of Congress in the establishment of the Joint Committee on Reconstruction. The *Herald* in December advised the President to keep Raymond's associates out in the cold if they had the impudence to present themselves at the White House with a candidate for the collector's post; let them wait "and see how the New York Congressmen vote on the question of reconstruction when the report of the Joint Committee comes before Congress."[75] Secretary Seward had forestalled a rebuff to Weed by persuading him not to ask for an interview with the President after Weed had come to Washington expressly for that purpose.[76] The Springfield *Republican*'s able Washington correspondent sent a report early in February that Johnson "means to hold the vacant place as a rod over New York republicans."[77] Senator Morgan had remained faithful in upholding the President's first veto; but in the interval between Raymond's reassuring report to Weed and Johnson's announcement of the appointment, the Senate on April 6, 1866, had upset the second veto with Morgan's vote counted against the President. In the House balloting three days later, Raymond vindicated his loyalty by supporting the veto, but the Republican representative from Seward's home district voted against the President. Montgomery Blair quickly seized upon this as evidence to persuade Johnson of Seward's perfidy: "He will not even allow Mr. Pomeroy the Representative of the Auburn District who is known to do nothing he does not sanction to sustain you."[78]

A week after Blair's letter, Johnson announced his decision. The office of collector went to Henry A. Smythe, President of the Central National Bank of the City of New York. In mid-December there had been a long interview between Smythe and the President, which had left the banker and his friends sanguine but without a definite commitment. Although Weed had received a confidential note some weeks later that Smythe was very much in the running, and although Smythe himself claimed that all parties advocated him from every city and nearly every state, he had apparently not been considered a major contender for the office.[79] The few references to Smythe in the Johnson letters before late March were brief and slighting. Smythe was characterized by a McCulloch ally as popular among his personal friends and a worthy citizen but physically infirm and one who "would add no positive strength to the administration."[80] In his December letter, Barlow had dismissed Smythe as "an excellent merchant (a connection of mine) and a good fellow," but "as for use to the Country he may be counted out as of no importance whatever."[81]

Smythe, who was Mrs. Barlow's cousin, had written Barlow in November asking him to "pull a string in my favor—I can get any number of merchants to back me—but politically I am nowhere—except that I am sound & loyal—but as you know I am no politician—do not like those who are—& would rather not get anywhere—than accomplish it through Weed & Co.,—or anyone who would expect to control or govern me. I should expect to serve my govt & the administration & to please the merchants & after that anybody that choses to be suited."[82] Barlow, however, had not chosen to pull any wires. Not until the end of March, apparently after further importuning from Smythe, did he write Montgomery Blair as he had "promised and said everything I could properly say under the circumstances."[83] What he could properly say was that Smythe was "one of the best fellows alive," "a friend of the President, and can be trusted," a "thousand fold better" than men such as Davies and Stebbins, but that he was not enough of a politician to be able to do the President "much real service." Barlow still preferred "an out and out democrat," particularly Shipman, but if this were unattainable Smythe's appointment would be the next best thing. He would "do very well if he knew that the President expected him to take advice. . . . I think Smythe has sense enough to know that in such matters Richmond's head is better than his own, though I still cling to the idea of Shipman."[84]

Montgomery Blair recognized that Barlow's letter was "dictated by private friendship" and did not constitute a political endorsement. He had not presented it to the President because he had been trying, on word from Richmond, to prevent an appointment if possible. "If however you & the Sachem say Smythe, why so be it—Smythe's brother in law Dr. E. C. Franklin [?] is a special friend of mine & I wd greatly rejoice to favor him."[85] After this cordial invitation to give Smythe clearance, Barlow did so, but with reluctance, making it clear that Richmond and his associates preferred Judge Shipman. To use his own characterization, made months later, Barlow had been "finally dragooned into writing."[86] Since his Connecticut friend, he inferred, would not receive the nomination, he asked for him the place of New York district attorney, recently opened by its incumbent's decease. As for Cousin Smythe, "well—if the President appoints him, we shall be satisfied & Harry will do as the President advises, provided he tells him plainly what he expects, and after Shipman we all prefer him, to Davies, who has no friend or influence anywhere, or to Depew or Littlejohn who are already sold, body & breeches to

Seward."[87] Montgomery read to the President that part of Barlow's letter concerning the collectorship; they discussed the matter at length, and Montgomery "did not conceal the fact that Smythe's appt would be agreeable to me on your account." Johnson "finally told me I might write you that Smythe wd be appointed. I think he had almost come to that conclusion before I saw him, but not quite."[88]

Meantime Smythe, chagrined at being kept waiting as the willing bride at the altar, had appealed in late March to Johnson's son-in-law, Judge Patterson. "It is said, there is no one near the President to strongly advocate me—may I ask *you* to speak for me?"[89] He had also stimulated a number of supporting letters: from Charles G. Halpine, an influential Irish Democrat and journalist-poet who had fought Tammany before the war, served in the Union forces, and now edited the *Citizen*, the newspaper of New York city reformers; from William S. Huntington of Jay Cooke and Company; from Robert J. Walker, former Mississippi senator, expansionist, speculator, and close associate of bankers; and from the prominent Democratic senator from Maryland, Reverdy Johnson. Smythe and his friends pushed his selection as the merchants' collector—businessmen would count his appointment "a noble recognition of their value to the body politic"—and as the man who could free the President from "cliques" and "wire pullers." Smythe pledged himself ready to unselfishly "*serve Andrew Johnson*," and no one else. The Democrat Walker emphasized Smythe's qualification as "a Johnson *Republican. . . .* The appointment of a democrat, will keep back wavering Republicans." Halpine gave assurances that the nomination would be "most acceptable" to the Democrats; Reverdy Johnson was certain that it would receive "the sanction of the South."[90]

It is clear that Smythe was not the choice of the Seward faction, though Weed at the last moment probably gave his assent to Smythe as a lesser evil than Judge Davies or a Democrat. Weed certainly accepted the appointment loyally and helped to secure Smythe's confirmation when that appeared in doubt. Morgan thought Smythe was incompetent and that the President had taken a great hazard, but did not oppose the nomination in the Senate.

In mid-June, following the appointment, Weed was reporting to Seward that Collector Smythe was well disposed but inexperienced; a few months later, however, Raymond was sending a quite different message. "I cannot explain it nor understand it—but Collector Smythe is *against us*." And Secretary McCulloch was giving Weed feeble consolation; he could "not imagine what influence was operative upon Smythe that he was still giving cause for complaint to the friends of the Administration."[91]

Though Smythe was presented as a Republican of Whig antecedents, his political past was so unknown and uncertain that in order to quiet Senatorial apprehensions Weed and Morgan had to obtain from him an explicit disavowal of the rumor that he had voted for McClellan and Seymour.[92] It is extremely doubtful that Smythe's denial, at least in respect to McClellan, was an honest one. In September, 1864, he had written his cousin giving advice meant to aid McClellan's candidacy and flatly stated, "I intend to go in for him, & to support him."[93] The *Herald* editorially interpreted the appointment as a Presidential signal that the fight for his Southern policy was to be made within the lines of the Republican party.[94] Yet Smythe had just been actively aiding the Democratic gubernatorial candidate in neighboring Connecticut, with the President's knowledge, probably with the President's approval, and perhaps at the President's instigation![95] The *Herald*'s news columns reported that while Weed was claiming control of the new collector, anti-Tammany Democrats and anti-Weed Radicals were busily contesting his pretensions.[96] This remarkably ambidextrous "non-politico" was accomplishing the feat, to credit his own report, of having "the strongest kind" of letters sent off to doubting senators from James Gordon Bennett, Thurlow Weed, and Horace Greeley![97] Within a few weeks the *Herald*'s editorial columns added a further incongruous note by asserting that all the cliques claiming Smythe had been outgeneralled by Richard B. Connolly, loyal son of Tammany and Mozart Hall, with "Alphabet Barlow" acting as his aide-decamp.[98]

Senator Morgan understood what had happened. "I shall make the best of it," he wrote Weed. "It is the President's appointment."[99] The chosen man, it would appear certain, had convinced the Chief Executive that "I have *but the two aims*—viz—to be an unexceptionable collector—& to serve and sustain the President *throughout.*"[100] Even to the discomfiture of those who had given the counsel, the President had prepared to grind his own ax upon his own grindstone. After the initial surprise and confusion, all factions might lay claim to the new collector, but like Senator Morgan and S. L. M. Barlow they were trying to make the best of it. Johnson had made free with his coattails, but he had held fast to the coat itself.

The New York collectorship episode is a revealing case study of the complications attendant upon the political use of appointments. It in no way suggests, however, that Johnson ignored the power of patronage nor that it was a negligible factor in politics prior to the August harvest of officeholders. Those who look to the "loaves and fishes" as determinants of politics might well consider the wonder expressed in a letter of late February, 1866, from a friendly Ohioan to the President. "It is a strange sight!" he wrote. "You have both patronage and principle with you; and yet there are more men, not fanatics, who appear to side with Congress as against your present policy."[101]

The crux of the difficulty, and the explanation of the puzzle, lay not in Johnson's handling of the patronage, but in the dissent of many Union-Republicans to the Ohioan's assumption that principle as well as patronage resided exclusively with the President. One such, the postmaster of Atchison, late colonel of the Kansas infantry and personal friend of the President, wrote in August to offer his resignation. He believed that the Republican party was not "all that it should be, & some of its members are rash & reckless," but he could not bring himself to give approval to the call for the Philadelphia Convention. Party policy as indicated by congressional approval of what was to be the Fourteenth Amendment he believed the most satisfactory basis attainable for a generous and just settlement of the Southern problem. Though in need of office, he wrote, "I cannot stoop to pretence. . . . I hold principle far, far above the benefits to be derived from holding official place, and if, as an honest and sincere Union-Republican

I cannot retain position under a Union-Republican Administration, I must give it up. And in regard to this you alone can decide."[102] Atchison's postmaster had taken a stand based on principle rather than patronage, but he had not yet repudiated the President. By the time he wrote, however, there was left little middle ground; with the fall campaign gaining momentum, the time was fast approaching when the choice must be either for Andrew Johnson or against him.

7 RESTORATION, RECONSTRUCTION, AND CONFUSION

THE OPPOSITION TO JOHNSON WHICH DEVELOPED OVERWHELMING strength between late February and early November, 1866, was in startling contrast to the wide and cordial support given the President during his first ten months in office. Many factors help to explain this apparent fickleness of public opinion. Of these, the one which has received least recognition from historians is the amazing ambiguity that characterized President Johnson's attitudes and policies up to the veto messages. Though in some degree the ambiguity persisted even beyond the vetoes, these marked the beginning of the end for that uncertainty in respect to the President's intentions which had enabled men of opposite convictions, prejudices, and aims to accept without rancor and generally with approval the President's policy toward the South. Before the vetoes, only a few had spoken out in sharp opposition to Johnson; their leadership had been rejected as lacking in that moderation and wisdom requisite for the great task of binding up the nation's wounds.

Despite the general approval of the President, there existed in the months prior to the vetoes an undercurrent of uncertainty and apprehension. The Democrats' chief organ, the *World*, awaited the President's December message to Congress for certain knowledge of whether or not "he will yield to the clamor of the revolutionists who insist that he shall reconstruct the Union, instead of restoring it." The Administration had as yet encountered "no ostensible and organized opposition," which in view of the "vehement antagonism of views known to exist among our citizens . . . is as remarkable a phenomenon as any in the history of politics." The annual message would terminate "the present unnatural state of things, in which men holding the most conflicting views on the most fundamental questions, are alike courting and claiming the President."¹ Still smarting from the November defeat in New York, Barlow was writing the Confederate General Richard Taylor: "Our people are rather more inclined to favor Johnson than when you left. They believe that his action has been taken in pursuance of a policy, looking solely to the restoration of the States in Congress & that he believes, no matter how erroneously, that he could not win in any other way. But as we shall have his message in ten days there is no use in speculation."²

Greeley's *Tribune* likewise awaited the message, counseling against acceptance of what the "Sham Democracy" represented to be the President's attitude and plan. "No other person can interpret the President so fairly and clearly as himself."³ The *Herald*'s Washington correspondent reported much speculation and solicitation about the message as members of Congress gathered for their first session under the Johnson administration.⁴ On the very eve of the message, a fellow journalist sent word to the Springfield *Republican* of "all sorts of reports and conjectures as to the probable course of the President." One Washington paper anticipated no material difference between the Chief Executive and Congress on the Reconstruction question; another saw a wide divergence.⁵ Through the deluge of editorial comment that followed the message ran a persistent reference to the "intense anxiety" and "popular suspense" with which the President's statement had been awaited by the public, North and South, Democrat and Republican.⁶ The people, stated one such editorial, "have been eagerly seeking explanation for many months."⁷ Another commented, "Wall Street has stood in almost silent expectancy; and everywhere have been presented those indications which mark a people swayed alternately by fear and doubt and hope."[8] Some papers issued extras to meet "the urgent desire of the public" to read "the anxiously expected document";[9] innumerable others curtailed their usual news and comments to make room for the complete text of the President's message. Distant papers were markedly appreciative of the Administration's forethought in sending out advance copies of the document.

Editorial response to the message paid tribute, time and time again, to Johnson's statement of his policy toward the South as "clear," "frank," "free from ambiguity," containing nothing "enigmatic or deceptive," without "evasion or equivocal opinions" on the issues at stake. True, there were a few dissenting voices that challenged its forthrightness; but convincing evidence of its disingenuous character appears not so much in their distrust as in the diametrically opposed interpretations placed upon the message even by those who extolled its clarity. The skillfull wording of George Bancroft, the historian and sturdy Democrat to whom the President entrusted the writing of the message, left an impression of frankness and complete definition. Johnson's decisions as to the substance of the document prolonged the tortuous ambiguity that held the nation in suspense.

Most Democratic papers found the message a vindication of the position of the Democracy, a repudiation of Radical doctrine, and a certain indication that warfare between Congress and the President lay ahead. Most Republican papers held that the message extinguished any danger of conflict between the President and the party; one even characterized its principles as "unmistakably Radical" and another asserted it could not ask "anything more radical of the President!"[10]

On more specific issues interpretation of the message was equally conflicting. On the one hand, it was seen as indicating a fast approaching end to military occupation and military trials. On the other hand, it was read as giving no assurance of the removal of Negro troops, as passing over the matter of military arrests, and even as leaving open an indefinite continuation of martial law as a threat to coerce Southern states against their will.[11] Here are some of the questions raised by the message and the answers, in substance, as given by the press.

Had Johnson indicated that his policy to date was a success and that he would adhere to it?

yes   He declares himself satisfed with the results of his policy and declares his intention to adhere to it firmly.[12]

no   Johnson does not say in all respects that his policy has been successful; he intends sterner methods so far as milder ones do not have the desired result.[13]

uncertain He says nothing as to the success of his efforts at restoration.[14]

Did he wish the immediate admission of the Southern states with ratification of the antislavery amendment as the only condition to their restoration?

yes   The President's position is clear; with the adoption of the Amendment nothing more is necessary and Congress should admit the Southern states forthwith.[15]

no   He extends to the rebels no invitation to share in government; so far from advocating the immediate and unreserved admission of the late rebellious states, he declares their functions suspended for any period thought necessary for the safety of the country.[16]

uncertain The President implies that he favors admission from states that have adopted the Amendment, but recommends nothing.[17]

Did Johnson support the test oath that disqualified former rebels from taking seats in Congress to which they were elected?

yes   The public can see from the President's position why he has manifested a strong desire that no objectionable men [i.e., rebel leaders] shall be elected in the South.[18]

uncertain The question of the test oath and admission of southern members he touches very gingerly.[19]

*Had the President turned over to Congress the decision in respect to
Reconstruction?*

> yes   He candidly leaves Congress an unrestricted field of ac-
>   tion; his previous course led us to hope that he would
>   insist upon rapid restoration but he abandons the entire
>   matter to Congress; nothing is more admirable than the
>   unreserved way the President has submitted the solution
>   of the reconstruction question to Congress.[20]
>
> no   Johnson has left no part whatsoever for Congress; such
>   states as have complied with his terms are clearly entitled
>   to their seats in Congress and any opposition would be
>   regarded by the President as unconstitutional and revo-
>   lutionary; the President assumes that it is for him alone
>   to decide what qualifies the states for admittance, Con-
>   gress has power only to judge the technical qualifica-
>   tions of members elect.[21]

Editorial writers generally accepted at face value Johnson's assertion that the freedmen must be protected in their property and
liberty and saw on the President's part a sincere concern for the
Negro's future. But they disagreed as to how he meant protection
to be guaranteed. Most believed that as distinct from the right to
grant suffrage, which the President assigned to the states, he held
that the national government had constitutional power to establish
and enforce the freedmen's rights as free men. Some saw this
protection attributed to Executive action, some to the courts, but
most commentators held that Johnson had invited Congress to
legislate on the matter. "Without any doubt any action which
that body may take towards accomplishing the proposed object,
will meet with the cordial approval of the President."[22] Some
readers of the message, however, saw in the President's words an
exclusive delegation to the states of all action to secure civil rights
for the freedmen, or even that such an advance in status must
rest upon the former slave's own record and the benevolence of
his late master.[23]

The support for the President that was widespread among
moderate Republicans, and not exceptional among those who considered themselves Radicals, depended in large measure upon two
related interpretations of his actions and his words. They read

them as granting to Congress a major share in formulating the conditions upon which the rebellious states would be received back into the body politic and as giving assurance that justice and equal rights, in all matters save suffrage, would be secured for the liberated slaves. These expectations of most Republicans were to prove unwarranted, but for this not they but the President was responsible.

In a close scrutiny of Johnson's policies and attitudes it is difficult to arrive at any more charitable conclusion than that the ambiguity so evident in the December message was consciously assumed. Perhaps it resulted from the instinctive reactions of the politician rather than from deliberate design. In either event full responsibility for misconception and subsequent disillusionment rests with Johnson.

Students of history have often seen in the conflict between Johnson and Congress a clash between the executive and legislative branches of government as to which was possessed of the legal power to deal with the seceded states. Yet Johnson himself did not claim that Reconstruction, or restoration as he preferred to designate the process, was an exclusively executive function. Such a claim would need to have rested on the war powers of the Presidency, an authority used by Lincoln to justify the Emancipation Proclamation. In the nearly nine months prior to the meeting of Johnson's first Congress, he established for the Southern states a procedure for restoration. When he came to explain this, however, he relied primarily upon pragmatic rather than upon theoretical justification. Military government, he said, would have been divisive, expensive, damaging to peaceful restoration, dangerous in the power of patronage and rule it entrusted to one man. Hence he had appointed civil provisional governors directed to call conventions and order elections. Though in effect the regime of the provisional governors was a military occupation, Johnson did not recognize it as such nor justify his course on the basis of the war powers of the Commander-in-Chief. When Congress met, he did not assert an exclusive authority over the South but did acknowledge the right of each House "to judge, each of you for yourselves, of the elections, returns, and qualifications of your own members."[24] This expression was diversely interpreted, as we have seen, but generally accepted as an invitation to Congress to participate in the Reconstruction process.

Had Johnson wished his attitude toward Congress to have been unequivocal, the message could easily have made his meaning explicit. Secretary Seward had sent to the President, probably at the latter's invitation, a draft for the message which left little room for doubt. The relevant passages of Seward's version read as follows:[25]

When such governments shall have thus been established, it will be as necessary as it will be just, and in harmony with the Constitution to receive Representatives from the insurrectionary states into the Congress of the United States. The power, however, in this respect, belongs, not to the executive department of the government, but to Congress. I leave it there with entire confidence in the wisdom, prudence and patriotism of the National Legislature. . . .

I have not at any time fixed, and it is not my purpose now to insist upon, or ask Congress to fix with exactness, upon a detailed scheme to be applied in all cases for the restoration of their political connection with the Union. On the contrary, I have held, and with the sanction of Congress, shall for the present continue to hold, through the agents of the national government in the several states, such control therein as would be sure to prevent anarchy, and at the same time favor the efforts which are being made by the people in those states to effect on their part, the restoration so much desired by all. I am anxious that the Executive department of the government shall be relieved, as soon as compatible with the public safety, of these responsibilities, which are as delicate as they are exceptional in their nature and foreign to the habits of our countrymen. I have thought it proper, however, for the executive department to insist upon three conditions, which are deemed essential preliminaries of a healthful, successful and permanent restoration. . . . With the fulfilment of these conditions, of which, relying upon the agreement of Congress, I still am hopeful, I shall be content, so far as depends upon the executive department of the government, to accept and recognize the lately insurgent states, as loyal members of the national Union, and their citizens as brethren in full standing within the national family and entitled to equal participation in its manifold and precious advantages and benefits.

Despite Seward's characteristically verbose writing, his passages clearly acknowledged that Congress was entitled to a role beyond that of technically passing upon the credentials of the members-elect from the South. Had Johnson wished to be equally explicit he would not have adopted as his own the phraseology of the final message. An explicit recognition of congressional authority, however, would have antagonized the Northern Democracy and the South.

On the other hand, Johnson could readily have made a clear statement of the theory dear to the Democracy: namely, that Congress had no right to decide whether the rebellious states were ready for readmission or to prescribe conditions. To have done so would have alienated a large part of the Union-Republican membership. Johnson chose to be ambiguous.

That Johnson avoided a clear statement as to congressional authority points up the fact that there was not an obvious and consistent Presidential theory of Reconstruction. The President's position did not rest upon a claim of exclusive executive jurisdiction. Nor was it consistent with the careful formulation later made by William Archibald Dunning, the father of modern historical scholarship in respect to Reconstruction. Dunning states that according to Johnson's theory, the seceded states, being indestructible as states, required only the removal by Presidential pardon of the disability attached to their officers and people by the fact of their having been insurgents. "With the removal of this disability, the *ante-bellum* status returned."[26] Under such a theory there would be no place for the imposition, either by the President or by Congress, of any conditions upon the states once they were reorganized by citizens who had received the grace of Presidential pardon.

Dunning's formulation is a reasonable interpretation of Johnson's statements in the December message as to the status of the Southern states. Johnson there held that a state could not secede, could not as a state commit treason, that by the attempt to secede, states "placed themselves in a condition where their vitality was impaired, but not extinguished—their functions suspended, but not destroyed." He said that he had exercised the power of pardon "exclusively vested in the executive," taking care to exact a recognition of "the binding force of the laws of the United

States" and of the "great social change of condition in regard to slavery which has grown out of the war."[27] But the President did not say either that he had no power to impose conditions upon the states or that he had not done so. Johnson *said* neither; but he *implied* both.

In respect to the antislavery amendment, Johnson stated that he had extended "an *invitation*" to the Southern states "to participate in the high office of amending the Constitution"; that it was not too much "to *ask* of the States which are now resuming their places in the family of the Union to give this pledge of perpetual loyalty and peace."[28] In other words, Johnson seemed to be saying, "I have required nothing beyond the terms of the pardon; in respect to anything more I have merely given friendly advice." Some two weeks earlier, in fact, Johnson had reassured the Mississippi legislature in almost these words that the Administration had no disposition "to dictate what their action should be but on the contrary, simply advise a policy" that would help restore normal relations.[29]

For Johnson to have implied that in directing the restoration process he had required nothing more than the amnesty or pardon oath was a patent fiction. Without examining in detail Johnson's dealings with the South, it is sufficient to state the indisputable fact that the President made clear to the formerly rebel states that as states they must (1) abolish slavery by organic state law and also ratify the Thirteenth Amendment; (2) declare null and void their acts of secession; and (3) repudiate all debts incurred in support of the rebellion. Held under military rule, with their future uncertain and apparently in the hands of the President, the secession states had little freedom of choice; conformity to Johnson's directives had been equivalent to acceptance of peace terms imposed by victor upon vanquished. A Washington correspondent had appraised the situation in a terse sentence: "The President is really dictator; that is, the southern people understand his strength, not only physical but moral and whatever he says must be done, they do."[30] Though some states were hesitant in acting, or did so with qualification, the explanation lies in the opportunity which Johnson's "kindly advice" approach seemed to present. His conditions, however, were substantially met; and they clearly did not represent the free decisions of Southern state conventions and legislatures.

Evidence that the actions desired from the states were recognized by the Administration as executive requirements, rather than advice to be freely accepted or rejected, is afforded by Seward's draft of the December message. The relevant passage is included in the long extract given above, but bears repetition: "I have thought it proper, however, for the executive department to insist upon three conditions, which are deemed essential preliminaries of a healthful, successful and permanent restoration." Seward then enumerated the conditions: each state must, first, abolish slavery by organic state law; second, accept the antislavery amendment; third, disallow and annul pretended secession and all debts resulting therefrom.

Seward's version of the message together with the course of events in the South during 1865 are conclusive. Johnson did not take his stand upon the basis of a clear and logical theory such as that seen by Dunning. Presidential actions were not consistent with it; Presidential words avoided its explicit statement. In itself, the lack of consistency implies no criticism, for Lincoln's distrust of "mere pernicious abstraction" as a guide to restoration of the South was eminently sensible in view of the unprecedented and extraconstitutional nature of the problem. Johnson, however, did not similarly disavow theory; rather, his words of December, 1865, *implied* a theory, but the implication did not square with the facts.

The impression given by the December message and earlier statements yielded a practical advantage to the President in his relations with the Democracy, North and South. Their potential protest against Presidential pressure during the process of Southern constitution-making, elections, and basic legislation was restrained by the fiction of "kindly advice" and "free consent." The South and its Northern supporters could bury animosity toward the President under the belief that his theoretical position was theirs. Their position, as emphatically stated by the *World*, was that the seceding states had never been "out of the

Union" and were entitled to all rights of states within the Union. This was the same position that Jeremiah Black had insisted the President must assume if he were to receive the support of the Democrats. The distinction between this and Johnson's position that the states had not seceded nor lost their character as states was, in fact, decidedly elusive. Indeed, though Johnson did not use the phrase in the formal exposition of his message, he is reported to have done so in private conversation; and it is a matter of record that he told a delegation from Virginia that he could not take the position that "a State which attempted to secede is out of the Union."[31]

The logical implication of the "not-out-of-the-Union" view was that the Southern states rightfully possessed all authority over their local affairs and all the rights of decision in respect to national matters which they had enjoyed before secession. This would preclude martial law, national interference in adjusting race relations, and any conditions preliminary to readmission of their representatives to Congress. Johnson's generalities about the Constitution and state rights enabled the Democracy to claim their conclusions as the logic of the President's own position and to press him for corresponding action. Johnson was unready to capitulate completely to the practical requirements that followed from the logic of the "not-out-of-the-Union" theory; neither was he prepared to deny the expectations which the Northern Democracy and the South derived from the conviction that he was in head and heart their champion. So long as the Democracy could hold to the fiction that nothing was required of the seceded states but loyalty, inconsistencies in the President's course could be condoned as politic diversions to outmaneuver the Republicans. The merit of the President's message, one Democratic paper commented, "consists of its generality. It leaves the President at liberty to finally side with the Democracy."[32]

Failure to recognize the ambiguity in the President's attitude toward Congress and the South has led to a distorted interpretation of an interesting episode that occurred at the opening session of the House of Representatives, December 4, 1865. Edward McPherson, Clerk of the House, omitted from the roll call all names of members-elect from the formerly rebellious states. When Horace Maynard of Tennessee rose to protest the omission of his name, he was refused recognition. This incident has been presented as a Radical conspiracy, a declaration of war against the President, the beginning of a Radical revolution.

Actually, the matter of the roll call had been under discussion in the public press for weeks. Wendell Phillips had raised the question in July when he stated forcefully his fear that Presidential pressure would result in McPherson's calling the names of all Southern members-elect and thus effect the immediate admission of the seceded states.[33] Long before Congress met, Bennett's *Herald*, together with the *World* and a number of other Democratic papers, were demanding that McPherson do just that. An act of March 3, 1863, directed the Clerk to make a roll of representatives-elect, and to place thereon the names of all persons, and such persons only, whose credentials showed that they had been regularly elected in accordance with the laws of their states or those of the United States. This was interpreted by the *Herald* and the Democratic press as permitting or requiring—their comments appear inconsistent as to the permissive or mandatory nature of the law—the inclusion of Southern members in the roll call of the House. They anticipated with delighted satisfaction that the Southern members would then wield the balance of power in the election of speaker and that once this was accomplished no requirements, not even the test oath, could interfere with the swearing in of representatives from the secession states. The Clerk of the House, exulted the *Herald*, "may have a golden opportunity for a brilliant *coup d'état* in support of President Johnson. . . . [He] may play a leading part in one of the most important revolutions of the nineteenth century."[34] Both the *Herald* and the *World* anticipated that before Congress met the case for roll call and admission would be made unassailable by the President's proclaiming the insurgent states restored to the Union, a proclamation that was not, however, forthcoming. The *World*, undaunted, pointed to the message of Benjamin Perry, provisional governor of South Carolina, as representing the views of the President; Perry had stated that it was the duty of the Clerk of the House to call the names of Southern members.[35]

The New York *Times*, on the other hand, raised the question of whether elections held under the Southern provisional governments would meet the conditions set by the law of 1863.[36] John Forney of the Philadelphia *Press* and Washington *Chronicle*, then loyally supporting the President, considered the Democratic expectations of McPherson "extraordinary" and cited precedents for excluding the Southern states from the roll call.[37] A. K. McClure, prominent Pennsylvania politician and publisher, interpreted the law as actually forbidding the Clerk to include members from the seceded states.[38] Greeley's *Tribune* saw in the demands of the Democratic journals an intent "to settle all questions of reconstruction" in a manner that would preclude Congress from any voice in their decision.[39]

In the midst of the controversy McPherson let it be known that he would not place the names of representatives from the formerly rebellious states on the roll of regularly elected members. The House itself must pass upon their claims; for him to do so, he quite reasonably held, would be to himself decide one of the most important questions before Congress.[40] Well before the legislators assembled for their first session, it was recognized that the names of the Southern members-elect would not appear on the House roll call. The *Times'* Washington correspondent, in fact, reported that the question of seating Southern claimants had almost ceased to attract discussion in view of the certainty that they would be excluded.[41] The Springfield *Republican* in commenting upon McPherson's decision, observed that the President had disavowed any desire to interfere with the action of Congress, that no Southern member would be seated until Congress had judged his state entitled to representation and himself both regularly elected and personally loyal, and that "Nobody can object to this."[42]

The omission of the secession states and their elected delegates from the House roll was neither unexpected, revolutionary, nor in defiance of the President. Had they been included, then indeed would the Clerk of the House have effected a *coup d'état*. He would have been pronouncing a judgment as to their status and their right to resume their places in the Union more explicit than any President Johnson himself had announced.

The establishment of the Joint Committee of Fifteen, like the omission of Southern names from the roll call, has been generally interpreted in accordance with the strictures of the *Herald* and the *World*. Two days before the opening of Congress, the Union-Republican caucus on motion of Thaddeus Stevens unanimously agreed to establish a committee to inquire into the condition of the seceded states and report whether they, or any of them, were entitled to representation; pending the committee's report, none of their members-elect would be seated. The caucus decision and the House action that followed have been seen simply as a skillfull and successful maneuver by Stevens, the Radical leader, to defeat the President by committing the entire Union party "knowingly or unknowingly . . . against the policy of the President."[43]

What has been overlooked is that this disposition of the problem of seating Southern representatives was first suggested in October by Samuel Bowles' Springfield *Republican*, a moderate, conciliatory Republican paper. The *Republican* welcomed the action of the House as an acceptance of its own proposal and as altogether "proper and prudent." It denied the Democratic charge that the move meant support for the theories of Sumner and Stevens. "On the contrary it implies a disposition to admit loyal representatives from loyal states on sufficient evidence." Admitting that Stevens might like to annul all that the President had done toward restoration, the paper asserted "all that the majority of the republican members want is evidence of the soundness of reconstruction as it stands, and security that the reorganized states will behave loyally and keep faith with the freedmen."[44]

Despite the apprehensions that preceded and the different interpretations that followed the President's December message, most Republicans believed that Johnson was willing for Congress to participate in the Reconstruction process. Many thought his actions and his words before Congress assembled indicated disappointment in the behavior of the states under provisional governments and a readiness to let their representatives, except those of Tennessee, stand waiting outside the doors of the House and the Senate, not indefinitely but for at least some little time.[45] The establishment of the Joint Committee was not a defiance of the President's wishes, as most Republicans interpreted them, nor did it create any fatal necessity for eventual conflict between Johnson and Congress. Cooperation and mutual adjustment were the earnest desire of the Republican majority; they intended to conduct the functions appropriate to the legislative branch of the government in friendship, and with accommodation. Johnson's vetoes, not Stevens' so-called maneuver, marked a beginning of the battle between Congress and the President. Only then did Johnson depart from the wide margin of ambiguity that had obscured a basic disagreement of purpose and principle.

The ambiguous nature of Johnson's statements and actions resulted in confusion not only at the nation's Capital, but in local politics as well. The fall campaign in New York, as we have seen, was replete with contradictory interpretations of the President's policy and with conflicting claims upon his support.[46] The Connecticut elections in the spring of 1866 are another example of confused practical politics. This state of affairs was, of course, intimately linked with Johnson's intention of creating a new national Johnson party. Though an expectation, it was not a reality nor even an officially acknowledged objective; meanwhile, local battles for office, in the traditional manner of American politics, were waged between the two established political parties.

In Connecticut, prenomination maneuvering began in November, 1865; and party conventions chose candidates and set forth platforms in mid-February, 1866, before the first veto. The Democrats wrote into their platform a strong pledge of support for President Johnson, approving the sentiments "which he has expressed against negro suffrage, the proposed amendments to the Constitution by the radicals, and his declared policy in favor of restoring the Southern States to their proper position in the Union, and the admission of their Senators and Representatives to the halls of Congress."[47] The Republican convention reconciled differences of opinion in committee and unanimously adopted resolutions that expressed confidence in both Johnson and Congress, and in their ability "to cooperate in securing . . . the extinction of the doctrine of Secession; the repudiation of all pecuniary obligations incurred in support of the Rebellion; the sacred inviolability of the national debt; the complete destruction of slavery in fact as well as in name; and the enactment of appropriate laws to assure to every class of citizens the full enjoyment of the rights and immunities accorded to all by the Constitution of the United States."[48] Then the convention adjourned with three cheers for Andrew Johnson.[49]

For governor, the Democrats chose James E. English, a substantial and respected former member of Congress who had voted in January, 1865, in favor of the Thirteenth Amendment. The Republicans selected General James R. Hawley, a staunch Union man, war hero, friend of the Negro, and one of the proprietors and editors of the influential Hartford *Press*. Gideon Welles, an old friend and intimate political associate of Hawley, considered him "really well intended and [as] fairminded as one can be who has been a zealous Abolitionist and is hopeful of political honors."[50]

Despite the harmonious nature of the Union-Republican convention, the campaign started off on a sour note that greatly embarrassed both Hawley and Welles. The Radical Hartford *Post* was smarting under the impact of a recent address by the President to a Virginia delegation in which he had equated "extreme men North" with Southern secession extremists and had stated that such Northerners stood in the way and "must get out of it."[51] The day after the convention, the *Post*'s leading editorial commended Hawley as "one of the men who, loving justice and devoted to the interests of humanity, is considered by President Johnson equally dangerous to the Union, with the rebels of the Southern States—one who must, in the language of the President, get out of the way." It continued, "The people of Connecticut by an unmistakeable majority, will demonstrate the impossibility of thus smothering the earnest convictions of thinking, progressive men."[52] The moderate Hartford *Courant*, widely believed to represent the sentiments of Republican Senator Dixon, took up the *Post*'s comment and demanded a statement from General Hawley. The *Post* replied by attacking the *Courant* for turning "grand inquisitor," defended its right to the free expression of its own opinion, and absolved Hawley from responsibility for anything except his own statements.[53] But the *National Intelligencer*, the Administration newspaper in Washington, was soon quoting the *Post* on Hawley, commending the Democratic endorsement of Johnson, and criticizing the Republican platform.[54] The whole Democratic press of Connecticut seized upon the opportunity to make political capital and to emphasize the Democratic view that English was a "Johnson man" and Hawley was not. The latter's embarrassment was increased by Johnson's veto of the Freedmen's Bureau Bill and the attack upon Sumner and Stevens in the President's speech of February 22.

In his paper, the *Press*, and in his own speeches, Hawley maintained a moderate tone, arguing that the entire Union party, Congress and the President included, were seeking the same *ends* and had no essential difference of *principle*, that the question at issue was one of *fact* as to the state of loyalty at the South, the submission of its bigoted elements to law and order, the protection and opportunity afforded freedmen for "anything like an equal chance in the race for life." The party was strong enough to admit and tolerate differences of opinion and to work out satisfactory decisions. Hawley pointed to the conditions and restrictions which Johnson had already imposed upon the South, challenged the Democrats to approve them, and accused his opponents of hypocrisy and self-seeking in their attitude toward the President.[55] Privately, the Union-Republican candidate was much troubled. He wrote Welles of his apprehensions and asked if it were not reasonable for the Union party to have some expression of good wishes from the Administration. "Let us deal honestly with one another," he told his old friend. "Perhaps I am blinded. I try to keep cool, but I do not see how any gentleman can fail to regret the President's speech on the 22nd. The *universal* feeling here is one of sadness and humiliation. Does he really mean to leave us entirely? . . . Who cares for scattered angry or weak utterances of Stevens and Sumner? They are not Congress nor the Union majority thereof. . . . For my life I cannot see the foundation for the President's hostility to Congress. He must have some personal friends and advisers who malignantly misrepresent all things. The whole loyal North was disposed not only to respect and support but admire and love him. But if Tom Florence & Co give him the coloring how can we be rightly judged?"[56]

No public endorsement came from the Secretary of the Navy. He did, however, write the editor of New Haven's leading Republican paper, clearly indicating that his views were not for publication, of his "personal regard for General Hawley," his own desire for the success of Administration policy and of those who supported it, and his "belief" that Hawley concurred and would act in conformity with that policy.[57] In his private diary, Welles confided his conviction that Hawley intended to support both the President and Congress, that the two would be difficult to reconcile, and that "if compelled to make an election he would be more likely at the present moment to do wrong, I fear, than right."[58] Welles rationalized his own conflict between loyalty to old friends and his desire for an uncompromising executive attitude toward Congress with the argument that the President should have made an issue with Congress in December. Since the Connecticut nominations had been made prior to a clear-cut issue, it was "too late now to change front or get up a new arrangement."[59]

Though restrained in his public statements, General Hawley was too honest a man to dissimulate. In response to a series of loaded questions at a public meeting, the General stated his views frankly. He recognized the force of many of the President's objections to the Freedmen's Bureau Bill, but admitted that had he been a member of Congress he would have supported the measure. He thought the President had spoken with provocation but with undue severity in respect to Sumner and Stevens, though he himself differed with some ideas of both, particularly with Stevens' plan for wholesale confiscations. He forthrightly supported suffrage for the Negro in Connecticut and expressed a personal desire for a constitutional amendment prohibiting discrimination on the basis of race, color, or religion; but he stated that he

did not favor extending the right of suffrage by Federal legislation. Making unmistakably clear his respect for Johnson, he said
that he was "nobody's man but his wife's." A truncated version
of the questions and answers was widely publicized by the Democrats as Hawley's anti-Johnson, pro-Negro "platform."[60]

The Democrats found much to stimulate their hope for victory, but they too had apprehensions as to the President's course.
Their candidate, English, came out unequivocally in support of
Johnson's veto and the speech of February 22, and also stated his
opposition to any further agitation on the question of Negro
suffrage, in Connecticut or elsewhere.[61] Under the banner of "The
Union, Johnson and English," a party rally wildly cheered when
the Republican postmaster of Hartford, E. S. Cleveland, deserted
General Hawley and spoke in favor of English as the candidate
who supported the President.[62] But privately, Democratic leaders
were writing Welles to complain of the President's silence, of
Postmaster General Dennison's letter of support for New Hampshire Unionists, of local officeholders' activities on behalf of their
opponents, of Republican claims that the Administration wished
the success of Hawley and spurned the votes of "Copperheads."[63]
In an attempt to relieve themselves of these handicaps, candidate
English made a pilgrimage to Washington and talked earnestly
with the President. Johnson was favorably impressed;[64] but, to
quote S. L. M. Barlow's report, "The President unhesitatingly
approves English, in private, but publicly his refusal to act, leaves
thousands in Conn. in the dark as to his real wishes."[65]

The rumors of Presidential support for English which his
Washington visit evoked, together with jibes from the Democratic press to the effect that Hawley was an anti-Johnson man
and opposed to the speedy restoration of the South, brought a
long and defensive letter to Welles from General Hawley. He
explained that in his speeches he always referred to the President
"in terms of the highest respect, while acknowledging . . . differences of opinion in the party." He desired, as a preliminary to
restoration, only to be "*very sure*" that the Southern states would
fulfill the conditions that had been "asked *by the President*"; re-
manding the South to a territorial status or "prolonging the ab-

normal & unnatural state of 'subjugated provinces' are ideas ab-
horrent to me." The Hartford *Times* and the New Haven
Register, Hawley assured Welles, were misrepresenting his position. Had the Secretary heard his statements on the stump, "I
KNOW that . . . while we might not agree *precisely*, you would not
find fault with my discretion, or my general principles."[66]

On March 20, Welles read the letter from Hawley to the
President.[67] The next day General Hawley was present in person
to talk with him and with Johnson. The Connecticut candidate
asked a letter of endorsement from his old friend, held a two-hour
interview with the President, and returned to tell Welles that he
was satisfied with Johnson's views and his intent to take no part
in a local election.[68] It is clear from subsequent correspondence
that Hawley hoped Welles would send a friendly commendation
for publication. But in answer to Hawley's request, Welles, in
effect, took the position that the policies of Congress and those
of the President were antagonistic, and that Hawley must make a
choice between them. He argued that Hawley's difficulties were
due to the nature of the platform resolutions adopted by the
Connecticut Republicans, and to Hawley's own failure to express
a preference for either Congress or the President. Also, according
to Welles, the letter Hawley had written him in February, after
Johnson's attack upon Sumner and Stevens, had expressed "some
apprehensions in regard to the President and some ideas respecting
the powers of Congress . . . [that] lean to the policy of the
radicals." If Hawley would send an avowal of his support for
the President's policy that would absolve him of the "ambiguity
and duplicity" of the Republican platform, then Welles could
"speak clearly, understandingly and explicitly to the President and
if deemed expedient to the public."[69] No reply came from General
Hawley, and no public statement was issued by Welles. Hawley
continued the campaign without departing from his position of
good will toward both the Republican Congress and the President.

The two candidates for governor were not alone in seeking
clarification from the President. Indeed, during the closing days
of the campaign, there were a series of interviews between John-

son and Connecticut politicos, both Democratic and Union-Republican. After each consultation, a reassuring report of the President's wishes was made public for Connecticut constituents; and these reassurances were as promptly denied by conflicting reports or interpretations of the same interview emanating from the opposite camp.[70] It was agreed that the President desired the success of "Union" candidates; but the Democrats labeled the Republicans "disunionists" and considered themselves the "Unionists." The Union-Republicans stoutly maintained that the Democratic interpretation was a ridiculous distortion of the President's view.[71] On the whole, the Democrats had the better of these exchanges, though in the end they lost the election by a very narrow margin.

The Hawley forces finally took the position that the President quite properly did not intend to interfere in a local contest, though his sympathies were still held to be with their candidate, and that they had asked for no interference on their behalf.[72] Toward the end of the heated contest, however, a sharp discrepant note was sounded in the editorials of Hawley's *Press*. "If Mr. Johnson considers Mr. English a better Union man than Gen. Hawley, he differs with his whole cabinet, with the entire republican party in Congress . . . and what is of more consequence to us than all else, *he differs* with THE REPUBLICAN PARTY OF CONNECTICUT which in lawful convention laid down its platform and with extraordinary unanimity chose Gen. Hawley as its candidate."[73] And a few days later, after questioning a report in the New York *World* that Johnson favored the candidates who supported his policy, the *Press* concluded, "The Union men of Connecticut are not, however, accustomed to vote under instructions from New York or elsewhere. There is too much of the spirit of old Put. in the Nutmeg State for that."[74]

There was good reason for this minor but unmistakable theme of asperity from the Union-Republicans. Evidence is now available that Johnson did, indeed, wish English to win. He was undoubtedly restrained by Welles and James F. Babcock, the most unreservedly loyal pro-Johnson men among Connecticut Union-Republican leaders, and probably also by Seward and by the distaste of other Cabinet members for any disassociation of the

Administration from the "War party."[75] The President, however, had not pursued a strictly "hands-off" policy. He had publicly refused the proffered resignation of Cleveland, the apostate Hartford postmaster, and sent written approval of "your political action in upholding my measures and policy."[76] The President's Kentucky friend and political advocate, General L. H. Rousseau, had spoken for English in the last days of the Connecticut contest. And just before the campaign ended, Johnson himself had sent a telegram which was triumphantly read at an "English and Johnson" rally. The President wired:[77]

In reference to the elections in Connecticut or elsewhere, . . . I am for the candidate, who is for the general policy, and the specific measures promulgated, of my administration in my regular message, veto message, speech on 22d February, and the veto message sent in this day. There can be no mistake in this, I presume it is known, or can be ascertained, what candidates favor or oppose my policy, or measures as promulgated to the country.

The implication could hardly be mistaken. General Hawley and the *Press* had openly differed with the President on the Freedmen's Bureau veto and the February 22 speech, and they were maintaining that the Civil Rights veto had no relevance for the Connecticut vote.[78]

Some weeks later, a key Democratic strategist wrote Welles that the English ticket would have won, "had we been favored with two weeks more, after that declaration of the President."[79] The accuracy of his diagnosis is questionable in the light of election results in other states the following October and November. Before then, however, even a man of Hawley's good will could no longer refuse to acknowledge a sharp conflict between the intentions of Congress and those of the President.

8 JOHNSON AND THE NEGRO

No uncertainty about the President caused more concern among Republicans, particularly those of the Eastern states, than his attitude toward the freedmen. As a people, Americans have always been alert to motives and intent behind matters judged of moral consequence; and both Johnson's contemporaries and historians have passed judgment upon his attitude toward the Negro. This raises a question which admits of no easy answer.

The December message, as we have seen, was generally received as reassuring. Sharp and bitter dissent, however, came from Wendell Phillips' *National Anti-Slavery Standard;* it found the tone of the President toward the freedmen "utterly repulsive."[1] The *Liberator*, William Lloyd Garrison's venerable weekly, also challenged Johnson's sincerity. Fair words, according to the *Liberator*, must be interpreted by acts; and it saw the President as working to place the governments of the Southern states in the hands of those already re-enacting Black Codes.[2] A more moderate and friendly challenge to the President, but one that, for this very reason, must have been the more disconcerting to its readers, was voiced by the Brooklyn *Daily Union:*[3]

If the nation is bound to defend the rights of the blacks, why has not the President incorporated such a defence in the conditions of re-admission? If justice only is the thing which can save us from suffering in the solution of the negro problem, why has the President quietly ignored justice just at the point where it becomes most absolutely essential that it should be observed? Just when the President proposes to establish each State securely and impregnably behind the banners of resumed Statehood, why does he leave the negro helpless?

President Johnson himself told a delegation of Negroes in February, 1866, that the "feelings of my own heart" had been "for the colored man"; that he had opposed slavery, first, because it had been a great monopoly that enabled an aristocracy to derive great profits and rule with an iron hand and, secondly, because of the abstract principle of slavery. But as a political leader in prewar Tennessee, Andrew Johnson, though an antagonist of the slaveholding aristocracy, had not been known as an opponent of slavery. A kindly master to the slaves of his household, he had on occasion spoken harsh words in respect to the Negro. It is clear that he regarded the whites as a race superior to the blacks, and that he harbored a deep antagonism to Northern Abolitionism.[4] Shortly after Johnson took office as President, the antislavery New York *Tribune* pointed out that the new Chief Executive would not be open to charges of "nigger-worship" since he had "always till now voted and acted as though Blacks had no rights which Whites are bound to respect."[5] Although the tone of the *Tribune*'s comment was friendly, its characterization may not have been altogether fair. During his wartime governorship of Tennessee, Johnson pledged to the Negro populace that he would be their "Moses"; he recognized that the war would kill slavery, welcomed its passing as the end of a disturbing element in the body politic, and loyally strove to implement Lincoln's desire that Tennessee should officially bury the institution.[6] He did not, however, attempt to prevent the exclusion of Negroes "not only from the ballot box, but also from the witness-box," a fact that the Democratic press later delighted in citing.[7]

In October, 1865, President Johnson went far toward repudiating the view associated with the Blairs and the Democracy, and one most obnoxious to Republican friends of the Negro, namely that "this is a white man's country." "This is your country as well as anybody else's country," he told a regiment of Negro soldiers who had gathered to pay him tribute. "This country is founded upon the principle of equality. . . . He that is meritorious and virtuous, intellectual and well informed, must stand highest, without regard to color."[8] Private letters to the President, however, strongly suggest that Johnson's views were close to those of the Democracy. A Tennessee friend remembered well "your remark, and that was, Gorham, I am for a *White* Man's Government in America."[9] Harvey Watterson, Johnson's trusted representative in the South, commended a general for command in North Carolina. "Like yourself, too, he is for a white man's government, and in favor of free white citizens controlling this country."[10] There is grave doubt that Johnson's private views were ever completely emancipated from his heritage of Southern racial attitudes. His private secretary, in 1868, noted in his shorthand diary that "the President has at times exhibited a morbid distress and feeling against the negroes." He made note of the President's querulous demand, on seeing a half-dozen Negroes at work about the White House grounds, whether "all the white men had been discharged." The secretary consoled the President with the comment that "the evident discrimination made here on behalf of the negroes, was sufficient to excite the disgust of all reflecting men."[11]

Johnson's public statements, even that to the Negro soldiers quoted above, seemed to carry an implication that colonization or separate Negro communities might well prove the ultimate solution of the Negro problem. The great question, Johnson told the colored regiment, is whether "this race can be incorporated and mixed with the people of the United States—to make a harmonious and permanent ingredient in the population. . . . Let us make the experiment, and make it in good faith. . . . If we have to become a separate and distinct people (although I trust that the system can be made to work harmoniously) . . . Providence . . . will point out the way, and the mode, and the manner by which these people are to be separated."[12] The December message also spoke of an "experiment in good faith" and cautioned against hasty assumptions that the two races could not live side by side. Some weeks later the President spoke with great emphasis to a Negro delegation of the mutual enmity between "the colored man and the non-slaveholders" and urged the Negro leaders, who had come with a plea for suffrage, to tell their people that they could "live and advance in civilization to better advantage elsewhere than crowded right down there in the South."[13] Although the Thirty-eighth Congress had attempted to put an end to colonization schemes, James Mitchell, who had been appointed Commissioner of Emigration by Lincoln in 1862, clung to his office. In the fall of 1865, Mitchell was actively canvassing political centers from New York to Wisconsin for support of colonization. He reported to President Johnson that he had found many men "anxious to go with us on the question of the separation of the White and Black races."[14] Men close to the President desired separation as the solution of the Negro problem, and Johnson himself may have viewed it with greater favor than his public comment indicated.[15]

Even on the question of Negro suffrage, where Johnson's position seems clearer than on most questions relating to the freedmen, there was room for uncertainty and contradiction. Before his proclamation of May 29, 1865, establishing a provisional government for North Carolina, he considered the possibility of imposing Negro suffrage upon the rebellious states with enough sympathy to kindle the hopes of men committed to this end. Once this first step toward restoration was followed in mid-June by a similar government for Mississippi without extending the vote to any portion of the Negro people, Johnson's policy was generally recognized as based upon the position that the question of suffrage pertained exclusively to the states. There was a lively difference of opinion, however, as to whether or not the President approved and desired extension of the suffrage to Negroes by state action. In a June interview with a white delegation from South Carolina, Johnson indicated that he feared the late slaveholders would control the Negro vote, if suffrage were granted, and use it against the poorer white men of the South.[16] A few days later Secretary

Welles, while defending the Administration's hands-off policy in respect to state suffrage, reassured Charles Sumner that there was not "on the part of the President or his advisers any opposition to most liberal extensions of the elective franchises."[17]

In the battle over Negro suffrage waged in Connecticut during the fall of 1865, the Democracy—as we have seen—identified their opposition with the President's cause.[18] Johnson's Connecticut Secretary of Navy, Gideon Welles, was reported in the local press as having expressed without hesitation "his opinion as decidedly opposed to negro suffrage," and this was used as evidence that "President Johnson is opposed to negro suffrage, as he is opposed to forcing negro voting upon the South." Connecticut Republicans, who were fighting hard for the liberalizing amendment to their state constitution, were alarmed at this damaging blow to the cause and appealed to Welles for a public contradiction. Welles declined to make a statement for publication but authorized a denial that he had "expressed any opinion on the subject of the constitutional amendment now pending."[19]

Just as the voters of Connecticut were deciding the issue with the Democrats and against the Republicans, a dedicated but conciliatory antislavery man from neighboring Massachusetts, George L. Stearns, sought from the President a direct answer to this now politically freighted question. In an interview which he later obtained permission to make public, Stearns heard from the President that were he in Tennessee "I should try to introduce negro suffrage gradually; first those who had served in the army; those who could read and write; and perhaps a property qualification for the others, say $200 or $250. It would not do to let the negro have universal suffrage now; it would breed a war of races."[20] This statement greatly pleased Eastern Republicans. Greeley's *Tribune*, for example, commented that judicious men would "rejoice that Mr. Johnson is willing to use even his indirect and unofficial influence that justice may be done to the blacks of the South." The *World* was not unduly disturbed. If the *Tribune* or anyone else can find satisfaction in Johnson's "private views which he steadily refuses to embody in official action we do not object. Give us his official acts, and you are welcome to his private sentiments."[21]

Much of Johnson's popularity among Southerners rested upon the conviction that the President alone stood between them and the dire fate of Negro suffrage. They relied not only upon his official policy in restricting elections under the provisional governments to whites but also upon unofficial assurances. Watterson during his stay in North Carolina had let it be known "in the right quarter" that the President would never be driven by "the Chases and Sumners" from the position "that the suffrage question belongs to the States alone."[22] Letters that reached the President made unmistakably clear the Southern aversion to an extension of the suffrage and the gratitude for his stand.[23] Like the *World*, Southerners could pass over Johnson's remarks to Stearns, approving a limited state grant of voting privileges to Negroes, so long as he left the question in their hands. The prediction of an Alabama Unionist proved erroneous; the statement in favor of qualified Negro suffrage, he wrote the President, "is enough for these southern people not only to condemn you while lieveing [*sic*] —but will try to blacken your future name and history."[24] The Alabaman was not in error, however, in assuming an overwhelming opposition to Negro voting in the South. In view of this attitude, which was undoubtedly clear to Johnson, the following sentence in his December message appears evasive and misleading:[25]

In my judgment, the freedmen, if they show patience and manly virtues, will sooner obtain a participation in the elective franchise through the States than through the General Government, even if it had power to intervene.

President Johnson's often cited recommendation to the provisional governor of Mississippi that the state grant limited suffrage to the Negro requires examination in a larger perspective than it has generally received. The Mississippi convention which met in Jackson on August 14, 1865, was the first such convention to assemble under Johnson's plan of restoration. On August 15, the President sent to Governor W. L. Sharkey a telegram urging abolition of slavery in the state constitution and the ratification of the pending Thirteenth Amendment. The telegram continued:[26]

If you could extend the elective franchise to all persons of color who can read the constitution of the United States in English and write their names, and to all persons of color who own real estate valued at not less than two hundred and fifty dollars and pay taxes thereon, you would completely disarm the adversary and set an example the other states will follow.

This you can do with perfect safety. . . . I hope and trust your convention will do this, and as a consequence the Radicals, who are wild upon negro franchise, will be completely foiled in their attempts to keep the Southern States from renewing their relations to the Union by not accepting their Senators and Representatives.

On August 20, Sharkey wired back that the convention would amend the state constitution to abolish slavery, but that the right to testify in court and the right of suffrage would probably be left to the legislature.[27] The President replied that he was "much gratified to hear of your proceedings being so favorable," and that "your convention can adopt the Amendment to the Constitution of the United States or recommend its adoption by the Legislature." He pointed out "the importance of being prompt and circumspect in all that is being done," since the Mississippi proceeding would "set an example that will be followed by all the other States." But not one word in the reply made reference to his previous recommendation for qualified Negro suffrage.[28] Four days later the President sent another telegram of commendation, promising an early removal of Federal troops and expressing his belief that if the other Southern states followed Mississippi's example the day of restoration was not distant. Again he omitted any mention of the suffrage issue. Governor Sharkey read this telegram to the legislature, which heard it with satisfaction.[29]

The convention soon adjourned, and Sharkey sent the President a report of its actions including its charge to the legislature to enact laws to protect the Negro in his rights of person and property. He continued, "How it will do this I cannot say, possibly it may allow the negro to testify. . . . The right of suffrage I do not think will be extended to them; indeed there is an inclination to limit the right of suffrage with the white man. In regard to the amendment of the Constitution of the United States prohibiting slavery I do not think the State ever will adopt the second article or provision of the amendment." He continued with complaints against the military and the Freedmen's Bureau and concluded by asserting that both he and the people of Mississippi thought they were entitled now to be relieved of martial law and "to be treated as though the rebellion had ended."[30]

In the face of this recalcitrant reaction to his recommendations and the almost peremptory request for complete self-rule, Johnson permitted his congratulatory message to remain without qualification, public or private. He did not, however, completely remand Mississippi to the inclinations of its people. Two weeks after the assembling of the Mississippi legislature Johnson renewed his pressure for ratification of the antislavery amendment in a telegram to Governor Sharkey of November 1, 1865, holding out the inducement that its adoption would "make the way clear for the admission of Senators and Representatives to their seats in the present Congress." Once again he abandoned the recommendation for an extension of the vote to qualified Negroes.[31] On the 16th, while a joint committee was considering the Amendment, the elected governor, Benjamin Humphreys, sought additional reassurances. He reported that the legislators appeared willing to permit freedmen to testify in courts if assured the Federal troops would be withdrawn, but they feared "that one concession will only lead to others. What assurances can I give on the subject?"[32] In his reply the next day, the President stated:[33]

There can be no other or greater assurance given than has heretofore been on the part of the President. There is no concession required on the part of the people of Mississippi or the Legislature, other than a loyal compliance with the laws and constitution of the United States, and the adoption of such measures giving protection to all freedmen, or freemen, in person and property without regard to color, as will entitle them to resume all their constitutional relations in the Federal Union. . . .

There must be confidence between the Government and the States —while the Government confides in the people—the people must have faith in the Government. This must be mutual and reciprocal, or all that has been done will be thrown away.

While refusing to make a definite commitment in respect to withdrawal of troops and while placing legislation to protect the freedmen under the designation of "concession required," in this same telegram Johnson gave the assurance, quoted earlier, that he was not dictating action but only offering kindly advice. Within ten days, the Mississippi legislature adopted a civil rights act for freedmen so inequitable that the Administration had to set aside certain of its provisions. The legislature also accepted the recommendation of its joint committee *not* to ratify the antislavery amendment.[34]

Thus, in the face of Southern hostility and defiance, Johnson completely discarded his Negro suffrage recommendation.[35] He had urged an extension of voting privileges, not as a matter of equity or of personal conviction, but as an expedient to outmaneuver the Radicals. Perhaps he felt confident of an early restoration without this concession. He did not repeat the advice of August 15, either to Mississippi or to any other of the Southern states. Greeley's "judicious men" might rejoice at the Stearns' interview of October 3 and hope that the President would use his "indirect and unofficial influence" for qualified Negro suffrage; but he had already tried and abandoned the effort. In his December message Johnson argued at length the case for state control of suffrage on the basis of history and the Constitution. He did not include the suggestion forwarded by his friend and political adviser, Lewis Campbell, that he recommend an end to suffrage restrictions which deprived of the vote men of any class—"white, black, or mixed"—who possessed virtue, intelligence and patriotism.[36] Most Republican advocates of Negro suffrage accepted Johnson's argument as sincere but took issue with his logic. It is not difficult to understand their view that Johnson had as much right under the Constitution to obtain an extension of suffrage from the rebel states as he had to establish provisional governments, insist that they abolish slavery, ratify the Thirteenth Amendment, and repudiate their acts of secession and war debt. Even the *Herald* had stated that the President undoubtedly had the power in closing up the rebellion to insist upon Negro suffrage but deemed it wiser to leave the matter to the states.[37] The correspondence between Johnson and the Mississippi governors illustrates the inconsistency and embarrassment in his "advice-not-dictation" posture, as well as the ineffectual character of his endorsement of limited suffrage for the freedmen.

Two other incidents throw some additional light upon Johnson's attitude toward Negro suffrage. On January 18, 1866, the House of Representatives passed by a large majority, though no Democrat voted yea, a bill striking the word "white" from the qualifications for voters in the District of Columbia. A preceding motion would have recommitted the bill with instructions to amend by extending the suffrage only to those who could read the Constitution or had served in the Union forces. These changes would have brought the measure in line with Johnson's position. The Union-Republicans split on this motion, but the Democrats to a man voted against it, thereby defeating a qualified extension of the suffrage.[38] The New York *Times* accused the Democrats of two aims: to stir up trouble between the Union party and the President, and to facilitate passage of a measure that could be used to agitate the Negro question in their constituencies.[39]

Johnson received word that there were enough votes in the Senate to defeat the bill and was requested to send for the senators who were "sound," tell them his views and unite with them for action.[40] His response is not a matter of record, but on January 28 he had an interview with his loyal Republican supporter, Senator Dixon of Connecticut, which was at once made public. Here he "expressed the opinion that the agitation of the negro franchise question in the District of Columbia at this time was the mere entering-wedge to the agitation of the question throughout the States, and was ill-timed, uncalled for, and calculated to do great harm." The interview dealt principally with his position in respect to amending the Constitution, a matter then engaging the urgent attention of the Joint Committee on Reconstruction and of Congress. Johnson held that any amendment at the time was of dubious propriety, would tend to diminish respect for the Constitution, and was quite unnecessary. However, if any were to be made, he knew of none better than the simple proposition that direct taxation be based upon the value of property and representation be based upon the number of voters. Such an amendment, he thought, "would remove from Congress all issues in reference to the political equality of the races" and leave to the states the absolute determination of "qualifications of their own voters with regard to color."[41] Johnson's reluctant approval for an amendment that would give to the South a choice between lessened representation and an extension of suffrage to Negroes represented the farthest limit of his support for a measure of Negro suffrage. In respect to the substance of the District of Columbia bill he avoided approval or disapproval, or any suggestion for its modification.

An amendment of the nature Johnson haltingly endorsed at the end of January, 1866, by then had no chance of obtaining congressional approval. The proposal that representation be based upon voters had been made by Robert Schenck, representative from Ohio, at the opening of Congress; it had been approved by Thaddeus Stevens and the Joint Committee on Reconstruction, but it had run into opposition from New Englanders. Their objection was that this formula would result in an inequitable decrease of representation for their section. Due to westward emigration New England's population, the current basis of apportionment, had a disproportionate number of women and children to men; also, the number of voters in the New England states was relatively less than in other states because of educational requirements for voting. New England objections had led to a revision of the proposed amendment retaining population as the basis of representation but providing a reduction wherever the franchise was denied on the basis of race.[42] The President's endorsement of the original proposal could have no practical effect except to embarrass the New England Radicals. A Johnson political strategist was urging in March that a vote be pressed on the representation-based-on-voters amendment. New England would reject it, and thereby "show the country that New England selfishness is not willing to accept any basis of representation that diminishes her political power"—this would "shut their mouths."[43]

Ten days after the interview with Senator Dixon, the President received a delegation of Negroes that included Frederick Douglass, who came to express the hope that their people would be fully enfranchised. In reply, Johnson spoke with emotion of the scorn which he insisted the slave had held for the poor white man and was the basis for a continuing enmity between Negro and nonslaveholder. The colored man had gained much as the result of the rebellion, he said, the poor white had lost a great deal; on what principle of justice could they be "placed in a condition different from what they were before?" It would commence a war of races; to force universal suffrage without the consent of the community would deny the "first great principle of the right of the people to govern themselves." Without recognizing any inconsistency in his devotion to the principle of government by consent of the governed, Johnson claimed for white Southerners the right to determine whether or not the Negro should vote. He made no allusion to the desirability of a beginning through a qualified franchise.[44]

The interview buried the hopes of those who still looked to the President for unofficial support in breaching the race barrier against Negro suffrage. It delighted many a believer in white supremacy. "I cannot forbear to express to you the great pleasure I felt on reading your remarks to the colored man," wrote an old friend. He continued:[45]

The principles you enunciated are the same expressed to me in a conversation I had with you last Autumn, and in which I fully agreed with you. You said to me then that every one would, and *must* admit that the white race was superior to the black, and that while we ought to do our best to bring them [the blacks] up to our present level, that in doing so we should, at the same time raise our own intellectual status so that the relative position of the two races would be the same. . . .

I am astonished, and more than astonished, at the persistency with which the radical idea of placing negroes on an equality with whites, *in every particular*, is pressed in Congress. . . . Until the tide of fanaticism, which is now in full flood, shall turn, as it must, unless sanity has departed from the people, we must place our trust in you to keep us safe "from the pestilence that walketh in darkness, and the destruction that wasteth at noon-day."

Men of like views might have looked with even greater confidence to the President as the bulwark against Negro "equality" had they been privy to Johnson's private reactions to the delegation headed by Douglass. According to one of the President's private secretaries who was present at the occasion, on the departure of the "darkey delegation" the President "uttered the following terse Saxon: 'Those d——d sons of b——s thought they had me in a trap! I know that d——d Douglass; he's just like any nigger, and he would sooner cut a white man's throat than not.' "[46]

Republican opinion was far from united in respect to Negro suffrage, but it was substantially agreed that the freedmen should enjoy all other rights and privileges pertaining to free men and citizens. On the matter of these civil rights, Johnson's pre-veto record seemed to indicate that here he stood squarely with Northern liberal opinion. There were grave apprehensions, however, that Presidential authority might prove inadequate to obtain from the South that measure of justice which was considered the freedman's due, or at least, obtain it in time to effect speedy restoration. During the meeting of the Mississippi convention in August, 1865, the New York *Times*, which enjoyed an unofficial status as spokesman for the Administration, gave warning in an editorial entitled "The Real Question as to the Future Political Status of the Negro." The "real question" was not whether the freedman should vote but whether he should be protected against injustice and oppression. The North would be watching to see that the convention did not proceed "upon the principle that the colored race are to be kept in a state of subordination, and made the subject of peculiar restraints and exactions." This would be "the great index" to whether or not restoration would soon be effected. "The government, anxious as it is to hasten this end, can make no concession here."[47] The *Times* was not happy with the work of the convention though it acknowledged that Northern doubts might be settled if the Mississippi legislature faithfully fulfilled the duties assigned it by the convention. But why, it asked, was so important a matter left to the faithfulness or unfaithfulness of legislators?[48]

Ever loyal to the President, and adhering to his position as they saw it, the editorial staff of the *Times* succinctly posed the difference that divided the President and the Republican Radicals. "President Johnson founds all his practical policy upon the presumption that the South is fit to be trusted. His radical opponents found theirs upon the presumption that the South is unfit to be trusted." Though the *Times* agreed with the President, there was yet a doubt and a threat in its comment. "When the contrary is shown, then and not until then, will the time come for a different policy."[49] The *Times* hoped for speedy reinstatement of the Southern states, but recognized that in Congress various questions would first be considered, particularly whether more complete securities should not be required for the protection of the rights of the freedmen.[50] As political activity accelerated under Johnson's plan of conventions, elections and legislative action, the *Times* hoped for a "clean sweep of the old black codes, and giving to the blacks substantially the same equality with the white men before the law, that prevails in the Northern states." No solid ground was left for opposition to admission of the formerly rebellious states, it asserted, save assurance that once reinstated in all their old municipal powers these would not be used to harm the freedmen; on this the government must find some kind of security in advance of readmission. The Southern people would not be put in unlimited control of the freedman until they had given proof that they would befriend and not injure him. As of mid-November, "no such proof has yet been given."[51]

The news from Mississippi in October and November was not reassuring. Where the question of Negro testimony had entered the local canvass for the legislature, the nonadmission candidates had won the elections. The defeat by a decided majority of a Negro testimony bill after the legislature convened was hailed by a local paper as a "Glorious Result," an honor to the legislators who had withstood "home threats" and "outside influences." "They have been importuned, threatened, reasoned with and implored to admit the negro to equality in our judicial tribunals, but the *representatives of the people* have frowned upon the proposition, and will never permit the slave of yesterday to confront his former master in the witness-box."[52] Henry J. Raymond, the

Times editor, was telling cheering Republicans in mid-October
that the President's plan included such provision in Southern constitutions and laws "as shall put all their citizens upon an equality
before the law."[53] Editorially, the *Times* reinforced the point by
stating that President Johnson had given "the power and influence
of his position without reserve" to securing for the freedmen
"all the great civil safeguards of person and property. . . . They
have made themselves felt in no small measure through his Provisional Governors and through the Freedmen's Bureau; and the
effects will be made palpable to all in the favorable enactments for
the freedmen, in the legislatures of the late rebel states, soon to
assemble."[54] To underscore the differences between the Democracy and the President, the *Times* pointed out that the former
held that for restoration the Southern states had only to reorganize "in accordance with their own will" while the President insisted that full rights were not restored until certain conditions
had been met including "effective laws . . . for the protection
of the natural rights of the freedmen."[55] In a rejoinder to the
Louisville *Journal*, which had criticized Northerners for meddling
with the status of the freedmen, the *Times* warned that the South
could disarm the "fanatics" by taking measures to secure the
Negroes in their civil rights, to educate them, and to prepare them
for responsible duties. *"If the South will not do this, the nation*
MUST. It cannot be left undone." The influential Louisville *Journal*
would do better to stimulate the Southern people to their duty
rather than waste its energies in denouncing Northerners.[56]

The New York Democratic convention, while embracing the
President and his policy, denounced any attempt by prolonging
military rule or denying representation to coerce the Southern
states "to adopt negro equality or negro suffrage" as tending to
subvert the principles of government and the liberties of the
people.[57] However, the Democracy's chief organ, the *World*,
recognized as an integral part of Johnson's program "entire equality before the law" for the emancipated slaves. It even urged
upon the South that it give Negroes the right to testify in
court, and pointed with pleasure to favorable reaction to its suggestion in Southern and Northern Democratic newspapers. "In

this fact is a conclusive refutation of the charge falsely made
against the Democratic party that they are willing to exclude
negro freedmen from that justice and *equality before the law*
which is their right. . . . We believe that we express the views of
President Johnson, as we know that we do the views of the
great mass of the Democratic party of the North, in saying that
this *equality before the law* ought not to be, and cannot prudently
be, denied to negro freedmen." [58] The *Herald* reinforced this
view of the President's position. "It is the simple policy of recognizing the emancipated blacks as *citizens*, entitled without delay
to all the rights and protection of other citizens in the civil
courts." An editorial subtitled "What the Southern States Have
to Do" listed civil rights for Negroes along with the requirements
of abolishing slavery, ratifying the Thirteenth Amendment, repudiating ordinances of secession, and recognizing an obligation to
share the national debt. The grant of limited suffrage was placed
in a separate category, not a "must," but a "wise" concession.[59]

Thus there was substantial evidence of Johnson's intentions:
the agreement of the *Times*, the *World*, and the *Herald;* the President's public telegram to Governor Humphreys, quoted earlier,
asserting that the Mississippi legislature must adopt measures to
protect freedmen without regard to color; the enforcement of
equal rights by the Freedmen's Bureau under the authority of the
President. Republicans generally could, and did, credit him with
the best intentions in respect to the freedman's civil status. Yet the
situation in the South generally, not just in Mississippi, was disturbing. The Southern states, under great pressure, were meeting
the President's conditions reluctantly and partially. The President
was quoted as saying that the "foolish Georgians were hindering
him in the carrying out of his plans a good deal more than the
worst of the northern radicals." The cruel part, continued the
reporter, is that this occurs just when the President and his friends
have been inculcating the idea of nonintervention in the South.[60]
Johnson's orders to provisional governors to retain their positions
even after elected governors were ready to take over authority
was interpreted as a stern Presidential answer to Southern obstinancy.[61] Contrary to the President's known wishes, Southern

voters were choosing men to represent them at home and in Congress who had held leadership in the rebellion. Reports abounded that with the liberal grant of pardons and the apparently official standing of the theory that the states were entitled to full rights within the Union, the earlier submissive mood of Southerners was turning to one of thinly disguised defiance. Private letters to the President, Secretary Seward, and Secretary Welles spoke with concern of this changing temper of "obstinancy and bitterness" in the South.[62] The provisional governors for North Carolina and Georgia had in desperation appealed to the President for support in obtaining repudiation of the war debts and general acquiescence in the Administration's program. Johnson had replied with strong telegrams that were used with effect upon lawmakers.[63] Florida had ratified the Amendment only after a pointed dispatch sent by Secretary Seward on behalf of the President.[64] Even with open Presidential pressure, South Carolina had refused to repudiate the debt and Mississippi to ratify the Amendment. Florida and Georgia had balked at declaring the ordinances of secession "null and void," either "repealing" or "annulling" them instead.

Resistance to giving the freedmen equal treatment under state laws was even greater. Some states reluctantly allowed Negroes to testify in civil courts in order to be free of the jurisdiction of Freedmen's Bureau courts; but even where this was done under Administrative agreement, lawmakers hesitated to act because of an overwhelmingly hostile public sentiment against receiving Negro testimony.[65] In the face of this reaction, and despite the sharp pressure in the case of Mississippi and more discreet pressures upon other states, certain of Johnson's reactions to the issue of civil rights, though not publicized at the time, were ominous. In Alabama both Provisional Governor Lewis E. Parsons and the Freedmen's Bureau administrator, Wager Swayne, were laboring to obtain from the convention an organic law to permit Negro testimony.[66] Governor Parsons reported difficulty to the President in mid-September and asked to be informed "by telegraph immediately, if you regard it indispensible [*sic*] to the interests of the people of Alabama that such a clause should be inserted."[67] No word came from the President. The convention merely enjoined the legislature to pass laws to protect the freedmen. Governor Parsons appealed again to the President. The important question "was and is whether it is necessary to declare in the Constitution that 'no distinction should be made on account of color, as to the competency of witnesses in this state.' There could be no room for cavil if that had been done. . . . But the individual members of Convention, some of them, were afraid of consequences to themselves if they put it in the constitution. If it had been done the fight [for restoration] would then have to be made on the precise line where I understand you to have placed it— viz—the right of the people of these states to declare who shall vote. . . . I beg to assure you that Alabama approves and will in good faith do all things necessary to sustain your policy with regard to her."[68] The Alabama convention remained in session for another week, but no answer to Governor Parsons' appeal arrived from the President. After the convention's adjournment, Johnson sent a brief telegram commending its proceedings as having "met the highest expectations of all who desire the restoration of the Union. All seems now to be working well, and will result as I believe in a decided success."[69]

From Tennessee also came requests, both unofficially in October and officially in November, that the President send a statement of his views on the subject of Negroes testifying in the courts. It "*would save infinite trouble,*" so great is "the enthusiasm you have kindled among the people."[70] Johnson finally replied on December 9. He would have answered sooner, he said, but thought his message which "would indicate my views, upon the subject of negro testimony, in all cases where they are parties, would be conclusive. It is to be regretted that our Legislature failed to make some advance at its present session upon this question."[71] Two points in connection with this reply are of special interest: first, the December message made no specific mention of Negro testimony; secondly, Johnson's formula as to the right of Negroes to testify where "they are parties" was much less comprehensive than Governor Parsons' version that "no distinction shall be made on account of color."

Johnson had made specific reference to Negro testimony in an interview granted to a distinguished white delegation from South Carolina October 13, 1865. The statement was reported as follows:[72]

The President thought many of the evils would disappear if they inaugurated the right system. Pass laws protecting the colored man in his person and property and he can collect his debts. He knew how it was in the South. The question when first presented of putting a colored man in the witness stand made them shrug their shoulders. But the colored man's testimony was to be taken for what it was worth by those who examined him and the jury who hear it. Those coming out of slavery cannot do without work. . . . They ought to understand that liberty means simply the right to work and enjoy the products of labor, and that the laws protect them. That being done, and when we come to the period to feel that men must work or starve the country will be prepared to receive a system applicable to both white and black. . . . But get the public mind right and you can treat both alike. Let us get the general principles and the details and collaterals will follow.

Johnson's advice is quoted above at some length, for this statement, like the December message, invited favorable reaction from men of fundamentally differing convictions. Republicans could seize with satisfaction upon the idea of "treating both alike"; Southerners could read into the reference to taking testimony "for what it was worth" an invitation to concede the form without the substance of equality before the law. After bitter battles, Southern legislators, during the period of Johnson's control over the Reconstruction process, conceded to the Negro the right to testify. They limited this, however, to cases in which he was a party and denied to the freedmen—Tennessee made the denial a specific proviso of its testimony bill—the right to sit as jurors.[73] Efforts made in the summer and fall of 1865 by Freedmen's Bureau officers to implement the President's desire to remand jurisdiction over Negroes to civil courts resulted, in a number of instances, in local courts permitting Negro testimony.[74] The results of local justice, however, did not provide substantive protection for the freedmen.[75]

Even more ominous for the future of the freedmen, and for future relations between Johnson and the Republican majority as well, was the concession made by Secretary Seward in the President's name in respect to the Thirteenth Amendment. Southern states were willing to recognize that slavery was dead, but they were not willing to ratify a constitutional provision that gave to Congress the power of enforcement. The fear was that under this authority Congress would pass legislation affecting the status of freedmen in the Southern states. Considerable opinion in and out of Congress held that the Amendment gave just such power to protect the rights of Negroes as free men. Even the *Herald* had stated editorially that the Amendment "in giving to Congress the 'necessary legislation' to carry the abolition of slavery into effect, gives to Congress some discretionary power touching the late slave codes of the State concerned."[76] Yet in a message to Provisional Governor B. J. Perry of South Carolina, November 6, 1865, Secretary Seward stated: "The objection you mention to the last clause of the constitutional amendment is regarded as querulous and unreasonable, because that clause is really restraining in its effect, instead of enlarging the powers of Congress."[77] South Carolina then ratified the Amendment with the following qualification:[78]

That any attempt by Congress toward legislating upon the political status of former slaves, *or their civil relations*, would be contrary to the Constitution of the United States as it now is, or as it would be altered by the proposed amendment, in conflict with the policy of the President, declared in his amnesty proclamation and with the restoration of that harmony upon which depend the vital interests of the American Union.

Alabama and Florida subsequently accepted the Amendment with the proviso that it did not confer upon Congress power "to legislate upon the political status of the freedmen in this State." Mississippi's consent was finally granted contingent upon qualifications even more extended than those of South Carolina. They included the explicit statement that the second section "shall not be construed as a grant of power to Congress to legislate in regard to the freedmen of this state."[79]

Clearly the Southern states were determined to obtain full control over the freedmen. In some instances there was open avowal of the intent, once restoration was complete, to repeal civil rights that had been granted under pressure and return the Negro to "his place."[80] Various provisions of the legislation in respect to Negroes under consideration or recently enacted in Mississippi, South Carolina, and other Southern states appeared to be flagrant attempts legally to remand the freedmen to an inferior status. Troubled Republicans found consolation in the President's reported characterization of his policy as an "experiment"; Democrats deprecated or denied the remark and insisted that the President would not be moved from his present policy.[81] The Administration gave assurances that it would stand by the freedmen, but it also had been thought to promise early withdrawal of military forces and Freedmen's Bureau jurisdiction in the South.[82] To the confusion and concern that marked the fall and early winter of 1865 was added Seward's curious and limiting interpretation of the enforcement clause of the Thirteenth Amendment.

As Congress began its labors there was much evidence to arouse fears that Southerners were not yet ready to meet the freedman in his new status with justice and without discrimination. The congressional majority approached the problem with confidence in the President's good intentions. But there were portents, not yet generally recognized, that Johnson's version of "the security of the freedmen in their liberty and in their property" might hold concessions to Southern prejudice that could not be reconciled with the Republican view that Negroes were citizens entitled to equality before the law.

9 THE PRESIDENT DECLARES WAR

"The fight is on!" This was the jubilant announcement sent by Samuel S. Cox, Democratic leader in the House of Representatives, to Manton Marble on the day following Johnson's veto of the Freedmen's Bureau Bill. "He [Johnson] is in great earnest. I am sure," Cox further advised the editor of the most influential Democratic paper in the nation, "that you cannot say too much now tho I have been very wary."[1] North and South and West, the Democracy rejoiced and prepared for battle under Johnson's banner. Moderate men in the Union-Republican ranks were confused and dismayed. "We had . . . a veto yesterday," the conciliatory Henry L. Dawes of Massachusetts wrote home to his wife. "Everything looks very dark and what is before us cannot well be seen."[2] And two days later he added, "The veto has made Congress very furious—and the war has begun which *can* end only in general ruin of the party."[3] Those who could not, or would not, recognize a second Sumter were soon shaken by the reverberation of further blasts—Johnson's February 22 speech and his March veto of the Civil Rights Bill. The second veto, the *Herald* trumpeted, "is in fact an emphatic declaration of war against the radicals. . . . The veto of the Freedmen's Bureau bill was but the distant thunder announcing the approaching storm. This veto is the storm itself. . . . It is a declaration of war against the radicals and their impracticable schemes, and Andrew Johnson, as in the rebellion, is the man to fight it through on his platform of the Union and the Constitution."[4] One Democratic paper greeted the Freedmen's veto as:[5]

GLORIOUS NEWS   PRESIDENT JOHNSON
THROWS HOT SHELL IN THE ABOLITION CAMP! !
THE FIRST GUN! !   LET HER BLAZE!

The war which President Johnson declared in February and March of 1866 brought to a climax the long-standing design to force the Radicals out of the Union-Republican party and inaugurate a reorganization of national parties. Much of the pressure for an assault upon the Radicals came from the Democrats, both the "regulars," who had opposed the war, and the War Democrats who had wholeheartedly supported the national effort. It is difficult to determine the exact expectation of the former group in their support of Johnson and their attack upon the Radicals. Some of their number clearly welcomed the prospect of a new Johnson party which would purge them of any guilt of association with the peace plank of the wartime Democracy. For them, the issue was the extent to which they would be able to control the new party. Others sought merely to split the Union-Republican ranks into an ineffectual opposition, regain political ascendancy with the support of a restored South, and use the presidential influence for their own party advantage. This use of Johnson's prestige and power might, or might not, include a tacit understanding that he would be offered the Democratic nomination for the Presidency in 1868. Others hedged, waiting upon events to decide whether they would transfer allegiance to a new Union party or gather up dissident Republicans into the old organization of the Democracy. Individual Democrats shifted from one expectation to another with the changing currents of the political scene. Both "regulars" and War Democrats, and Conservative Republicans as well, sought for themselves a central role of power in postwar politics.

The drive to isolate the Radicals had gained momentum since the convening of Congress. Even as that body assembled for its first session since victory, Democrats were scheming to "precipitate the fight with the Radicals." An intimate was informing Marble, the *World*'s editor, that "I have inspired Cox to set things in train (if he can do it so convertly as not to seem officious) for launching some sort of thunderbolt immediately on the reading of the message to set the Radicals on fire and kindle a conflagration. . . . I hope a fight may be brought on in such a way that only the Radicals may take part against us. If the President will give us a good pretext for fighting the Radicals under *his* banner, we can get them wild, widen the breach by an exciting debate, and all will come out right."[6] The wartime Democratic governor of New York, Horatio Seymour, was soon advising Montgomery Blair that the "President must strike" at the Radicals.[7] Through the correspondence and comment respecting the long, sharp contest over the appointment to the vacant New York collectorship there flowed a pervasive expectation of impending political realignments in which the winner of that patronage plum would be expected to play a key role.[8]

As the weeks passed, Democrats, and even some Union men ready to join forces with them under Johnson's leadership, grew restive. "Action is what the Democratic party requires from the President before putting its entire faith in him," read an editorial of the Newton, New Jersey, *Herald and Democrat*, "and any new party got up to sustain him, must show that his *actions* sustain his sentiments. A veto on any of the unconstitutional acts of the present congress would be vastly more effectual than all the addresses he has ever made since he became President."[9] Lewis D. Campbell, Johnson's Whig-Republican political lieutenant, wrote from Ohio that "the sooner you cut yourself loose from them [the Radicals] the better for you and for the country."[10] What was needed, in Campbell's view, was the organization of a party on the basis of the President's policy. "The *Union party* as an organization is rapidly going under. *Burnt brandy* won't save it. . . . He [Johnson] must sooner or later accept the *fact* that the great Union party has fulfilled its mission."[11] By the end of January, the Springfield *Republican*'s Washington correspondent was reporting that the President and Senator Dixon of Connecticut "have gone into a scheme to smash up the radicals . . . and to prepare the way for the great Johnson party which (according to Doolittle, Cowan and others) is to grow out of the ruins of the present two political organizations"[12] The *National Intelligencer*, which was already beginning to be recognized as spokesman for the Administration,[13] commented four days before the veto that the day was "not now distant" when a spontaneous movement of the people in behalf of the President might lead to "A JOHNSON PARTY."[14] The *World*'s position was more ambiguous, but left the door open for such a development. While ridiculing Bennett's call for a new Johnson party and joyfully citing past election figures to support the contention that the Democracy, the "Party of the Past," would be the "Party of the Future," the *World*'s editor also praised Johnson's fitness "for the double work of a disintegrator and a reorganizer." The President was "the nucleus around which the party of the future is to crystallize," since he enjoyed "contact and sympathy with all that is sound and healthy in every considerable party."[15]

Two days before the final passage of the Freedmen's Bureau Bill, John Cochrane, War Democrat of New York, wrote the President that the Democratic masses were "restlessly expectant of the period when an overt act by you, in resistance of systematic Congressional encroachment, shall enable them to muster into your service."[16] Two days after the passage of the bill, Edward Bates, Lincoln's conservative Attorney General, sent off a long letter denouncing the intended extension of the Freedmen's Bureau jurisdiction and reassuring the President that in a split between the Administration and the Radicals the latter would be "trodden out like so many sparks on the floor."[17] A Democratic leader in Pennsylvania, eager to secure an endorsement of the President at the approaching state Democratic convention, damned the Freedmen's Bureau Bill and sent word that "Considerations of this kind weigh with our Delegates. . . . I hope you will veto that Freedmans Bill."[18]

John Cochrane may not have anticipated that the "signal" so

eagerly awaited would be the veto of the Freedmen's measure, for he had counseled that in any conflict there should be not "even the colour of an inference that your line of policy is unfriendly to the negro."[19] All was in readiness, however, whatever might be the "overt act," particularly in the key political state of New York. There Cochrane was ardently engaged in consultations with Dean Richmond, the upstate Democratic boss, with Bennett of the *Herald,* and with General J. B. Steedman of Ohio, one of Johnson's most trusted military politicos. Dean Richmond, Cochrane reported, was awaiting developments in Washington and wanted the President to know that whenever he was in a position to accept the cooperation of his Democratic friends, support would "not be delayed." Bennett was urging the feasibility and importance of "a coalition between the moderate Republicans and the loyal Democrats." General Steedman had promised to confer with the President "upon the propriety of holding a large meeting here in behalf of your policy and to write me the result. Whenever you think it seasonable you must be aware that a formidable demonstration can be made."[20] Cochrane and Bennett held that pro-Johnson voters, rank-and-file Democrats, and Union men—mostly former Democrats—would have a preponderance of 50,000 in New York and a proportional majority in the central and northwestern states, and that the "logical sequence" of their organization would be the "reproduction of your power in 1868."[21]

The anticipated "signal" may have been the ousting of Secretary Stanton from the Cabinet and his replacement by General Steedman as Secretary of War. Within a week, at the end of January and the beginning of February, letters of recommendation for General Steedman reached the President from Dean Richmond, Samuel J. Tilden, George H. Pendleton of Ohio, Horace Greeley, and Augustus Schell, the affluent and influential brother of Seward's friend Richard Schell.[22] A change in the post of Secretary of War could have signaled a new direction not only in respect to personalities and patronage but also in regard to the role of the army and the Freedmen's Bureau in the still-occupied South; for the Secretary's office held a large measure of influence over the conduct of those arms of the national government. Rumors of Stanton's exit from the Cabinet, however, proved premature, probably in large part because he had powerful support from the Seward-Weed forces.[23] Another possibility to which some Johnson men looked hopefully as the cleaver by which the Radicals could be severed from the Union ranks was the bill passed by the House, but later buried in the Senate, to extend suffrage to Negroes in the District of Columbia.[24] The issue of Negro suffrage would have afforded to Conservatives a tactical advantage. Johnson was ready to veto the District of Columbia bill had it passed the Senate.[25]

In contrast, a veto of the Freedmen's Bureau Bill held certain disadvantages. The bill was identified not with the Radicals, but with the moderate leadership in Congress, and it enjoyed overwhelming support among Republicans in and out of Congress. Rumors of an impending veto alarmed Republicans friendly to the President. They feared such action would be received as an indication that the Administration was not determined to protect the Negro, and they saw in it a potential rupture between the President and the Union party which would disastrously shatter the latter.[26] On the other hand, unlike the question of suffrage in an area clearly under congressional jurisdiction, the freedmen's bill afforded an opportunity for a direct statement on Reconstruction policy. In addition, a veto of the measure would allay the bitter resentment of the Bureau in the South and the stock Democratic complaint in the North against the "unconstitutional" interference of the military in civil affairs. The leading Democratic organ, the *World*, had denounced the Bureau bill in a comprehensive indictment; and not one Democrat had voted for the measure in either the Senate or the House.[27] The veto also gave Johnson an opportunity to flatter James Gordon Bennett, whose editorials were belaboring the bill and calling for a Presidential veto.[28] When the President's message was released, a telegram went from the White House to James Gordon Bennett, Jr.: "Your Saturday's article in reference to the Freedmen's Bureau Bill is highly approved. Veto message has just gone in."[29]

The Tennessee President was particularly sensitive to opinion and pressures from the border states, and letters that reached his desk during January and February made their demands articulate and unmistakable. They wanted an end to the Freedmen's Bureau, to military jurisdiction, and to the suspension of *habeas corpus*. The governor of Kentucky threatened that unless the Bureau "be taken away" he himself would take the lead in compelling the Negro to leave Kentucky or starve. His threat was to convene the state assembly and procure an act making it a crime for any white person to lease or rent lands or houses or to employ in any way any Negro or mulatto.[30] Johnson undoubtedly knew, without waiting to be told, that his support in the border states would be in jeopardy unless he took some step toward removing the Freedmen's Bureau and restoring *habeas corpus*. "I say to you frankly if that is not done," wrote a Kentucky state senator, "you will not get a cordial endorsement from Kentucky."[31] A few days later his belligerent admonisher hailed the veto message "with infinite satisfaction and approval."[32]

The President was well aware that the Bureau was as unpopular in the deep South as in the border states. He had been for some time under much pressure from leading men of South Carolina who were hostile to the Bureau and the provisions of the new bill, particularly those in respect to the Sea Island lands.[33] Benjamin F. Perry, Johnson's provisional governor and now senator-elect from South Carolina, made clear the Southern position toward the Bureau bill in a letter to the *National Intelligencer*. Trumbull's bill was "a monstrous injustice to the planter," a "demoralizing influence on the freedman," "ruinous" to the culture of Sea Island cotton, a startling extravagance that would tax the poor white men of the North "to support the vicious and vagrant Southern negro." Perry returned from Washington with confidence that Southern representatives would soon be admitted and that "the radicals will be utterly defeated and routed."[34] Just prior to the veto, Southerners were cheered by a series of reports that the President was holding firm against any congressional requirements preliminary to admission of their representatives; and they were anticipating "an approaching crisis.[35]

Despite much speculation by contemporaries and historians, it is extremely unlikely that Johnson experienced any real indecision as to his course once the Freedmen's Bureau Bill had reached his desk. Two days after the passage of the measure, and eleven days before the veto message, "the clerks & so on, down in the Executive office" were "unanimous . . . in declaring that Johnson will veto the Freedmen's Bureau Bill."[36] Among the Presidential manuscripts there have been preserved six working papers for the message. All are arguments *against* the bill, apparently solicited by the President.[37] There exists in the Johnson Papers not one such brief in support of the measure. The contention that the veto was a last-minute decision dependent upon the action of the Joint Committee on Reconstruction in respect to Tennessee has been convincingly refuted by Eric McKitrick.[38] Johnson's action has also been attributed to irate reaction to Radical provocation, such as the remarks of Stevens, Sumner, and Wendell Phillips. Such a hypothesis ignores too many aspects of the contemporary scene—the plans for party reorganization, the pressures upon Johnson for some such action as the veto, the moderate rather than Radical sponsorship of the bill, and the large measure of deference and concession which most Republicans in and out of Congress still offered the President. Sumner and Stevens, let alone Wendell Phillips—with their sharp words and their desires for Negro suffrage, confiscation, and prolonged territorial status for the South—did not speak for the congressional majority. And it was the congressional majority that had spoken for the freedmen's bill. Clearly, Presidential hostility to the extreme Radicals cannot alone explain the veto. Neither can it be attributed solely to Johnson's constitutional principles, for they were not so consistent and sharply defined as to constitute a compelling necessity for so sweeping a rejection of the bill.[39] The weight of evidence, including a comparison of the final message with the drafts from which it was prepared, indicates that Johnson's first veto represented a considered decision. In view of the letters that had crossed his desk and the comments of the press, it was a decision Johnson could not possibly have made without giving thought to its political impact. It would strengthen his ties with the Northern Democracy and the South, force an issue with those of the Republicans who he considered his opponents, and signal the beginning of a major political realignment under his leadership.

William H. Seward's role in the veto message is of particular interest in view of his pre-eminent position in Johnson's official family, his early identification with a generous policy toward the South, and his long-standing interest in a reorganization of parties. The Secretary's policy of refraining from political comment in his personal letters[40] sorely handicaps the inquiring historian. We know that Seward supported the veto in Cabinet meeting,[41] and that he later defended it skillfully in an effective public appearance in New York City. These facts reveal little. Fortunately, there is another source of information—Seward's own draft for the veto message. This paper, and other Seward draft messages, have long been available in the Johnson manuscripts at the Library of Congress, but their authorship was unknown. The type of paper used and the characteristic manner of writing on alternate lines were the identifying clues.[42] It is unlikely that Seward composed his draft for the veto, which is written in the presidential first person, without prior consultation with the President; hence we cannot be certain whether Seward advised that the measure be rejected, or simply acquiesced in Johnson's decision. There is much, however, that Seward's version does reveal.

Seward's central argument was that the enlargement and extension of the Bureau at that time was unnecessary, although he acknowledged that future developments might require additional legislation to prolong the Bureau. He interpreted the existing law as maintaining the Bureau in force until a full year after a formal declaration of peace, an announcement which had not yet been made, and expressed hope that by the end of that year the necessity for the Bureau would have ceased. Seward made little use of any other argument against the bill, though in passing he gently criticized its extension of the Bureau both as to time, which he considered indefinite, and as to jurisdiction, which included all parts of the United States containing refugees and freedmen. He also pointed out that martial law and military tribunals should be used only on occasion of absolute necessity and that the fiscal condition of the country required "so far as possible" severe retrenchment. He had kind words for the Bureau, making reference to its "beneficent operations" and the "care and fidelity" with which it had been administered.

Seward also raised the general problem of restoration. His draft expressed pleasure that the bill contemplated a full restoration of the several states. Here his reference was to the bill's provision for terminating Bureau jurisdiction over freedmen's civil rights in any state fully restored "in all its constitutional relations to the United States," and enjoying the unobstructed functioning of the civil courts. He added, however, that the bill was "vague and uncertain in defining the conditions which will be accepted as evidences of that full restoration," and continued:

It is hardly necessary for me to inform the Congress that in my own judgment most of those states so far at least as depends upon themselves have already been thus fully restored and are to be deemed as entitled to enjoy their constitutional rights as members of the Union. Since Congress now proposes to make so important a proceeding as the prolongation of the Freedmen's Bureau dependent upon a restoration in some sense which differs from the one entertained by the Executive Department it would seem to be important that Congress and the President should first agree upon what actually constitutes such restoration.

He ended the draft on a similar note:

Without trenching upon the province of Congress I may be permitted in explaining my own course on the present occasion to say that when a state at some previous time comes not only in an attitude of loyalty and harmony but in the persons of representatives whose loyalty cannot be questioned under any existing constitutional or legal test that in this case they have a claim to be heard in Congress especially in regard to projected laws which bear especially upon themselves.

In short, Seward's draft of the veto message both in referring to the bill itself and in stating the Presidential theory of restoration was gentle and conciliatory. Unlike the official message, it did not make a slashing indictment of the military jurisdiction through which the Bureau was to operate in the future, as it had in the past, to protect the civil rights of freedmen whenever

they were discriminated against by "local law, custom, or prejudice." Unlike the official message, it did not criticize the bill for
providing relief for destitute freedmen and lands for the building
of asylums and schools and for rental to those who could not find
employment. Neither did it object to the provision that freedmen holding lands under Sherman's order on the Sea Islands be
confirmed in their possession for three years, with the proviso that
any such land could earlier be restored to its original owner if
the Bureaus' commissioner procured for the freedmen occupants,
with their written consent, other lands for rental or purchase.
Nor did Seward's draft imply, as did the President's official message, that special protection for the newly freed Negro was in
effect discrimination against white men.

A comparable divergence between Seward's approach and that
of the President is apparent in the references to Congress and the
restoration process. That part of the official message incorporated
much of Seward's wording but changed the order and emphasis,
omitted phrases, and added comments. The result was a virtual
Presidential fiat to Congress. The right of each house to judge
the qualifications of its members, read a critically important sentence, "cannot be construed as including the right to shut out,
in time of peace, any State from the representation to which it
is entitled by the Constitution."[43] Because the President was
chosen by all the states, Johnson asserted that he as President
stood in a different relationship to the country than did any member of Congress; it was his duty to present the "just claims" of
the eleven states not represented in either House of Congress. He
closed the message with what was in effect a challenge to Congress
to submit the issues he had raised to the "enlightened public
judgment" of the people.

Seward's draft for the veto was a statement to which the moderates of the Republican party, and even many men known as
Radicals, might have accommodated without too much strain.
Johnson's veto included a few passages that could be interpreted
as conciliatory if taken out of the context of the message as a
whole, but in essence it did not invite Congress to negotiate but
defied Congress to act. The message still held a measure of that

ambiguity so characteristic of Johnson's actions and statements during the previous months, but only a small measure.[44] To most Democrats and Radicals who were his contemporaries, and to historians who look back upon the course of events, the ambiguity was resolved. Only Republicans who were moderate and trusting, timid or self-interested, or more Democrat than Republican in their view of race and their attitude toward states' rights and Federal power—only such men clung to the illusions with which the President's December message had been so generally and hopefully received. The surprising fact is that their number was considerable. Seward's influence was in part responsible, for he publicly interpreted the President's veto in the spirit of the one which he had written and would doubtless have preferred.

It is evident from Seward's draft that the Secretary had some share of responsibility for the veto of the Freedmen's Bureau Bill. Also, this document confirms what would seem apparent from his earlier and later public statements and action: namely, that Seward wished the rebellious states to be promptly readmitted to their old seats in Congress in keeping with his wartime contention that the government had no intent to "subjugate" them, but only to restore the Union.[45] In this essential commitment to a policy of speedy reunion and reconciliation, Seward's position coincided with that of the Democracy. In other respects, however, his arguments in the draft message conceded little to Democratic contentions and attitudes. We can be certain, in view of the political activities of Thurlow Weed, that Seward and his political manager were still planning a reorganization of parties; we cannot be equally certain that they welcomed a veto of the freedmen's bill as the starting signal for realignment. If such were the case, Seward clearly did not wish that signal to carry the boom and destruction of cannon fire in defense of the entrenched positions of the old Democracy.

Andrew Johnson, in contrast, went far toward accepting and defending the position of the Democrats. He did not, it is true, go so far as to voice the Democratic argument that any federal action on behalf of the freedmen by the Federal Government was an invasion of state and local rights. The common ground which he, but not Seward, held with the Democracy was of considerable extent. It is evident in the following aspects of the official message: the sweeping nature of the condemnation of the bill and by implication of the Bureau itself; the omission of any kindly word for the Bureau or of any assurance of its continuation; the emphasis upon violation of the constitutional rights of white men by the Bureaus' jurisdiction over cases involving discrimination to Negroes; the argument that a federal "system of support of indigent persons" was contrary to the Constitution; the contention that the message would keep the freedmen in a state of expectant restlessness; the assurance that the Negro could protect himself because his labor was necessary to the Southern economy; the censure of the Sea Island provisions as a violation of the property rights of Southern owners; the stress upon the immense Federal patronage and expense that the bill allegedly would make mandatory; and lastly, the oblique appeal to race prejudice.

The President's veto was greeted by a series of "spontaneous" demonstrations, mass meetings, and resolutions of support and approval. The 22nd of February, Washington's birthday and a holiday, resounded with the firing of cannon and the oratory of prominent public figures celebrating the "patriotic and statesmanlike act of the present chief executive."[46] The largest, noisiest, and most successful of these meetings was held in New York's Cooper Institute, and it was Secretary Seward's show. Thousands were reportedly unable to find room within the hall, and minor orators were hurriedly enlisted to entertain the crowds outside the building. Within, the hall was gay with patriotic decorations, music, and a huge portrait of Andrew Johnson. Making his first public appearance in New York since the assassination attempt upon his life, Seward in his entrance upon the stage was "greeted with the most rapturous applause, the whole house rising and cheering vociferously."[47] The "eloquent scar" across his cheek, the "broken voice," added to the drama of the old Republican's appearance to explain and support Johnson's action. He spoke leaning with his left arm and his body against the rostrum, yet his delivery was reported as reaching at times as high a "pitch of animation and vigor" as ever it had shown in the prewar years.[48]

Seward assumed a light touch in his oratory, evoking laughter by his sallies, reassuring his audience that "There are no dangers, there are no perils, there is no occasion for alarm." The country was safe, the difference between Congress and the President was only a "dispute between the pilots," all honest, all well meaning, all seeking the same port. President and Congress agreed that the freedmen could not be abandoned during the transition from war to peace. The President thinks the transition period is nearly ended, that there is no necessity for an indefinite extension of the Bureau; "for that reason" he vetoed the bill. Seward explained that the Bureau would continue under the original law for another year; if Congress then found it still needed, Congress could take "the necessary steps." The President ought not to be denounced, in the absence of any necessity, "for refusing to retain and exercise powers greater than those of any imperial magistrate in the world!"[49]

The meeting was page one news in the New York press, and most of the editorial comment was an enthusiastic endorsement. The chief voice of dissent came from the columns of Greeley's *Tribune*. It conceded that Seward's speech was "ingenious, and in some points able" but objected that Seward like the other speakers ignored the real questions in the controversy. These were two: whether the late rebel states had shown such signs of returning loyalty as to make it prudent to restore all their suspended rights; and whether the nation ought not to interpose "a fixed, absolute and impassable barrier" between the freed Negroes and "the few Southern Whites who seek to oppress them."[50] The *Herald*'s Friday treatment was warm, including pleasant references to the "distinguished" Secretary of State; its Saturday comments became critical of Seward's optimism, his "incapacity to practically comprehend the vital questions which agitate the country."[51] The first reaction of the *World* to the triumphant performance of the man so long and bitterly assailed in its columns was caustic:[52]

Secretary Seward's speech to the repentant Republicans at the Cooper Institute last night was pitched in the key of his famous ninety day prophecies.

The Ship of State has out-breasted the storm and is now in the haven of rest. There is no cloud in the future; the Union is fully restored; it does not much matter whether Congress or the President prevail—all will come right in the end. In short, according to the Secretary—

> "Everything is lovely
> And the goose hangs high"

The query is, if everything is so serene, why was the meeting held? and why did Mr. Seward come all the way from Washington to give it his countenance?

Seward was a "rose-water statesman"; "the greater affairs of the world are moved by the passions; but Mr. Seward is passionless, and therefore blind." Yet his speech would do great good, "not as he intends by uniting and reconciling, but by hastening the division and disintegration of the doomed Republican party."[53] On second thought, however, the *World* softened its tone and joined the general chorus of acclaim for the meeting. Seward had been speaking for readers in Europe, which was quite within his province; the point of the meeting was that the "respectable Republican gentlemen" who ran it "have *indorsed* [*sic*] Mr. Johnson in his fight with the Radicals in Congress . . . have proclaimed the present Congress to be a Rump Congress, and the Radicals . . . to be *Disunionists*." The *World* would accept them, presumably even Seward, as "new recruits" and after their fortitude had been tested, even advance them "to the post of honor."[54]

Seward and Weed clearly had no intention of playing the role of penitent sinners turned novitiates under the rule of the *World*. They recognized, as Weed wrote Senator Morgan a few days after the meeting, that "We are in a crisis."[55] Both Weed and Wakeman, the Seward politico who held the office of surveyor of the port, had sent Seward urgent appeals to address the meeting. "It is deemed important that you should be present," wired Wakeman on the 19th.[56] "Can you come to our meeting," read Weed's telegram of the 20th; "I have reflected well and hope you can come."[57] "Our meeting" was designed not just to rally support for the President, but in the discreet words of the official call "to promote harmony in the public Councils of the Country."[58] It was Weed and Seward's most important public move to keep the pro-Johnson movement under their control; to do this, not only did they need to maintain some good Democratic contacts, but most importantly they also needed to retain a substantial following among *Republicans*. With Democrats pledging unqualified allegiance to the President, their leaders were in a position to assert authority as commanding generals. Seward and Weed had to assemble all the political strength they could rally to counter this danger and particularly "to promote harmony" in the Republican ranks.

The roster of vice presidents, officers, and speakers for the Cooper Institute meeting included not only Seward's faithful among the New York Republicans but also such leaders of the dissident faction as William C. Bryant, editor of the *Evening Post*, David Dudley Field, and George Opdyke. James Gordon Bennett was there also. Democrats were not excluded; Daniel S. Dickinson, prominent War Democrat sent a letter which was read from the platform, and Francis B. Cutting, a prewar ultra-Southern Democrat who had supported Lincoln and the war effort, was permanent chairman of the meeting. Although there appeared nowhere in the proceedings the name either of Fernando Wood or of his brother Ben, editor of the *Daily News*, the enthusiastically warm response of the *News* to the meeting suggests that this extreme wing of the New York Democracy had not been overlooked by Weed and Wakeman in their preparations for the meeting. The roster, however, did not include the most prominent War Democrats such as Dix and Cochrane, nor did it contain the names of leaders among the regular Democrats such as Tilden and Barlow.

Preserved among the Seward papers is an anonymous printed lampoon of the meeting.[59] This opens with a scene in a back room at Washington, just before the veto, where Seward, Weed, and Richard Schell were planning the New York meeting. Weed urged the need to obtain strength from the Union War Democrats; Seward was made to reply:

Yes, and they are ready to help us on; but you must remember that they may impress the President *too* strongly and claim our places. This point must not be lost sight of. Will not lesser lights answer our purpose and make us stronger, rather than jeopardize our future!

We have no evidence to indicate whether Weed asked Dix to participate and he refused, as the skit implied, or whether the most prominent War Democrat of the state was deliberately omitted from the list of sponsors. As for Tilden and other close associates of the *World*'s editor, the ungracious attitude of that paper toward the meeting suggests that they were not among the especially invited.

Contemporaries variously assessed the political complexion of the Cooper Institute meeting. The hostile *Tribune* thought the meeting "bore the unmistakable marks of a good old-fashioned Democratic gathering."[60] The *World* jibed that the crowd consisted of repentant rank-and-file Republicans and "the entire corp of anxious officeholders in the city of New York."[61] Bryant's *Evening Post* reported that it was a respectable gathering composed of men of all parties, "old democrats, old whigs, old free-soilers, and old conservatives."[62] Bennett's *Herald* agreed that the meeting was composed of "our most respectable classes," although "we believe that they all belong to one political party."[63] Seward's organ, the New York *Times*, characterized the occasion as one "for the suppression of everything like mere party and partisan feeling."[64] The urbane George Templeton Strong commented in his diary that it was a " 'Conservative' meeting. . . . got up by men of weight, political purity, and unquestioned loyalty, Republicans and War Democrats."[65] Despite these conflicting opinions—indeed, in view of the particular political orientation of each—it is evident that the meeting was largely Republican in complexion.

This was clearly shown in the formal resolutions and accompanying address which were presented by David Dudley Field. Although unqualified in approval of Johnson's position, they emphasized that the participants in the meeting, and also both Congress and the President, were agreed that the freedmen must have "all the civil rights of any other class of citizens . . . they

must have equality *before the law*." Field stated that the only dividing question was whether the freedmen should have the
suffrage. He summarized with remarkable equity and lack of
rancor the arguments on each side of this question, and then took
his stand against suffrage. Those who argue that the Negro could
not be protected in his rights without the franchise, Field pointed
out, forget the power given to Congress by the enforcement
clause of the Thirteenth Amendment and also forget that the men
and women of the South have a sense of justice.[66] The emphasis
upon the Negro's civil rights had a distinctively Republican
flavor.

Seward and Weed had scored a local victory at the Cooper
Institute. Their support from Greeley's former allies within the
Union-Republican party, however, could be retained only so long
as there was confidence in Johnson's readiness to protect the
freedman as a citizen. Nor did their success on February 22, any
more than their triumph in the election of the previous November, bring a capitulation from Democratic rivals among the friends
of the President. After the meeting, Seward wired his son, the
President, and Senator Morgan an almost identical message: "ALL
RIGHT AND SAFE THE WORK IS DONE THE TROUBLE IS ENDED."[67] But all
was not safe and the work had not ended. John Dix sent off an
emissary to Johnson;[68] Tilden utilized the influence of Montgomery Blair to warn the President that he could not succeed if he
placed "an *exclusive reliance on the republican machine*."[69] Pressure mounted from the Democrats in respect to the New York
collectorship, and it was directed primarily against the Seward-
Weed forces.[70] Weed reassured Seward that he was "in frequent
communication with leading Democrats (not Copperheads) who
are preparing the way for political reconstruction." For success,
however, "the new organization" must be "based on the Conservative Plan in the Union Platform."[71]

Other than in New York City, it was the Democracy which
dominated the movement to celebrate and endorse the President's
veto. Democrats showered the President with individual letters
and joint resolutions of approval, some direct from party conventions. In meetings "irrespective of party," they sought to place

Conservative Republicans, and especially Republican officeholders, conspicuously on the front rows, while keeping direction of the proceedings in their own hands. Often Republicans balked at the prospect of appearing on programs which to them seemed calculated merely to reinvigorate their old foes—the Copperheads and Peace Democracy.[72] The most persuasive argument against such meetings came from the conciliatory but principled John A. Andrew, former governor of Massachusetts, in reply to the elder Frank Blair, who had asked Andrew's support of a Johnson meeting:[73]

> Seeing so clearly as I do, the duty of us all, of endeavoring to meet the present and coming emergencies, in the spirit, and in the manner of calm, patriotic, liberal minded statesmanship, I am opposed to public meetings, called in support of, or the interest of, any man, leader or party. All the men whose names are made prominent in a controversial way, will have to yield something of what they may have said. . . . And in this remark, I include President Johnson. . . .
>
> Now, if one set of men get up meetings for Paul, another set will get up meetings for Apollo. The result will be antagonism, not patriotism.

The calm approach that Andrew desired to the problem of the freedmen and of restoration had been made more difficult by Johnson's own speech of February 22, in which he had named Sumner, Stevens, and Wendell Phillips as traitors and intimated that the Radicals were bent upon his assassination. Democrats hailed the performance. General George McClellan, the Democrat's 1864 presidential candidate who was vacationing in Europe, was so pleased with the speech that he came to the conclusion that "the least the country can do for him [Johnson] is to make him the next President," and encouraged his political friends in the States to initiate such a movement.[74] Conciliatory Republicans attempted to explain it away as an intemperate emotional outburst under provocation. Both Seward and Weed, however, wired Johnson congratulations on his speech;[75] yet observers noted a marked differences of approach between the Secretary and the President. A friend wrote Seward that he had read his speech with gratitude; "but what shall I say of the speech of the President!"[76] Bryant's *Evening Post* remarked sadly that Johnson seemed to forget what Seward had emphasized, that the difference between the President and certain leading Republicans "is a question of methods and not one of different ends." The *Post* trusted that Johnson would apologize for the "shocking imputation that Stevens, Sumner and others were seeking to incite assassination."[77] Johnson himself never repudiated his statement; indeed, he subsequently insisted in connection with the Connecticut gubernatorial election that those who wished his support must sustain the controversial speech as well as his various messages to Congress.[78]

Johnson's veto and speech aroused excitement, concern, and indignation among Republicans. John W. Forney of the Washington *Chronicle* and Philadelphia *Press* had been publishing strong statements of confidence and denouncing Democratic efforts to "fabricate opinion" for the President.[79] With the announcement of the veto, he turned upon Johnson with bitterness. He revealed that despite his earlier declarations of faith in the President, he had been apprehensive when Johnson had failed to declare for the Union party prior to the New York and Pennsylvania elections, had received Democratic leaders "almost in state," and had for a time made John Van Buren a "daily confidant." The veto would, according to Forney, postpone or defeat "every essential amendment of the National Constitution," remand the freedmen to new horrors, lead to the merciless proscription of "independent and earnest men," and to the "resuscitation by federal patronage of the entire Copperhead party." The nation's leading Radical paper, the Chicago *Tribune*, which had long since lost its early confidence in Johnson, now attacked relentlessly, not hesitating to accuse the President of "deep hypocrisy" in respect to Negro rights and of deliberate intent to cement the loyalty of Southern states whose votes he expected to make him President. The *Tribune*'s attack was echoed by a number of papers of the Midwest, where there was an acute awareness that Vallandigham, the notorious Ohio Copperhead, was claiming the President as a convert to his platform. Greeley's *Tribune* was firm in opposition, but spoke more in stern sorrow than in anger.[80] These papers accepted the challenge of the veto.

More of the Republican press, however, refused to acknowledge the Presidential declaration of war. They did not damn the veto entirely but saw in it a balance of valid and invalid argument, some tipping the scale for Johnson, others against him. A number accepted the Seward position that the difference between Executive and Congress was a matter not of ends, but of means. There was a general expectation that a modified version of the Bureau bill would receive the President's assent. Many papers ignored the President's denial to Congress of any authority to set conditions before a restoration of the former rebel states to full participation in the nation's councils. With notable exceptions, the pervasive tone of the Republican press was one of respect, a refusal to follow Forney and the Chicago *Tribune* in impugning the motives of the President. The dominant sentiment among Republicans was still one of accepting Johnson as *their* president and scorning Democratic claims that he was theirs or that a chasm had been opened between the Chief Executive and the Union-Republican party.

Evidence of this moderation and openness to conciliation is certain beyond question. The *Herald*'s Washington correspondent sent word that the Republican caucus held the evening after the President's speech was a "singular" affair, without the passion and "spicy time" anticipated. A majority had not been willing "to declare an open war against Andrew Johnson." He predicted that since the congressional majority would not declare war then, when excitement was at its height, they would not be able to do so later, for with time the moderate men of the party would be increasingly "inclined to go with Johnson."[81] The *World* cynically remarked that "the Radicals rather than give up the offices, are preparing to surrender at discretion."[82]

The President still enjoyed the support of influential and articulate moderates, notably that of Senator John Sherman and Governor Jacob D. Cox of Ohio. Governor Cox had talked with the President and released a reassuring letter to the press. Samuel

Bowles, editor of the highly respected Springfield *Republican*, was in Washington and sent home reports of "A Lull in the Conflict at the Capital." He saw in the conversation between Governor Cox and the President a basis for "cooperation and harmony"; meantime, "Congress is doing nothing and saying nothing to aggravate matters."[83] By March 8, Senator Morgan was reporting to Weed: "We are gaining here, but our friends in the Senate were very angry for some time."[84] A week later, Representative Dawes was writing his wife that there would probably be no open rupture during the current session of Congress.[85] Henry Ward Beecher's support of the President in the Freedmen's Bureau veto must have led many an old Abolitionist to suspend judgment.[86] Charles Sumner, the most uncompromising of the Radicals, was weakening in his opposition to anything short of equal suffrage. Indeed, Wendell Phillips, in apprehension, tried to persuade Sumner that "this is no time to consult *harmony*." Phillips disparaged not only Doolittle and Raymond, avowed Johnson supporters, but also Senators Trumbull and Fessenden, moderates, and Henry Wilson of Massachusetts, a Radical, as examples of "cowardly Republicanism."[87] A compromise program for restoration of the Southern states suggested by Senator William M. Stewart of Nevada was receiving wide support.[88] Senator Trumbull believed that his Civil Rights Bill, which would protect Negro rights through regular court procedures rather than the extralegal agency of the Bureau and the Army, had the approval of the President. In short, to quote an authority on the work of the Joint Committee on Reconstruction, there was "much peace talk in and out of Congress."[89]

The conciliatory reaction of Republicans generally, the flood of approving letters that reached his desk, the overwhelming support indicated by the numerous press clippings which his staff assembled—all these may have given Andrew Johnson an unwarranted confidence that he was "master of the situation." To be certain, letters and clippings were weighted heavily by Northern Democratic opinion and Southern jubilation. The President, however, was not unmindful of the Democracy and the South; and neither the South nor the Democracy wished compromise and reconciliation between the President and the congressional majority. Andrew Johnson chose war, not peace. On March 27, 1866, he returned Trumbull's Civil Rights Bill to the Senate with a Presidential veto.

10 CIVIL RIGHTS: THE ISSUE OF RECONSTRUCTION

JOHNSON CHOSE TO RENEW WARFARE WITH A BATTLE OVER FEDERAL protection for the basic civil rights, not including suffrage or officeholding, of the slaves now made free men by the Thirteenth Amendment. The veto of the Civil Rights Bill, officially entitled "An Act to protect all persons in the United States in their civil rights, and furnish the means of their vindication," reopened the conflict between Executive and Congress. The second veto, like the first, can be viewed as an accommodation to the sentiment of the South and of the Northern Democracy.[1] Not one Democratic vote had been cast for the bill in either House. A few days after its passage, George W. Morgan, the Democratic candidate for governor defeated by Jacob D. Cox in Ohio the previous fall, sent the proceedings of a pro-Johnson meeting and the message: "We are looking for another veto."[2] The elder Frank Blair wrote Johnson a letter with four pages of argument against the bill. His objections were all directed to the heart of the matter: under the bill, as Blair saw it, the states would be able to make "no discrimination between *Whites* & Black," a result he considered disastrous. "No man can advocate an amalgamation of the white & black races and so create a mongrel nation. . . . The policy of the country must therefore be a gradual segregation of the Races. This will be attempted by the legislation of the States now filled by negroes." These states must retain such rights, for example, as that to send black convicts to penal colonies outside the country while retaining white convicts in local workhouses. They must be able to induce manufacturing companies into the South by educating the rising generations of the white race while restricting the blacks "to the ruder trades and to the producing of the raw material." Blair concluded the long letter:[3]

An infinite variety of municipal regulations grow up in the economy of states to advance the interest of the Race who made the Govt & to whom it belongs by making discriminations Congress forbids. Has it a right to do it?

Although stated with typical indiscretion, Blair's position represented widespread opinion at the South and among the Northern Democracy.

In contrast, eminent Republicans who had supported the President after the Freedmen's Bureau veto, ardently desired Presidential approval of civil rights legislation. Henry Ward Beecher, invoking the privilege of one who had "suffered, as being a friend of President Johnson," urged Johnson to sign Trumbull's Civil Rights Bill. The *"thing itself* is desirable," it would harmonize feelings, strengthen "your friends' hands," frustrate those who had tried to create the impression "that you have proved untrue to the cause of liberty," meet the prevailing "deep tide of moral feeling."[4] Governor Cox wrote from Ohio pleading for approval, even if it meant that the President must *"strain a point."* The people looked to the purposes of the bill: namely, to give the freedmen "the same rights of property and persons, the same remedies for injuries received and the same penalties for wrongs committed, as other men— This they approve, and they know that you and I and all true Union men have constantly desired this result." Though many of the provisions for enforcement were objectionable, Governor Cox argued that they were still *"civil* provisions . . . not the unrestrained despotism of military power which was embodied in the Freedmen's bureau bill."

If the Southern people would "do right themselves," by breaking down "the distinctions between classes," the law would be of little "practical moment . . . a dead letter." Executive approval of a bill, the Ohio Governor counseled, "by no means implies full assent to a measure," only that its objectionable features are not so "gross" as to make it an executive duty to interpose. The long letter made an appeal based upon practical politics. Cox had found the Ohio Democracy hypocritical in their support of the President; inasmuch as they had no disposition "to abandon their organization as a party," no real help could come from them except "as we convert *individuals*." Approval of the Civil Rights Bill would make Johnson with "our Western people," "fully master of the situation," would remove any possibility of opposition in Union ranks to other Administration measures, and would greatly assist in "holding together our State organizations, but this is a consideration I would not feel like urging upon you."[5]

On the eve of the veto, aware of its imminence, Thurlow Weed wrote Seward a letter meant for the President's eye. If the Civil Rights Bill were to be vetoed, the President must make a point of his long-standing "paternal regard for a race whose changed condition" required such legislation. "If he manifests a desire that the Negroes shall be protected in all that concerns his personal rights and material welfare the People will go with him."[6] Seward himself sent a hurried and unsigned note to the President: "If you can find a way to intimate that *you are not opposed to the policy of the bill* but *only to its detailed* provisions, it will be a great improvement and make the support of the veto easier to our friends in Congress."[7]

As in the case of the earlier Freedmen's Bureau Bill, Secretary Seward's attitude toward the Civil Rights Bill is revealed in a draft message prepared for the President.[8] Once again, Seward was conciliatory where Johnson was hostile. He objected at length to certain aspects of the bill, "rather questions of form than questions of substance," particularly the enforcement provisions; but in effect, Seward invited Congress to frame a new bill that would eliminate objectionable features yet effectively safeguard civil equality for the Negro through the Federal judiciary. The object of the bill, "to secure all persons in their civil rights without regard to race or color," received Seward's explicit approval, as did the status of citizenship for the freedmen. So far from challenging the right of Congress to pass such legislation, he pointed to a constitutional basis for the bill in the enforcement clause of the Thirteenth Amendment and in the privileges and immunities clause of the original Constitution. He tried to counter apprehensions that a guarantee of civil rights would open the door to congressional legislation granting suffrage to the Negro. Qualifications for voting and officeholding, according to Seward, would be left with the states, "precisely as if the bill were not enacted into law."[9]

In all these aspects, Seward's attitude was in sharp contrast to the position taken by Johnson in the official message. This is true despite the fact that the President borrowed liberally from Seward's draft.[10] Johnson challenged the assumption that the newly emancipated slaves were qualified for citizenship.[11] By indirection, he defended discrimination by state law on the basis of race. He raised the objection that if Congress had the power to abrogate state discriminations in respect to certain civil rights, it would also have the power to decide who should be juror, judge, and voter. He affirmed that Congress had no power over states, as it did over territories " 'to make rules and regulations' for them."[12] The weight of argument in the President's message, as this quotation indicates, was against the position that Congress possessed authority to pass civil rights legislation; it implied that such legislation would be an invasion of the reserved rights of the states. The message, however, did not squarely face the basic question of congressional authority. At one point, the President referred to the enforcement clause of the Thirteenth Amendment as presumably the authority by virtue of which the bill gave Federal courts exclusive jurisdiction over cases involving discrimination. Without agreeing or disagreeing with that presumption, he continued, "It cannot, however, be justly claimed that, with a view to the enforcement of this article of the Constitution, there is at present any necessity for the exercise of all the powers which this bill confers."[13] Toward the close of the message, the President included a strong states'-rights statement drafted by Secretary Welles. This passage condemned the bill's provisions generally as an interference with municipal legislation that would destroy the Federal system of limited powers and intrude upon the reserved rights of the states.

Seward had ended his draft with a Presidential promise to approve "any bill that should provide, in harmony with the convictions I have expressed, for the protection of the civil rights of all classes of persons throughout the United States by judicial process in conformity with the Constitution of the United States." In a slightly more qualified version, Johnson added Seward's conclusion to his own veto. In the context of the message as a whole, however, it was a meaningless concession.

Despite the ambiguous concluding promise, Johnson's message when compared with Seward's draft clearly indicates that Presidential opposition to civil rights legislation was a matter not of form but of substance. In fact, Johnson refused to make any substantive concessions to moderate Republicans, Seward included, who desired a federally enforceable status of civil equality, short of voting and officeholding, for the former slave. Conclusive evidence can be found in the letters of Senator Edwin D. Morgan. Senator Morgan, it will be recalled, was closely associated with Seward and Weed. He had voted to uphold the Freedmen's Bureau veto; even after the veto of the Civil Rights Bill, he counseled against hasty condemnation of the President and made known his desire that "the great body of those with whom I am politically associated will continue acting together, and acting with the President."[14] He refused to bend before the pressure of "the malcontents," insisting that "the President means to do right."[15]

Morgan was ill during this period, but he was much concerned about the civil rights measure and kept in touch with Seward. On the 26th, the day before the veto, he sent an urgent note to Seward requesting information. "I am all in the dark as to what is going on and I want much to know more than I do concerning the Veto which it is said will be sent to the Senate perhaps today."[16] Secretary Seward sent Morgan's plea to the Executive Mansion with the notation: "Have the President please read and enable me to answer Gov. Morgan." The penciled reply to Seward read: "It will not go in before tomorrow—Mr. Moore will be over to see you."[17] The President's secretary, however, apparently did not appear. He wrote Seward that the President had directed another copy of his message to be made and expected that "it would be prepared in time for your examination this evening. He finds, however, that but little progress has been made, and fears that if he arrests the work he will not be able to obtain a correct copy in time for the Cabinet meeting tomorrow morning. He therefore directs me to say that it will be ready for you at any hour in the morning that you may designate."[18] This correspondence suggests not only Morgan's apprehensions and his desire to act in harmony with the President, but also a Presidential reluctance to discuss the message privately with Seward on the very eve of its release. In view of what we now know of Seward's position and its variance with that of the President's, the report of the Cabinet meeting next morning, March 27, which Welles noted in his diary, is of special interest. Welles wrote, "Seward said he [had] carefully studied the bill and thought it might be well to pass a law declaring negroes were citizens, because there had been some questions raised [on that point] though there never was a doubt in his own mind."[19] This passage suggests that Seward made a final, but ineffectual, plea for a major modification of the position Johnson had taken.

Between the veto and the vote upon it in the Senate, Senator Morgan conferred with the President in an attempt to secure "an understanding in relation to a new 'Civil Rights Bill,' free from Constitutional objections, and that will afford all necessary protection." He was convinced that this would achieve "harmony, in the party; and unity in the Nation."[20] At first he was hopeful. Thurlow Weed, whom Morgan kept informed of his position and activities, sent words of encouragement and counsel. Morgan's statement of his support of the President had quieted apprehensions among friends in New York and Albany. "Pray do not let the Friends of the Administration be kept in a negative position," Weed continued. "You need *affirmative* ground to stand on. The president can be invincible if to wisdom he adds calmness and *tact*."[21]

On April 6, in a dramatically close vote, the Senate overrode Johnson's veto of the Civil Rights Bill. Senator Morgan, to the applause of the galleries, cast his vote for the bill and against the President. Two days later he sent Thurlow Weed an explanation. He had made "most earnest efforts with Mr. Fessenden and with the President to have a compromise bill agreed upon and passed. It looked hopeful at one time but failed. The difficulty really was the President's objections to the *first* section of the bill. It was then *this* bill or *nothing*. . . . It is unfortunate perhaps that the bill was not signed. But if it had been returned with the President's objections to the second section *only* we could have got along with it very well and maintained ourselves which is a matter of *some* consideration." Morgan argued that with the issue out of the way in the elections, the President would be in a better position than if the bill had been defeated.[22] The first section of the bill, to which Morgan referred as crucial in the negotiations with the President, was the section granting Negroes citizenship and equal civil rights.

Other personal letters of Morgan repeated and elaborated his explanation to Weed. Had the President disavowed objections to the "*Principle* and pointed out the defects of the *details*, the Senate would have amended and passed the bill without any break or serious trouble, as we all knew that the *second* section was objectionable. But the first section declaring the Blacks Citizens, we could not and would not give up."[23]

When the Civil Rights Bill was returned to the Senate, Lyman Trumbull rose to voice the conclusion of a moderate man who felt a profound obligation to the newly freed Negroes of the South:[24]

Whatever may have been the opinion of the President at one time as to "good faith requiring the security of the freedmen in their liberty and their property" it is now manifest from the character of his objections to this bill that he will approve no measure that will accomplish the object.

Ironically, the *Herald* agreed. Ten days earlier its editorial columns had characterized the bill as "a practical, just and benefi-

cent measure," in no way conflicting with the "declared opinions and policy of President Johnson";[25] now it jubilantly greeted
the veto as the signal of a political revolution:[26]

The objections submitted against the first section of the bill, however, are those which mark the impassable barrier between him and
the ruling radicals of Congress. He is opposed to the recognition at
present, by law, of the blacks as citizens of the United States, and he
is opposed to any further legislation by Congress affecting the domestic affairs of the several States. . . .

Just after the veto, the conciliatory Henry L. Dawes, who had
harsh words for the President's extreme opponents, wrote his
wife that Johnson had deprived "every friend he has of the least
ground upon which to stand and defend him."[27]

No oratory of Charles Sumner, no lash of Thaddeus Stevens'
tongue nor of his reputed political whip, could drive the Republican majority in Congress into sustained open warfare with the
President. This accomplishment was Johnson's own. By refusing
Presidential support to any program that would effectively secure
equality before the law to the four million slaves whom the
national government had made free, he fatally alienated the reasonable men who wished to act with him rather than against him.
For some, the principle of equal status was decisive; for others,
the prospect of repudiation by their Republican constituencies
may have been sufficient reason. Johnson might have called for
modified civil rights legislation or asked for a constitutional
amendment to put beyond question the right of Congress to
secure for the freedmen civil equality.[28] He did neither.

By giving countenance to the Democratic claim that the Civil
Rights Act was unconstitutional, Johnson helped to destroy any
possibility that the civil rights issue, as Senator Morgan had
hoped, would be removed from the political arena. When Congress subsequently formulated its own amendment, with the
vital section one on citizenship and equal rights, Johnson might
have accepted it in whole or in part, or he might have used it as
a point of departure for compromise. Instead, the President made
clear his disapproval of any constitutional amendment whatsoever
before the South had been fully restored to a voice in national

affairs.[29] It was obvious at the time, as it is evident in retrospect, that no civil rights amendment could have received the requisite two-thirds vote of both Houses of Congress with the South fully represented. Neither in March of 1866, nor later, did Andrew Johnson give to the moderates of the party that had elected him any alternative with which they might spare the nation a dread conflict between Congress and the Chief Executive.[30]

In declaring war upon the Radicals, Johnson chose to make as well an issue with moderate Republicans. His action on the Civil Rights Bill, like that on the Freedmen's Bureau Bill, cannot be explained on the sole basis of Radical provocation or constitutional principles. It must be viewed in the context of pressures from the Democracy, North and South, and of plans to precipitate a reorganization of national parties that would result in a new or transformed Union party under his personal leadership. Yet a new or transformed Union party would be only the Democracy in disguise unless it could command the support of moderate men in the Republican ranks. Whether Johnson wished the substance or only the appearance of a new amalgam, we cannot know. If the former, his unyielding attitude on the civil rights issue was a major blunder. He may have been blinded by his own racial attitudes or by his victory in the battle over the Freedmen's Bureau Bill. Contemporary evidence, however, should have made unmistakably clear the near unanimity of Republican public opinion on behalf of some national guarantee of equal civil rights for the freedmen.

The advice of Henry Ward Beecher, of Governor Cox, of Thurlow Weed, and of Secretary Seward indicated the importance of the civil rights issue to continued support from rank-and-file Republicans. Even Senator Cowan in advising the second veto cautioned the President to "Be careful to put it distinctly as a question of *power*—not of policy—indeed it might be recommended to the States with propriety."[31] It will be recalled that John Cochrane, who had labored so diligently to prepare the way for a Johnson party centered about the War Democrats, had sent similar advice. He had cautioned Johnson that in the approaching conflict with his "disguised enemies" it would be

essential that the line of Presidential policy could not be interpreted as unfriendly to the Negro. "That concession to public
opinion" would enable Johnson to carry the North.[32] R. P. L.
Baber, a diligent Johnson political lieutenant, wrote from Ohio
both before and after the veto to Senator Doolittle, Secretary
Seward, and the President about the strategy needed for success
in the approaching congressional elections. A central requisite was
"Some effective and Constitutional law to enable the Freedmen
to enforce in the Federal Courts, rights denied them in the State
Courts, as to the protection of person and property."[33] Russell
Houston, an old personal friend who had acted as an intermediary
between Johnson and the New York Democracy, wrote Johnson
from Kentucky advising that the President's supporters in Congress take the lead in advocating a civil rights bill that would not
be unconstitutional or inappropriate. "It is important to you and
to the country, that when the issues now being made, shall go
before the people, you should appear as you are and have been,
the advocate, the friend and the promoter of the freedom of all
the people of our Country whether of one race or another. . . .
Under ordinary circumstances, I might say that no legislation on
the subject was necessary, but under present circumstances, I
think differently."[34] A New Jersey representative wrote the
President to explain that his vote on the Civil Rights Bill did not
indicate any desire to desert the Administration. "Whilst a different course would not have sustained you practically it would have
been a violation of my own sense of right, and in decided contra-
vention of the will of our friends whose opinion I have ascertained
by personal observation during my stay at Trenton last week.
They strongly desire protection to the freedmen and fear the
States would be slow to accord it."[35]

Private letters to Secretary Seward and to Senator Morgan bear
eloquent testimony to the importance of the civil rights issue.
Seward's public defense of the Freedmen's Bureau veto evoked
from an old friend and political supporter words of harsh but
sorrowful repudiation. "Had any one predicted even a single year
ago you would in so brief a period be found side by side with
the Hoods, Vallandigham, Pearce, Buchanan, Voorhees, Brooks,

Davis and other aiders and abetters of the rebellion, I should have deemed him as a libeller. . . . [Your friends] have the painful mortification of seeing you co-operating with your life-long enemies and the enemies of Freedom, Justice, Humanity and the Union, to fasten upon the country a system of slavery ten times more odious and cruel than that which the Army of the Republic has destroyed."[36] After the second veto, another former admirer wrote: "Your former friends are all deserting you. . . . Your reconstruction policy is believed by the people fatal to the true interests of liberty and the life of the Nation. Justice to the loyal whites of the South and the Freedmen is justice to the nation, so the people believe."[37] The pastor of New York's Trinity Church wrote to commend Morgan for sustaining the Civil Rights Bill. "That Bill seemed to us to be the necessary Legislation to give vitality to the late Amendment to the Constitution of the United States and to make freedom a real thing to the emancipated. . . . It is high time to assert by Legislation, the Union and Nationality of this great Country, and to maintain the citizenship of every native born American."[38] Another minister expressed satisfaction in the passage of the law for much the same reasons: "If our people are not to be protected by national law in the Civil Rights that are secured even in the empires of Europe, with what face can we stand up among the free nations of the world?"[39] A New York banker succinctly stated the issue: "The Freedmen's Bureau Bill involved a question of expediency about which earnest Union men might differ—the Civil Rights Bill however stood upon a different basis. The people whose rights as Citizens are sought to be protected by the Bill, were entitled to receive from the Government a law that would secure to them the practical enjoyment of those rights."[40] A New York lawyer congratulated Morgan upon his vote: "I am not radical but I am confident you will never regret the aid you gave to common humanity in sustaining that bill."[41]

The response of the press also indicated that Republican opinion was committed to some form of civil rights action. Republican papers were much more united in their support of Congress than had been the case after the first veto. Bryant's *Evening Post*, which had supported the President earlier, now regretfully dissented. The moderate and conciliatory editor of the Springfield *Republican* reluctantly concluded that the Civil Rights Bill must be passed over the President's veto "or the hope of any special legislation for the protection of the freedmen must be abandoned."[42] A few days later, at the very time when Senator Morgan was seeking compromise, Bowles wrote an extended analysis of the political situation. The President's purpose, according to the Springfield *Republican*'s editor, had been to drive off from the Republican party a small faction of extreme radicals and consolidate the mass of Republicans with War Democrats of the North and loyalists of the South into a powerful party that would bring the Union "peace and prosperity" and "give him a triumphant re-election." Even after the February 22 speech, the President might have held half the Republicans, "led Congress to his plan of reconstruction," and gained a larger power with the country than he had ever before possessed. The veto of the Civil Rights Bill, however, "instead of driving off from him a small minority of the republican party, or even the half of it, drives off substantially the whole of it. There is but one voice among republicans on this point. . . . If Mr. Johnson is to stand by the doctrine of that document, he must inevitably part company with all the great body of his old supporters, and rely for his friends upon the northern democrats and the reconstructed rebels of the South. . . . For though they might give up everything else; waive universal suffrage, concede the admission of southern Congressmen, abolish the test oath, grant general amnesty, they cannot give up national protection to the weak and minority classes in the South."[43] The *Democrat and Free Press* of Rockland, Maine, gave a similar warning. "Mr. Johnson is mistaken if he supposes that fanaticism is at the bottom of the movement to give the negroes the rights of free men. It is not fanaticism, but cool judgment; it is not sustained by the few, but by the great mass of those who fought down the rebellion."[44] The Columbus, Ohio, *Journal* commented that by the veto, the President "had done more to strengthen the supporters of Congress and to determine the policy of the wavering, than months of argument."[45]

Even the Republican papers that remained friendly in their attitude toward the President made clear their own support for some form of national guarantee of the freedmen's rights. A few reconciled their own attitude with that of the President by pointing to his concluding promise, the one Johnson had incorporated from Seward's draft, and insisting that the President was not opposed to Federal protection. Most of the Republican press, however, saw the veto as drawing a sharp line between the position of the President and that of their party.[46]

What had been taking place in the Republican party since the close of the civil conflict was a gradual metamorphosis, similar to the one that had taken place during the war. The war years transformed the Republicans, a political amalgam originally united on the principle of opposition to the extension of slavery, into a party committed to the destruction of slavery. This objective had been formally embodied in the party platform of 1864. The platform, however, had not included a plank supporting equal legal status for the freed slaves, despite the fact that such a plank was offered and considered. By the winter of 1865, Republicans generally had expanded their repudiation of slavery into a condemnation of legal discriminations which by then seemed to them the last vestiges of slavery. Important elements within the party held that the freedmen's rights must include an equality of suffrage, but on this more advanced position, Republicans were not yet agreed. They had, however, come to identify Republicanism with a defense of basic civil rights for the freed slave.[47] Sometimes this identification of Republicanism with the principle of equal status before the law was stated explicitly; sometimes it was expressed through generalizations that invoked liberty, freedom, or humanity. A characteristic argument, advanced by one Republican paper, was that if the position on equal civil rights embodied in Johnson's veto message were correct, then "all the principles of democracy and freedom upon which our creed of Republicanism rests are false and we must recant them."[48] When Republicans accused Johnson of treachery to the Republican party and Republican principles, or with greater forbearance simply asked that he give them some unmistakable evidence so that they might "continue to confide in him as a *Republican*,"[49] they were identifying their party with the principle of equality in legal status for all freedmen.

Thus what had once been an advanced, or "Radical," position within Republican ranks, by 1866 had become accepted and moderate. To most opponents of equal civil status, however, the principle still appeared "Radical." Herein lies one clue to the confusion in the use of the term "Radical" which plagues any serious student of the period. The term is inescapable; yet a man labeled a "Radical" by one set of contemporaries or historians is often found designated a "moderate" by another group of contemporaries or historians. All would agree that Charles Sumner, Thaddeus Stevens, and Wendell Phillips, extreme men though not of one mind, were the prototypes of Radicalism. The term *radical*, however, has often been used to identify, and castigate, all Republican opponents of Andrew Johnson. Many of these men were almost as critical of Sumner, Stevens, and Phillips as were their Conservative adversaries. Few followed Stevens in his demand for confiscation; most were ready to abandon or drastically compromise Sumner's aim of Negro suffrage. Though they wished to proceed with caution, there was no strong desire among them for an indefinite postponement of restoration by reducing the South to the status of "territories" or "conquered provinces." In other words, many Radicals were moderate men. The Radical opponents of President Johnson were united in one demand—that of national protection for the freedmen. On other issues of Reconstruction they held widely divergent views.

It has sometimes been assumed that a common economic attitude united Radicals and marked them off from pro-Johnson men. This assumption is demonstrably false. Some were protariff men, some antitariff men; some advocated cheap money, some upheld a sound gold standard; some were spoilsmen, others were among the spoilsmen's bitterest critics.[50] In 1865 and 1866 substantial members of the business community were as often found in the ranks of the President's supporters as in those of the opposition.[51] John A. Dix, a key figure in the Johnson movement, was president of the Union Pacific. A twenty-thousand dollar reception and dinner at the famed Delmonico's, at the opening of Johnson's ill-fated Swing-around-the-Circle, was attended by many of the most powerful figures of New York business and finance.[52] As late as September, 1866, the New York *Times,* in an editorial entitled "Business and Politics—the Conservatism of Commerce"—spoke of the "great unanimity of the commercial and business classes in supporting the conservative policy of the Administration, and in opposing with their might the schemes of the Radical Destructives."[53]

Nor were the Radicals distinguishable from the general run of Union men, as is often claimed, by vindictiveness toward the South or clamor for the heads of "traitors." Indeed, New York's outstanding Radical leader, Horace Greeley, was a leading figure in the movement for amnesty and forgiveness. Henry Wilson, Radical senator from Massachusetts, wrote to Johnson in support of a plea for the parole of Clement C. Clay of Alabama.[54] Even Thaddeus Stevens offered his services in the defense both of Clay and of Jefferson Davis.[55] The feeling against Southern leaders of the rebellion, which found expression both in a stubborn indignation at the prospect of their speedy return to the halls of Congress and in an emotional demand for Jefferson Davis' trial and conviction, cut across the division between pro-Johnson and anti-Johnson men. Thus in December, 1865, the House passed a resolution supporting the stringent Test Oath of July, 1862, as binding without exception upon all branches of government. Only one Republican registered opposition.[56] A few days earlier, without a single dissenting voice, the House had declared treason a crime that should be punished; thirty-four Democrats joined the Republicans in voting "yea."[57] In June, after the break with the President, a resolution calling for the trial of Jefferson Davis passed by a vote of 105 to 19, with no Republican voting against it. Six of the seven Conservatives who had broken with the majority of their party to support Johnson in the Civil Rights veto, registered their approval of this demand.[58]

The only common denominator that united the Radicals of 1866, and the only characteristic they shared which could logically justify the term *radical,* was their determination that the rebel

South should not be reinstated into the Union until there were adequate guarantees that the slaves liberated by the nation should enjoy the rights of free men.[59] It is true that Johnson's opponents believed Congress should have some voice in Reconstruction and that they were profoundly disturbed by the prospect of a restored South, united with the Northern Democracy, immediately controlling the destinies of the nation. They were also extremely sensitive to any patronage moves that might seem to indicate Johnson's support of the Democracy or an intent to punish Republicans for failure to agree completely with the President's position. These attitudes, however, can hardly be termed radical; and they were not decisive factors with most of the men who broke with the President after the veto messages. Possibly, without the civil rights issue, one of these points of friction might have generated warfare and become the dividing line between Johnson's opponents and his supporters; but this is extremely doubtful. The testimony of such men as Samuel Bowles, Thurlow Weed, Jacob D. Cox, and John Cochrane must be given weight. They believed that the President could achieve his goal of speedy restoration and renewed fellowship between North and South if only he endorsed some effective national guarantee of the freedmen's civil rights as citizens.[60] One of the most distinguished students of congressional Reconstruction, thoroughly sympathetic to Johnson, concluded that the moderate leadership in Congress desired just three conditions and would have settled for two: a guarantee of "the negroes' civil rights" and recognition of "the prerogative of Congress."[61] Since executive action alone could not guarantee the South's permanent acquiescence in the freedmen's newly gained rights, such security could be had only by way of the second condition, acceptance of some congressional action in the matter. In other words, the two conditions were inseparable; Johnson's consent to the first would have automatically fulfilled the second. Had Johnson come to terms with the moderates on the civil rights issue, the truly radical men of the party would have been clearly distinguishable from Republicans generally; and the true "Radical" would have faced the choice of compromise or defeat. Instead, except for a handful of Conservatives who totally accepted

Johnson's leadership, "Republican" tended to become synonymous with "Radical."

The Democracy had a major responsibility for the blurring of distinction between the terms *Radical* and *Republican*. Even before the vetoes, they had tended to stigmatize the entire Republican leadership in Congress as "Radical"; after the vetoes, they delighted in maligning the Freedmen's Bureau Bill and the Civil Rights Act as parts of a sinister Radical design to defeat Johnson's plan for speedy restoration. This was good political strategy. Political expediency and propaganda, however, are not a complete explanation. In the eyes of Democrats, North and South, the claim of "equality," in any form, for the newly freed Negro was indeed radical, an outrageous postwar version of prewar Abolitionism. Both before and after the vetoes, one finds expressions in the Democratic press and in private letters of the period which indicate an unmistakable identification of "Radical" with "Abolitionist." Thus, a Tennessee judge, complaining about the interference of the military, started to write that this was "just what the abominable Abolitionis [*sic*]" desired, then crossed out "Abolitionis" and substituted the word "Radicals."[62] It is true that Northern Democratic spokesmen and responsible Southerners at times urged upon the Southern states full equality in civil proceedings; but they did so because this appeared to them not only an inescapable concession to Republican opinion but a necessary condition for Presidential support as well. Moreover, so long as exclusive state authority were maintained, concessions made by state action before restoration could be undone by state action after restoration.

There is a certain validity in the Democratic equation that denied the historical differences between oldtime Abolitionists, postwar extremists, and those moderate Republicans of 1866 who upheld equal civil rights for the Negro. Between pro-Johnson Conservatives and anti-Johnson Radicals—whether the latter were moderate or extreme—the dividing line was marked by a distinction in race attitude. Wide differences existed on each side of the line, and there were those who took their places in each camp for reasons primarily of political expediency and advantage. Yet by

1866 all Radicals accepted, indeed most held as an article of faith, a nationally enforceable equality of civil status, even though their attitudes might differ in respect to equality of suffrage and equality of social status for the Negro. The position of Johnson supporters varied from extreme racism to an uncomfortable accommodation to the probability that legal discrimination and inequitable treatment for the freed slave would follow upon an unrestrained local autonomy in race relations. The anti-Johnson side attracted men with a deep sense of concern and responsibility for the freed slave; the pro-Johnson ranks drew men who thought national responsibility had ended with the destruction of property rights in human beings. The latter preferred to base formal argument upon aversion to centralized government, a defense of states' rights, respect for the Constitution, and devotion to a reunited Union. But behind such arguments there most often lay some shade of that prejudice of race which still divides the nation.

The racist tendency among Northern Democrats hardly needs further demonstration. If evidence is desired, it can be found among the editorials with which the veto messages were greeted. Johnson does not believe, wrote one New England Democratic editor, "in compounding our race with niggers, gipsies and baboons, neither do we . . . [or] our whole Democratic people."[63] A Washington paper editorialized:[64]

The negro is to have full and perfect equality with the white man. He is to mix up with the white gentlemen and ladies all over the land . . . at all public meetings and public places he is to be your equal and your associate. . . . How long will it be if Congress can do all this before it will say the negro shall vote, sit in the jury box, and intermarry with your families? Such are the questions put by the President.

The *Ohio Statesman* declared it was no crime for the President to "esteem his race as superior to an inferior race. In this hour of severe trial, when the President is endeavoring so to administer the government that the white man shall not be subordinated to the negro race, will not the white man stand by him."[65] The Radicals, commented a Pennsylvania paper with satisfaction, "now find that President Johnson regards this government as the White man's."[66] One set of huge headlines read:[67]

ALL HAIL!
GRAND AND GLORIOUS!
GREAT VICTORY FOR THE WHITE MAN
REJOICE, WHITE MAN REJOICE!
THE HOUR OF YOUR DELIVERANCE HAS COME
SATAN IS BOUND
RADICALISM REBUKED
TAXPAYERS RELIEVED
PRESIDENT JOHNSON TURNS OUT TO BE
A FULL BLOODED WHITE MAN
HAS VETOED THE FREEDMEN'S BUREAU BILL
'THE NEGROES HAVE TO WORK'

The limitations of Andrew Johnson's own benevolence toward the freedmen have already been explored.[68] A word more should be added as to the overtones of race prejudice apparent in his veto message. These may have been unintended expressions of his own bias or, more probably, deliberate appeals to the race prejudice of others. The first veto offended much less overtly than the second, although it called forth at least one protest against its appeal to "a low prejudice against color."[69] The offending passage was the argument that Congress could hardly appropriate moneys for relief, lands, and schools for the freedmen when it had never considered itself authorized "to expend the public money for the rent or purchase of homes for the thousands, not to say millions of the white race who are honestly toiling from day to day for their subsistence." The Civil Rights veto claimed that "the distinction of race and color is, by the bill, made to operate in favor of the colored and against the white race." It also raised the emotion-laden subject of intermarriage between whites and blacks, although the matter had little relevance to the President's argument. And in a passage clearly not intended as a compliment, it equated "the entire race designated as blacks, people of color, negroes, mullattoes, and persons of African blood" with Chinese, Indians, and "the people called Gipsies."[70]

The racist attitudes of the Blairs and of James Gordon Bennett, men whose influence with Johnson was very considerable, have already been sufficiently established.[71] The attitude of Conservative Republicans who stood with the President is less evident and requires examination.

Though not without criticism of the President, Gideon Welles agreed more completely with him than did any other member of the original Cabinet. Welles alone thoroughly approved of the Civil Rights veto. What he criticized in Johnson's conduct of affairs was *too little* of the very qualities most other critics have thought the Tennessean had in excess—inflexibility and boldness. The fact is that Welles at one end of the Republican spectrum was at least as dogmatic and extreme as was Charles Sumner at the other. An old Jacksonian Democrat, Welles's narrow views of national power and states' rights were unaffected by his adherence to the Republican party. Qualified only by fading personal loyalties and a stout defense of the war effort, his sympathies throughout the postwar period were with the Democrats. A sanctimonious curmudgeon, whom history has largely taken at his own self-evaluation, Welles had kind words for few men. Even so, the sustained animus and distortion that he directed against the Radicals in his famed diary are particularly malicious.

With a record of having broken with the Democratic party over slavery and of having ordered the wartime Navy to protect runaway slaves and to enlist Negroes, Welles's hostility toward the Radicals might be thought to have arisen entirely from his states'-rights views. This, however, was not the sole explanation. In the diary, Welles revealed a marked distaste for the "ingrained Abolitionism"[72] which he thought motivated Johnson's opponents. He was also frank in stating that he was "no advocate for social equality, nor do I labor for political or civil equality for the negro. I do not want him at my table, nor do I care to have him in the jury-box, or in the legislative hall, or on the bench."[73] The Washington correspondent of the Springfield *Republican*, while unconvinced by rumors that Welles had told his Democratic friends in Connecticut that he was opposed to Negro suffrage just before the state was to vote upon the question, thought it quite likely that Welles, who "never was very radical on the slavery question . . . retains many of his prejudices against the colored people."[74] Welles agreed with Sumner that there was "a dreadful state of things South" and that "the colored people were suffering"; but his own concern was for the whites who had also passed through a terrible ordeal and had hardship enough without "any oppressive acts from abroad."[75] Sumner told Welles that he, New England's representative in the Cabinet, misrepresented New England sentiment;[76] in this judgment, Sumner was most certainly correct.

Senator Doolittle of Wisconsin, the strongest pro-Johnson Republican in Congress, was not without compassion for the Negro, but his view of future race relations precluded any possibility of equality. Before and during the civil conflict, Doolittle had been acutely aware of the race problem and the difficulty of its solution. In his opposition to the extension of slavery, a key consideration was the desire to save the western lands for white settlers. He had been willing that the North should join in paying the expense of colonizing Southern Negroes in Latin America, and he had developed a strong feeling of resentment against the Abolitionists.[77]

In the fall of 1865, Doolittle proposed as a solution of the Negro problem that a part of Texas, and perhaps of Florida as well, be ceded to the Federal Government for a segregated freedmen's territory. His object was to attract the entire Negro population of the South to these exclusively Negro territories by the offer of free homesteads. Only thus, in his view, could they "save themselves from being trodden under foot by the advancing tide of Caucasion emigration from Europe and from all the North."[78] Short of such a territorial haven, Doolittle apparently thought that the problem would be resolved only by the passing away of the Negro due to his excessively high death rate in freedom.[79] He believed that rather than the comprehensive freedom given by the Thirteenth Amendment, it would have been far better for the slaves had their emancipation been gradual, with those born after a certain date made free at twenty-one or even thirty years of age.[80] After the veto of the Civil Rights Bill, the Wisconsin legislature instructed Doolittle, who had not voted on its original passage, to support the measure. When he refused to do so, the legislature called for his resignation.[81]

The draft argument of Senator Edgar Cowan of Pennsylvania for Johnson's veto of the Freedmen's Bureau Bill is revealing. In it there is no kind word for the freedmen nor for the Bureau. Cowan viewed with distaste not only the military jurisdiction which the bill authorized but also the fact that it went "the whole length of putting the negroes upon the same footing precisely as the whites as to all *civil rights and immunities*." He not only argued a want of power on the part of the Federal Government to purchase lands for the relief of destitute freedmen or to establish school buildings for their benefit, but added:[82]

The people were willing to emancipate the slave in order that he might have a chance to take care of himself—but they will be very unwilling to pay for his maintenance and support out of the public purse—and they say justly that if he is unable to cope with his neighbors, in the battle for life—he must be content with the fate which awaits him and not expect them to feed him at the nation's expense.

After the first veto, it is clear that Cowan recognized that general opinion in the North was not altogether in accord with his own. He urged Johnson to veto the Civil Rights Bill, but warned that the President's public opposition to the measure should not include an attack upon its principle of equal status.[83]

Cowan had been one of the three Republican senators voting against the Civil Rights Bill on its passage in early February, before the first veto; the other thirty-three Republicans who voted supported the measure.[84] On the Freedmen's Bureau Bill a few days earlier he had registered no vote, but in the course of discussion, when he had referred to himself as a friend of the Negro, Senator Henry Wilson had sharply attacked his record. "Why, Sir, there has hardly been a proposition before the Senate of the United States for the last five years leading to the emancipation of the negro and the protection of his rights that the Senator from Pennsylvania has not sturdily opposed. . . . He has made himself the champion of 'how not to do it.' "[85] A sympathetic student of Cowan's public career quotes Wilson's speech at length, and then comments, "These were strong words yet underneath them there was much truth."[86] The following May, Cowan was arguing that the men who were repudiating the Union-Republican platforms of Chicago (1860) and Baltimore (1864) were not those who stood by the President, but those "who go away after false lights, who wander in dangerous places, who cook up Freedmen's Bureau and civil rights bills."[87]

About James Dixon of Connecticut, the third of Johnson's Republican supporters in the Senate, we have little evidence. In October, 1865, he wrote the President that "the People desire justice to the Negro but they are tired of the perpetual reiteration of his claims upon their attention to the exclusion of all other interests. Moreover, as you will see by the recent vote of Connecticut on the question of extending suffrage to the colored population, there are grave doubts as to his fitness to govern the country, even *here*."[88] These words do not sound like those of a man with a deep concern for the Negro and his status. The same implication appears in an attack upon Senator Dixon by a fellow Connecticut Republican, who publicly accused him in 1863 of caring only for power. "I was forced to the conclusion that his [Dixon's] sympathies were not with his own section, but were with the Southern oligarchy. . . . That he hated republicanism for its humanity, and its self-sacrificing devotion to principle."[89]

The Thomas Ewings were among the most influential of Johnson's political counselors. Both father and son had a staunchly antislavery prewar record; yet the elder Ewing was known as a conservative Whig and Republican, not "as one of the 'earnest' or 'progressive' men of his time."[90] That the want of "earnestness" characterized his view of the Negro would seem evident from Ewing's notes for a public statement in 1867. In arguing against Negro suffrage in the South, he maintained that in the North "the popular mind cannot be excited to enthusiasm in favor of negro equality, social or political." Neither laborers, mechanics, nor professional men would admit a Negro man or woman on terms of equality to their parties, dinners, or dances, for the consequence would be mixed marriages. The feeling might be "vulgar prejudice, but if so, I am content to acknowledge myself therein essentially vulgar—I would be most unwilling to have a black daughter in law." According to Ewing, some Republicans thought that Providence would interfere and bring about Negro suffrage because it was founded on eternal justice, but God knew when he created man what was good for his creatures. "It is not probable that he will by a special miracle suddenly change his nature—his instincts, his prejudices and his passions, in order to adapt him to any man's or any party's purposes."[91]

Two intimate associates of Ewing's were brought into Johnson's Cabinet in 1866 on his recommendation, Henry Stanbery as Attorney General and Orville H. Browning as Secretary of the Interior. Though a Republican, Stanbery described himself to Democrats in 1868 as having been an "old guard" Whig who ceased to be one only when that party ceased to exist. Apparently he had not voted for Lincoln: "My last vote was given to that party [Whig] in the Presidential contest of 1860."[92] He was the author of those passages in Johnson's Civil Rights veto which appealed to race prejudice by interjecting the question of mixed marriages.[93] According to Gideon Welles, Stanbery told Cabinet members in 1867 that as a member of the Ohio legislature he had voted against Negro suffrage, and that he would do so again were he in Ohio.[94] Before the Supreme Court in 1875, it was Stanbery who argued the famous case of U.S. *vs.* Reese, thereby helping to set aside the Civil Rights Enforcement Act of 1870.[95]

Stanbery's colleague in the Cabinet, Orville Browning, had been an antislavery man, but one of the most conservative variety, an outspoken opponent of Abolitionists.[96] During the war he deplored Lincoln's action in issuing the Emancipation Proclamation.[97] The Thirteenth Amendment, in Browning's opinion, merely gave the slaves personal freedom and did not confer other rights "not necessary incidents of personal liberty, and not necessary for its enjoyment"; and he was opposed to further legislation or constitutional amendment to secure additional liberties. "If the general government will take its hands off, and let the thing alone, it will soon adjust itself upon a better and more satisfactory basis for all parties, than it can ever be forced to do by Federal interference."[98] Even after the ratification of the Fifteenth Amendment, Browning was numbered among those who opposed suffrage and nonsegregation for the Negroes in the conviction that, as an "inferior" race, their legal equality would threaten Anglo-Saxon institutions.[99]

Alexander W. Randall, who came into the Cabinet along with Stanbery and Browning, had been a vigorous war governor of Wisconsin, and then as Assistant Postmaster under Lincoln had assisted effectively in mending the President's political fences in preparation for his re-election in 1864.[100] Retaining that politically strategic post under Johnson, Randall was soon recognized as an active political lieutenant of the new President. In the Cabinet reorganization of 1866, he was raised to the rank of Postmaster General. While a young man in Wisconsin politics, Randall had helped prepare a proposal for Negro suffrage to be submitted for referendum in connection with the revision of the state constitution, an action which made him highly unpopular and kept him out of politics for some time.[101] Although associated with the Free Soil Democracy, he is said to have taken little part in its activities because of his opposition to the radical ideas of its leaders.[102] There is little evidence of his racial attitudes during the Johnson period. To judge from his position as reported by Gideon Welles, Randall was equivocal and politically minded rather than either prejudiced or deeply concerned in respect to matters touching equality for the freedmen.[103]

Hugh McCulloch, Secretary of the Treasury under both Lincoln and Johnson, believed firmly in the superior intelligence and energy of the white race.[104] He was reported to have said that "so far as the pretended equality of races was concerned," history showed that the Anglo-Saxon race in contact with an inferior one must "dominate or exterminate."[105] Like many another resident of Indiana, he was opposed to granting the vote to the Negroes even in the Northern states.[106] Charles Sumner, who found it difficult to condone the position of Seward and Welles on the question of Negro suffrage in the South, was inclined to more charity toward McCulloch as one "imbued with the pernicious folly of Indiana."[107] McCulloch was aware that Johnson's veto of the Civil Rights Bill, together with his February 22 speech, had "turned not only the Republican party but the general public sentiment of the northern states against him"; yet he had wanted the Administration forces to make an open attack upon the proposed Fourteenth Amendment.[108] In his reminiscences written more than two decades after the struggle between Johnson and Congress, when the Reconstruction amendments were the law of the land, McCulloch characterized the Negroes as "an alien race" and held that the Federal Government should abstain "from all interference with local affairs" on their behalf. Once outside "interference" was discontinued and "colored people understand that the government, by their emancipation, had done for them all it can do, and that hereafter their welfare and elevation must depend upon their own efforts, the great problem of what is to be the political future of these states must be worked out by the joint action of the two races."[109]

Lewis D. Campbell, perhaps Johnson's most active personal political emissary in the West, was a man who had only scorn for the prewar Oberlin antislavery movement and its underground railroad activities.[110] An ardent opponent of Negro suffrage in Ohio as well as in the South, he held that in crushing secession, slavery had been only an *incidental* casualty and that there was no basis for the idea being promulgated by "wild one-idea fanatics" that the mission of the Union party was "to advance the interests of the *black* man and disregard those of the *white* man."[111] Campbell's perception was so limited that when Sumner, during a private interview with the President at which Campbell was present, expressed concern for the freedmen, the Ohioan saw in Sumner's attitude only the shedding of "crocodile tears."[112]

The support given to the President by Seward and by Raymond is of special interest. Neither man was a party to that prejudice of race so common among adherents of Johnson's cause. Raymond broke with the pro-Johnson movement during the campaign of 1866; Seward remained loyal to the President until the bitter end. A definitive historical understanding and evaluation of Seward, if ever one can be reached, must wait upon a comprehensive modern study of the man. His prewar national repute was based upon his public identification with the opposition to slavery as a moral wrong; he had rallied devotion to himself and to the Republican party by his appeal to "the higher law" and the "irrepressible conflict." Whatever part the pull of oratory or of political ambition may have played in calling forth Seward's ringing phrases, there is no reason to think that they cloaked hypocrisy or an antislavery stand concerned only with the interest of white men. Seward's ardor may have weakened since the days when his words stirred the nation. There had been the cruel defeat of his presidential aspirations, due in considerable part to the very effectiveness of his phrases; there was the death of his wife, which severed a close personal tie between Seward and the moral intensity of antislavery sentiment.[113] The uncertainty of conjecture is compounded because in the postwar years, as we have noted,[114] Seward did not wish to reveal even in private his innermost convictions and intentions. Yet he retained more than compassion for the former slaves. He believed in their right to citizenship and equal status before the law—even equality of suffrage—though for the attainment of the latter, in his characteristically sanguine way, Seward would rely upon some vague development of the future rather than upon Federal authority.[115] It was Seward's adamant opposition that prevented an open attack upon the proposed Fourteenth Amendment, a position favored by the President, in issuing the call for the Philadelphia Convention to mobilize the pro-Johnson forces for the election battle of 1866.[116] After the Radical victory, the paper which Seward submitted as a basis for the President's message to Congress was conciliatory, leaving open an avenue for accommodation to congressional policy.[117] It was this draft message, its authorship unknown, which has been interpreted, erroneously, as evidence that Johnson in November, 1866, first decided not to oppose the Amendment further, then changed his mind, revived the quarrel with Congress and urged Southern states not to reconsider their refusal to ratify.[118] Not Johnson, but Seward, sought conciliation; and there is nothing to suggest a change of mind on the part of the Secretary of State.[119]

With these attitudes, why did Seward defer to Johnson? Why did he not like other moderates of similar sympathies break with the President? Why did he open himself to bitter repudiation by old friends and to political isolation, a fate which must at least have loomed as an ominous possibility by late spring of 1866?[120] Again, we cannot say with certainty; but a number of considerations come readily to mind. Seward believed that he had already made a major contribution to the cause of freedom by his part in the abolition of slavery and the treaty with Britain to suppress the slave traffic. With these great ends accomplished, and his always hopeful view of the future, perhaps he felt, as Weed had implied in explanation to an English friend's concern for the freedmen, that what "the Freedmen must suffer while the relationships arising between capital and labour are being adjusted" was a minor evil, to be borne with rather than publicly fought.[121] And the consequence of an open fight, the surrender of his post as Secretary of State without assurance of some other major position in national affairs, would have been a hard and selfless decision.

Since the days of battle for the Thirteenth Amendment, Seward had been committed to a reorganization of parties that would attract the support of Southerners and of Northern Democrats by a speedy and generous restoration of the secession states. He had undoubtedly been influential in directing Johnson toward that objective. Indeed, opinion in Congress in 1866 viewed him as the "head and front of the new party movement," though by the end of July he was thought to have given it up for "reconciliation between the President's particular friends and the body of the Union party."[122] And the President, while withholding full support for Seward's strategy as to both practical politics and basic policy, nevertheless deferred to him to an extent that would naturally have evoked Seward's loyalty and also his hope for a political victory that would renew his national influence and prestige. Then there was the Secretary's concern with the record and the achievement of his stewardship of foreign affairs. These were delicately balanced in 1865 and 1866, and he may well have felt that his departure from the Cabinet would lead to a dangerously adventuristic policy toward Mexico such as the Blairs had been urging. Or he may have been concerned lest any recognition on his part of basic disunity in the country weaken the nation's position abroad. In addition, Seward together with Stanton had become the symbol of Johnson's refusal to embrace the Democracy unconditionally.[123] To the Secretary, this role may have appeared not mere symbol but substance. What other man in the Cabinet could offset the full pressure of the Democracy? And if they were not kept at arm's length what might not be the consequences? The possible result was a matter of patronage and party power, but not that alone. There were extreme programs of action in the air, defiance of Congress with a denial of its legitimacy, recognition of a national legislature with Southern representatives seated by force if necessary. Contemporaries feared another civil war, more fratricidal than the first.[124] The possibility of such dire consequences may have stirred Seward's very real sense of devotion and responsibility to the nation.

Which considerations weighed with Seward, whether he viewed them as politician or statesman or something of both, we cannot know. But in his papers for 1868 there is an interesting passage, not revealing, but suggesting much. It appears in the draft of a response to an affectionate letter from a friend, a reply that was a far from modest affirmation of his historic role as "first secretary to the President." The passage reads: "The Government has been seriously endangered first by ambition on one side and the reckless passions on the other. I have been *felt* if not always *seen* in saving it from both. Only four months of trial remain, before the Government and the Constitution thus saved are in a constitutional way to be delivered into the keeping of a new administration when I shall be entitled to my discharge."[125]

Although Raymond voted to uphold Johnson's veto of the Civil Rights Bill, his entire course shows a consistent concern to protect the basic rights of the freedmen. In the summer and fall of 1865, the New York *Times* editorials made this objective abundantly clear and identified it with the President's policy. Raymond's paper even found no difficulty in accepting the principle that color should not be a basis for exclusion from the voting franchise, although it did not favor the national government's forcing Negro suffrage upon the South.[126] It had hoped that the President might sign the Civil Rights Bill. The critical first section, with its "absolute equality of civil rights," was, according to the *Times*, "unquestionably just and right"; the objection was to the arbitrary enforcement provisions of the second section.[127] This position was very close to Senator Morgan's.[128]

Raymond was the Administration leader in the House, Chairman of the Union (Republican) National Executive Committee, and a close ally of Seward. These political commitments constituted a very formidable restraint upon his championship of equality for the freedmen. Yet in the House of Representatives, the *Times* editor voted "yea" on the roll call for the Fourteenth Amendment. The fact that no enabling legislation accompanied the passage of the Amendment, which would have made clear that its ratification was a condition for readmission of the rebellious states, helped Raymond reconcile his vote for the Amendment with his support of the President, who publicly opposed any prerequisite to the return of Southern representatives.[129] Raymond had considered the object of the Freedmen's Bureau Bill of "utmost importance" and explained that he had not supported the Civil Rights Bill because he, along with Bingham and others, thought that it was not warranted by the Constitution. He had introduced an alternate proposal to declare all persons born in the United States citizens, entitled to the privileges and immunities of citizenship. All the main principles of the Fouteenth Amendment he considered "eminently wise and proper."[130]

It was the desire to placate Raymond and to insure the support of the *Times* for the pro-Johnson movement which broke down the intent of Welles, Cowan, Doolittle, Browning, and McCulloch to include an open attack upon the proposed Fourteenth Amendment in their call for the Philadelphia Convention.[131] For that meeting, Raymond prepared an address which recognized the need for the enlargement of Federal powers in respect to the freedmen's rights, and also the power of Congress and the states to make such amendments; but this part of his statement evoked sharp opposition and was deleted.[132] The resolutions adopted by the convention stated that it was the desire and purpose of the Southern states that all inhabitants should receive "equal protection in every right of person and property," but omitted any statement that might be interpreted as acquiescence in Federal authority over civil rights unless by amendment after the admission of the Southern states and with their free consent.[133] This was the most that Raymond could achieve in his effort to gain Southern agreement to the principle of "equal protection by law, and by equal access to courts of law, of all the citizens of all the states, without distinction of race or color."[134] He himself was ready to accept the provisions of the Fourteenth Amendment as the platform of the party, and he felt that the President had "made a great mistake in taking ground against those amendments."[135] Johnson's defeat in the fall elections of 1866 was interpreted by Raymond as a popular decision in favor of the principles of the Amendment, particularly "the absolute equality of civil rights to all the people of the United States."[136]

Although Raymond's break with Johnson did not come over the civil rights issue, his defection to the opposition was consonant with his basic convictions in respect to equality of citizenship for the Negro. Most other key Republican moderates who took their stand against Johnson shared those convictions. Senator John Sherman had long been troubled by the probability that freedmen would be oppressed if they had no share of political power. As for the Civil Rights Bill, he wrote, "I felt it so clearly right that I was prepared for the very general acquiescence in its provisions both North and South. To have refused the negroes the simplest rights granted to every other inhabitant, native or foreigner, would be outrageous."[137] The veto was a major factor in Sherman's repudiation of Johnson, whom he had hitherto defended. "The President's course on the Civil Rights Bill and constitutional amendment was so unwise that I could not for a moment allow anyone to suppose that I meant with him to join a coalition with the rebels and Copperheads."[138] Senators Lyman Trumbull of Illinois, James Grimes of Iowa, and William Fessenden of Maine were all men of moderation and principle, able to withstand terrific pressures, as their votes against Johnson's conviction on impeachment charges later made amply clear; their principles included a commitment to basic civil rights for the freedmen. All three wished to work with the President rather than against him, but, to use Welles's characterization of the latter two men, "their natural tendency would I knew incline them to the opposition. They are both intense on the negro."[139] The same might be said for other moderates, for Governor John Andrew of Massachusetts, for Henry Ward Beecher, for Samuel Bowles of the Springfield *Republican*, for John Bingham of Ohio, for Henry Dawes of Massachusetts, for James Hawley of Connecticut, and for General O. O. Howard of the Freedmen's Bureau.

The case of the two influential Midwestern governors, Oliver P. Morton of Indiana and Jacob D. Cox of Ohio, is not so clear. Both were chief executives of a citizenry much given to discrimination against the Negro and closely divided between Republicans and Democrats. Although Cox had strong convictions in respect to the evil of slavery and took great satisfaction as a military officer in freeing refugee "contrabands," he disappointed antislavery men who had hoped that his early Oberlin training and his close relationship to Charles G. Finney would bring support for Negro suffrage. Such support Cox refused, and instead issued a public statement proposing separation of the races in the Southern states, with schools, homesteads, and full political privileges for the Negroes.[140] Later in advising Johnson to accept the Civil Rights Bill, Cox stressed political expediency; but he also assumed that the President as well as himself and "all true Union men" believed in the principle of equality before the law—that it was "right."[141] While still supporting Johnson, he accepted the Fourteenth Amendment, expressing privately his approval of all parts of the Amendment except the disqualifying clause of the third section.[142] In the campaign of 1867 to amend the Ohio constitution, he argued for Negro suffrage since it had already been forced upon the South.[143]

Governor Morton was a political enemy of Radicals in Indiana; and his public opposition in September, 1865, to making Negro suffrage a condition for Southern restoration was widely publicized and enthusiastically received by pro-Johnson men. An examination of his speech discloses not an opposition to Negro suffrage as such but the argument that Indiana was in no condition to urge voting privileges for Negroes in the South when the state itself discriminated so grossly against the "many very intelligent and well qualified" colored people within its own borders. Morton pointed out the restriction not only upon their political power but also upon their testimony in court, their access to public schools, and, if they had come into the state since 1850, their legal right to make valid contracts. He spoke highly of the fighting record of the Indiana colored regiment and pointed to the ironic fact that half the men who composed it could not legally come back into the state. The tone of the address was not one of defending discrimination but one of gently criticising his fellow Hoosiers. As for Southern freedmen, Morton believed that they should have time to acquire property and obtain a little education, and then "at the end of 10, 15, or 20 years, let them come into the enjoyment of their political rights."[144] The governor was clearly in advance of state sentiment in advocating for Negroes the benefit of schooling and the right to testify in court. His sponsorship of the repeal of the state statute which excluded their testimony finally resulted in the elimination of that discrimination.[145] It was Morton who warned Johnson that a veto of the Civil Rights Bill would separate the President and the Union-Republican party, that if he did not sign the measure the two men could not again meet in political friendship.[146] Morton's decision to oppose Johnson was no doubt essentially a political one, but his attitude toward the Negro was not identical with that of the President.[147]

Behind conciliatory Republican leaders whose personal attitudes might in other circumstances have enabled them to accept a solution which would leave the future status of the freedmen in the hands of Southern whites, there was the pressure of mass Republican opinion. The overwhelming preponderance of Republican sentiment was behind a national guarantee for basic civil equality, short of suffrage, for the freedmen. This sentiment is unmistakable in newspaper editorials and private correspondence;[148] it was also reflected in the congressional vote on what was to become the Fourteenth Amendment. In the Senate, Republicans divided thirty-three to four in its favor. The "nays" were those of Senators Cowan, Doolittle, Norton of Minnesota and

Van Winkle of West Virginia. Senator Dixon was absent and not voting. In the House, 138 Republican votes were cast for the Amendment; not a single Republican voted against it.[149] This vote was taken *before* Johnson made clear his political intentions by issuance of the call for the Philadelphia Convention.

After the Civil Rights veto, Republican opinion had crystallized in a determination to set further conditions before accepting Southern representatives back into the counsels of the nation, but not just any conditions.[150] The matters dealt with in sections two and three of the Fourteenth Amendment, namely the basis of future Southern representation, the granting of suffrage to the Negro, and the degree of proscription of Confederate leaders were negotiable; the question of equality before the law, federally enforceable, was no longer open to compromise. The issue of civil rights and national protection for the freedmen was not, as has sometimes been implied, the product of campaign propaganda and exaggeration, nor even of the shocking impact of the Memphis and New Orleans riots. The civil rights issue predated those developments.

Although in deference to Seward and Raymond the pro-Johnson leaders had attempted to evade discussion of the Fourteenth Amendment, it was generally recognized as being at stake in the ensuing campaign. After Radical victories in the states that voted in September and early October, pressure was put upon the President to accept the Amendment. As early as September 19, Bennett in the *Herald* foresaw defeat unless the President would "take up" the proposed Fourteenth Amendent and "push it through all the still excluded Southern States as rapidly as possible" with the kind of pressure he had used in behalf of the Thirteenth Amendment. Bennett at last deplored the condition he had done so much to provoke, "the widening of his [Johnson's] conflict with the radicals to a conflict with Congress." He now viewed the Amendment as "not a radical measure, but a measure of the republican conservatives of Congress."[151] When Samuel S. Cox asked the President about the rumors that he would modify his oppositition to the Amendment in keeping with "the poplar [*sic*] current," Johnson "got as ugly as the Devil. He was regularly mad. . . . There's no budge in him. Browning's letter is his view."[152]

S. L. M. Barlow's attitude toward the Amendment's role in campaign strategy is pertinent. He was much opposed to the President's yielding unless the Johnson forces should suffer defeat in New York. In that event, he thought the President might be "compelled to yield on the Constitutional amendment, but to yield to the pressure now, before our election, would destroy him & be in gross bad faith . . . as we are making a good fight & cannot now change our course."[153] If faced with defeat in November, however, Barlow thought Johnson could say to the South, "While I have not thought the ratification of the amendment necessary . . . the Northern people have decided otherwise— You must be represented. . . . Ratify the amendment therefore." Barlow explained that Johnson could "be supported in this, if necessary, *after* November, not only here but by the ablest presses of the South in New Orleans, Mobile, Charleston & Richmond— To change *now* would deprive him, practically of every paper and every voter—The Radicals would not be won back to him and he would lose the whole power of the democratic party."[154]

Browning's letter, to which Representative Cox referred, is additional proof of the importance of the Amendment as a campaign issue. It is also, and more importantly, added evidence that the opposition of the pro-Johnson forces to the Amendment was not merely limited to a distaste for section three, which denied Southern leaders state and national office. The heart of Browning's argument, approved by the President, was that section one, the civil rights guarantee, would restrict the states in functions properly their own. It would subject the "authority and control of the States over matters of purely domestic and local concern . . . to criticism, interpretation and adjudication by the Federal tribunals, whose judgments and decrees will be supreme."[155]

Johnson's refusal, despite great pressure and much advice, to capitulate on the Fourteenth Amendment after his election defeat cannot be attributed alone to his stubborn nature. The explanation that he decided for conciliation, then reversed course on the basis of the Radicals' behavior, is exploded by the identification of the early conciliatory draft message as the work of Seward.[156] Another factor entered into policy considerations, the hope of ultimate victory and the tactical advantage to be gained by encouraging extreme action on the part of the opposition with a view to ultimate popular reaction against it. Doolittle wrote Browning on November 8: "The elections are over and we are beaten for the present. But our cause will live. If all the states not represented refuse to ratify the amendment . . . the extreme Rads will go . . . for reorganizing the southern states on negro suffrage. . . . That will present the issue squarely of forcing negro suffrage upon the South and upon that we can beat them at the next Presidential election."[157] A short time later, Weed was writing Seward that he had rebuffed Senator Morgan's suggestion of an organization in Congress against "extreme men." Weed explained, "I think that if the pressure should be withdrawn the Radicals would hang *themselves*."[158] From Ohio the prediction reached the President that "If Congress resorts to rash and violent means to carry out the destructive purposes of the radicals, their own party will break to pieces."[159] From New York came more positive advice: "Are those proposed amendments to be adopted, changing the whole nature of our government. I trust not. I think a year or two of Radicalism more, will satisfy the country that the principles contained in that old instrument are too dear to us to be frittered away. . . . I believe that with you standing firmly on the ground you have assumed and each state organizing her conservative men on the Philadelphia platform, two years more will have seen the end of the Radical race."[160] Analysts of the 1866 election returns pointed out to the President that if the potential vote of the unrepresented South were added to the Conservative vote in the North, a large majority of the nation supported the President and opposed the Amendment, and that ultimately the President must triumph.[161]

Raymond's editorials in the *Times* had urged the President to accept the decision of the people in favor of the Amendment, and either to recommend its ratification by the Southern states or to stand aside while they made a settlement with Congress upon the basis of its principles. By the end of December, however, Raymond had come to the conclusion that Johnson's opposition to the Amendment was unyielding. The President, he explained, intended to hold to his earlier position in the conviction that his policy would ultimately prevail. Johnson believed that the Supreme Court would set aside any conditions Congress might impose upon the South or, failing such a resolution of the conflict, that the use of military power to enforce congressional policy would become so "expensive, odious and intolerable" that the voters would expel from power the party responsible for such a policy.[162]

The losses which the Radicals sustained in the state elections of 1867 seemed to justify the President's hope of victory and the strategy of no compromise. News of the defeat of the Radicals in Connecticut's April election of that year was received by Johnson as "the turn of the current" and by Welles as "the first loud knock, which admonishes the Radicals of their inevitable doom."[163] Welles believed that the returns from Pennsylvania and Ohio in October "indicates the total overthrow of the Radicals and the downfall of that party."[164] In November, 1867, Johnson celebrated the election results by a victory speech before a group of serenaders in which he held that "the people have spoken in a manner not to be misunderstood."[165] The President's "stubbornness" of the previous November seemed to have prepared the way for success in the presidential election of 1868. The hope proved an illusion; but the hope was present, and died hard.[166]

In refusing to accept the equal rights provisions of the Civil Rights Act or of the Fourteenth Amendment, Johnson won lasting gratitude from white Southerners to whom the concept of equality between the races was anathema,[167] and this despite the ordeal of military government and immediate universal Negro suffrage which they in all likelihood would have been spared had Johnson's course been different. But with this decision, the President lost the confidence and respect of moderate Republicans. Lyman Trumbull and John Sherman both felt a sense of betrayal in Johnson's veto of the Civil Rights Bill. "Besides," confided Sherman to his brother, "he [Johnson] is insincere; he has deceived and misled his best friends."[168] The confidence in Johnson's assurances of justice for the freed people, which characterized Republican opinion, except that of extreme Radicals, in December, 1865, turned to distrust. No longer were misgivings directed toward Presidential policy alone; they came to embrace the President's intention and integrity, and corroded his public influence. "The truth is," Senator Fessenden wrote to Senator Morgan in mid-1867, "Mr. Johnson has continued to excite so much distrust that the public mind is easily played upon by those who are seeking only the accomplishment of their own purposes."[169] By standing adamant against a federally enforceable pledge of minimum civil equality for the Negro as a prerequisite to restoration of the secession states, Johnson precipitated a great issue of moral principle central to the battle over Reconstruction; and he brought upon himself an unparalleled humiliation.

NOTES

CHAPTER I

THE SEWARD LOBBY AND THE THIRTEENTH AMENDMENT

1. New York *Herald*, Dec. 5, 1864, Jan. 7, 1865; New York *Tribune*, Jan. 10, 1865; *The Independent*, Dec. 19, 1864, Jan. 15, 1865.
2. J. G. Randall and Richard N. Current, *Lincoln the President: Last Full Measure* (New York, 1955), pp. 308–12; Isaac N. Arnold, *Life of Abraham Lincoln* (Chicago, 1909), pp. 358–59; John G. Nicolay and John Hay, *Abraham Lincoln: A History* (10 vols., New York, 1890), X, pp. 84–85; Mallory, *Cong. Globe*, 38 Cong., 2 sess., p. 179 (Jan. 9, 1865). *See also* the episode related by Charles A. Dana in *Recollections of the Civil War* (New York, 1899), p. 176, which Earl S. Pomeroy has related to the Thirteenth Amendment. "Lincoln, the Thirteenth Amendment and the Admission of Nevada," *Pacific Historical Review*, XII (Dec., 1943), pp. 362–68.
3. New York *Herald*, Jan. 10, 1865, Jan. 11, 1865, Jan. 12, 1865; New York *Tribune*, Jan. 12, 1865, Jan. 13, 1865; Washington *National Intelligencer*, Jan. 13, 1865.
4. New York *Herald*, Jan. 28, 1865; New York *Times*, Jan. 28, 1865, Jan. 31, 1865; *The Independent*, Jan. 30, 1865.
5. *The Independent*, Feb. 9, 1865.
6. Johnson of Pennsylvania, in repudiating two Democratic colleagues who had spoken for the Amendment, *Cong. Globe*, 38 Cong., 2 sess., p. 524 (Jan. 31, 1865).

7. Coffroth of Pennsylvania, *ibid.*, p. 523 (Jan. 31, 1865).

8. The two were Alexander H. Coffroth of Pennsylvania and William Radforth of New York.

9. *Collected Works of Abraham Lincoln* (Roy P. Basler et al., eds., 9 vols., New Brunswick, N.J., 1953–1955), VII, p. 451 (July 18, 1864).

10. T. S. Faxton to Weed, Aug. 10, 1864, Weed MSS, University of Rochester Library; E. D. Smith to Seward, Aug. 22, 1864, Seward MSS, University of Rochester Library; Glydon G. Van Deusen, *Thurlow Weed: Wizard of the Lobby* (Boston, 1947), p. 310; James Ford Rhodes, *History of the United States* (7 vols., New York, 1896–1919), IV, pp. 514–15.

11. Copy in Seward MSS, Aug. 24, 1864; Raymond to Lincoln, Aug. 22, 1864, Lincoln to Raymond, Aug. 24, 1864, and notes on conference, *Collected Works of Abraham Lincoln*, VII, 517–18.

12. Dana to Raymond, July 26, 1864, George Jones MSS, New York Public Library.

13. Seward's speech Sept. 3, 1864, Auburn, New York, in George E. Baker, ed., *Works of William H. Seward* (5 vols., Boston, 1884), V, pp. 491–504.

14. Italics are McCulloch's. McCulloch to Seward, Sept. 8, 1864, Seward MSS.

15. Henry T. Cheever to Seward, Sept. 10, 1864, with accompanying letter from John D. Baldwin, Seward to Baldwin, Sept. 24, 1864, *ibid.* (Seward's letter is a letterpress copy. Where a letter cited is obviously a copy, in this or other MSS collections, we have not so designated it.)

16. New York *Times*, Dec. 7, 1864; quoted in Washington *National Intelligencer*, Dec. 12, 1864.

17. *Cong. Globe*, 38 Cong., 2 sess., p. 179 (Jan. 9, 1865).

18. *Ibid.*, p. 216 (Jan. 11, 1865). Both Mallory and White were Democrats and voted against the Amendment.

19. The paper was so characterized by the Washington *National Intelligencer*, Dec. 21, 1864.

20. New York *World*, Jan. 9, 1865; reprint in Washington *National Intelligencer*, Jan. 13, 1865.

21. New York *World*, Dec. 21, 1864.

22. Mallory, *Cong. Globe*, 38 Cong., 2 sess., p. 179 (Jan. 9, 1865); Wood, *ibid.*, p. 194 (Jan. 10, 1865).

23. Philo S. Shelton to Weed, Jan. 22, 1865, Weed MSS; New York *Herald*, Jan. 10, 1865.

24. Samuel S. Cox, Democratic Congressman from Ohio, in his *Three Decades of Federal Legislation, 1855 to 1885* (Providence, R.I., 1886), p. 329.

25. Bilbo to Seward, May 1, 1866, Seward MSS; *see also* Bilbo to Lincoln, Jan. 26, 1865, Lincoln MSS, Library of Congress.
26. Ethel Ames, *The Story of Coal and Iron in Alabama* (Birmingham, Ala., 1910), pp. 363–64. We are indebted to Mrs. Gertrude M. Parsley, reference librarian, Tennessee State Library and Archives, for this reference and also for a careful check of local histories, biographical works, and archival materials. Few traces of the man remain, despite his active political and social role.
27. Bilbo to Seward, Jan. 26, 1865, Seward MSS.
28. Vouchers of March 25, 1862, Nov. 6, 1862, Aug. 22, 1868, Bilbo to Surgeon Scott, May 20, 1862, Bilbo to Johnston, Dec. 5, 1861. Recommendation to Jefferson Davis, n.d., Confederate Citizens' File, War Department Collection of Confederate Records, National Archives.
29. Bilbo to Johnston, Dec. 5, 1861, *ibid.*
30. Testimony of Bilbo in Confederate States vs. H. J. Higgins or Wiggins, March, 1862, *ibid.*
31. Greeley to Lincoln, Nov. 16, 1864, Lincoln MSS.
32. Bilbo to Seward, May 1, 1866, Seward MSS.
33. Bilbo to Johnson, Jan. 10, 1865, May 17, 1865, Johnson MSS, Library of Congress.
34. Bilbo to Seward, n.d., filed Nov. 30, 1864, Seward MSS.
35. Draper to Lincoln, No. 12, 1864, Grinnell to Lincoln, Nov. 12, 1864, Greeley to Lincoln, Nov. 16, 1864, Lincoln MSS.
36. Bilbo to Lincoln, Jan. 26, 1865, *ibid.*
37. Bilbo to Seward, Jan. 11, 1867, Seward MSS; *see also* Bilbo to Seward, Dec. 23, 1864, *ibid.*, and Bilbo to Johnson, May 17, 1865, Johnson MSS.
38. Bilbo to Johnson, May 17, 1865, Johnson MSS.
39. Bilbo to Seward, Nov. 2, 1865, March 21, 1866, May 1, 1866, May 22, 1866, Seward MSS.
40. Bilbo to Seward, Jan. 20, 1865, Department of State, Miscellaneous Letters, National Archives.
41. Dix to Seward, Jan. 20, 1865, Seward to Dix, Jan. 20, 1865, Union Provost Marshal's file, War Department Collection of Confederate Records.
42. Lincoln to Dix, Jan. 20, 1865, *ibid.*, also printed in *Collected Works of Abraham Lincoln*, VIII, p. 226.
43. Bilbo to Lincoln, Jan. 26, 1865, Lincoln MSS.
44. Bilbo to Seward, Nov. 2, 1865, Seward MSS.
45. Bilbo to Seward, Jan. 11, 1867, *ibid.*
46. Hudson C. Tanner, *'The Lobby' and Public Men from Thurlow Weed's Time* (Albany, New York, 1888), pp. 372–75.

47. George O. Jones, *To the Merchants and Property-Owners of New York City; The Causes which Are Driving Commerce from your Doors, Forcing Trade into Other Cities, Destroying the Value of your Property, and Impoverishing the Country*, (pamphlet, n.d., n.p., [New York? 1872?]).

48. New York *Tribune*, July 28, 1890, Oct. 10, 1894, and obituaries, Jan. 18, 1895 in *ibid.*, New York *Herald*, and New York *Times*.

49. Bilbo to Seward, Feb. 1, 1865, Seward MSS.

50. Paul A. Chadbourne and Walter B. Moore, *The Public Service of the State of New York* (3 vols. in 4 parts, 1882), II, Pt. 1, p. 151.

51. *Biographical Directory of the American Congress* (Washington, 1928), p. 1351; Homer A. Stebbins, *A Political History of the State of New York, 1865–1869* (New York, 1913), pp. 53, 90, 178–79, 208, 360; DeAlva S. Alexander, *A Political History of the State of New York* (3 vols., New York, 1906–1909), III, pp. 226–27, 297, 488.

52. Chadbourne and Moore, *The Public Service*, II, Pt. 1, p. 151; Nelson to Seward, Nov. 20, 1866, Seward MSS.

53. *Biographical Directory of the American Congress*, p. 1069; Stebbins, *Political History of the State of New York*, pp. 323, 367.

54. John W. Forney, *Anecdotes of Public Men* (New York, 1873), p. 70.

55. Latham to Seward, Feb. 23, 1861, Jan. 25, 1864, Aug. 20, 1864, Seward MSS.

56. *Ibid.*, Jan. 25, 1864.

57. *Ibid.*, Aug. 20, 1864.

58. Roy F. Nichols, *Disruption of American Democracy* (New York, 1948), pp. 79, 174, 424.

59. *Report on Abstracted Indian Trust Bonds* (36 Cong., 2 sess., *House Report* 78, Serial 1105), pp. 217–28.

60. Latham to Seward, Jan. 25, 1864; Letterhead, Latham to Seward, Aug. 20, 1864, Seward MSS.

61. The records of the War Department, National Archives, failed to reveal Berret's name as an officer of the United States. During his campaign for the office of mayor in 1858, Berret was referred to as "Col." Washington *National Intelligencer*, June 1, 1858.

62. W. B. Bryan, *A History of the National Capital* (2 vols., New York, 1916), II, pp. 486–87; *War of the Rebellion, Official Records* (128 vols., Washington, 1880–1901), Series 2, II, pp. 229, 237, 596–99.

63. Draft of a letter from Lincoln to Berret, April 22, 1862, probably never sent, *Collected Works of Abraham Lincoln*, V, pp. 195–96.

64. Sketch of Berret by William J. Rhees, in *The Smithsonian Institution 1846–1896: The History of its First Half Century* (George B. Goode, ed., Washington, 1897), pp. 82–83.
65. Schell to Seward, Sept. 9, 1865, also his letter, n.d., filed Sept. 31, 1865, Seward MSS.
66. *War of the Rebellion, Official Records,* Series 2, II, pp. 156, 597.
67. Henry J. Raymond later sought a Washington office for a Mr. Barnett (or Barrett or Bennett), whom he described as one of the editors of the *National Intelligencer* "under its *new regime*," Raymond to Seward, March 22, 1865; in 1867 Berret, together with Thomas C. Pratt, presented a claim on behalf of the *National Intelligencer,* memorandum August 1867, Seward MSS. Berret was listed in *Boyd's Washington and Georgetown Directory* of 1865 and 1866 as a lawyer in the *Intelligencer* building.
68. Latham to Seward, Jan. 7, 1865, Jan. 9, 1865, Seward MSS.
69. Bilbo to Seward, Feb. 1, 1865, *ibid.*
70. Obituary, New York *Times,* Nov. 11, 1879. For Schell, see also obituaries of same date in the New York *Herald,* New York *World,* New York *Tribune,* and the sketch by Oliver W. Holmes of a younger brother, Augustus Schell, in the *Dictionary of American Biography.*
71. New York *Times,* Jan. 12, 1876, March 22, 1876, May, 4, 1876, May 6, 1876, June 10, 1876.
72. New York *Herald,* Nov. 11, 1879.
73. *Ibid.,* New York *Tribune,* Nov. 11, 1879.
74. Schell to Seward, Nov. 20, 1861, Seward MSS.
75. Schell to Seward, Oct. 24, 1862, Nov. 29, 1862, Dec. 23, 1862, Feb. 19, 1863; Schell to F. W. Seward, Dec. 13, 1862, *ibid.*
76. Schell to Seward, Jan. 12, 1863, Feb. 11, 1863, Feb. 21, 1863, Oct. 8, 1863, Oct. 15, 1863, June 27, 1864, Aug. 12, 1864, Aug. 26, 1864, *ibid.*; Schell to Weed, Aug. 6, 1864, Aug. 20, 1864, Weed MSS.
77. New York *Herald,* Nov. 11, 1879.
78. Bilbo to Seward, n.d., filed Nov. 30, 1865, Seward MSS.
79. New York *Herald,* Jan. 24, 1865.
80. Rochester *Democrat,* April 8, 1865.
81. Bilbo to Seward, Nov. 2, 1865, Seward MSS.
82. Bilbo to Seward, Dec. 12, 1864, *ibid.*
83. Sidney D. Brummer, *Political History of New York State during the Period of the Civil War* (New York, 1911), p. 25; Stebbins, *Political History of the State of New York,* p. 26.
84. Bilbo to Seward, Dec. 20, 1864, Seward MSS.
85. Jones to Seward, Dec. 20, 1864, *ibid.*
86. Possibly relevant is the fact that Pomeroy, early in 1864, had called for the organization of a new party on Radical principles

including support of an anti-slavery amendment, and also the fact that Pomeroy's public career was shot through with charges of bargain and corruption.

87. Cox, *Three Decades*, p. 310.

88. Two letters, Latham to Seward, Jan. 7, 1865, Seward MSS; Cox did talk with Seward, *Three Decades*, p. 310.

89. Latham to Seward, Jan. 9, 1865, Seward MSS.

90. Bilbo to Seward, Jan. 10, 1865, *ibid.*

91. Bilbo was apparently mistaken; Nelson was named a member of the New York Democratic State Central Committee in September, 1865, and may have held a similar position in January.

92. Fernando Wood was the political boss of New York City's Mozart Hall, an extremely prosouthern faction of the state Democracy; he was also a member of the House, speaking and voting against the amendment.

93. New York *Herald*, Jan. 11, 1865; New York *Times*, Jan. 12, 1865.

94. New York *Times*, Jan. 12, 1865.

95. Harry J. Carman and Reinhard H. Luthin, *Lincoln and the Patronage* (New York, 1943), pp. 119–21, 236.

96. Latham to Seward, Jan. 12, 1865; Forney to Seward, Jan. 11, 1865; Forney to Hart, Jan. 11, 1865; Forney to Seward, Jan. 13, 1865; Seward MSS.

97. *Cong. Globe*, 38 Cong., 2 sess., pp. 238–42 (Jan. 12, 1865); New York *Herald*, Jan. 13, 1865.

98. Samuel S. Cox, *Eight Years in Congress from 1857–1865* (New York, 1865), p. 397, and his *Three Decades*, p. 321.

99. William Van Zandt Cox and Milton H. Northrup, *Life of Samuel Sullivan Cox* (Syracuse, New York, 1899), p. 95; Seward's speech of Oct. 31, 1868, Baker, *Works of William H. Seward*, V, p. 554. A footnote indicates that Cox was understood to have persuaded other Democrats to vote for the amendment, although he voted against it. In a letter to Manton Marble, Cox denied the report that he had urged James English, Connecticut Democrat, to vote for the amendment; he stated, however, that he "did not dissuade any one from voting for it." He thought that only with the slavery question buried was there hope "for Democratic ascendancy." Cox to Marble, Feb. 13, 1865, Marble MSS, Library of Congress.

100. Bilbo to Johnson, Jan. 14, 1865, Johnson MSS.

101. Bilbo to Seward, Jan. 14, 1865, Seward MSS.

102. Bilbo to Seward, Jan. 23, 1865, *ibid.*; Bilbo to Lincoln, Jan. 26, 1865, Lincoln MSS.

103. Schell to Seward, Jan. 23, 1865, Seward MSS.
104. Schell to Barlow, Jan. 23, 1865; Schell to Kinne and Carver, Jan. 18, 1865, Barlow MSS, Huntington Library.
105. New York *World*, Dec. 19, 1864; Washington *National Intelligencer*, Dec. 21, 1864.
106. Italics in the original, New York *World*, Dec. 21, 1864, Dec. 30, 1864.
107. New York *World*, Jan. 9, 1865.
108. Bilbo to Seward, Jan. 26, 1865, Seward MSS.
109. Barlow to Cox, Feb. 9, 1865; Barlow to Wadsworth, Dec. 28, 1864; Barlow to M. Blair, Jan. 10, 1865, Jan. 16, 1865; M. Blair to Barlow, Jan. 12, 1865, Barlow MSS.
110. Barlow to Belmont, Feb. 14, 1865, *ibid.*
111. New York *Times*, Jan. 9, 1865, Jan. 28, 1865, Jan. 31, 1865.
112. New York *Herald*, Jan. 28, 1865. The *Herald* had supported the amendment earlier, *see* Nov. 29, 1864, Dec. 5, 1864.
113. Bilbo to Seward, Feb. 1, 1865, Seward MSS.
114. New York *World*, Jan. 24, 1865.
115. This account is based upon *Cong. Globe*, 38 Cong., 2 sess., pp. 523–31 (Jan. 31, 1865); Cox, *Eight Years in Congress*, pp. 397–98; *Collected Works of Abraham Lincoln*, VIII, pp. 246–52, 274–85; and newspaper reports of Washington correspondents, particularly in New York *Times*, Feb. 1, 1865, New York *Tribune*, Feb. 1, 1865, and *The Independent*, Feb. 9, 1865. Cox wrote the *World*'s editor that he would have liked to vote for the amendment had it been possible to do so and keep faith with Democratic friends and place no obstacle in the way of reunion. He thought that the amendment would be fatal to negotiations with the southern commissioners. Cox to Marble, Feb. 1, 1865, Feb. 2, 1865, Marble MSS. *See also* David Lindsey, *"Sunset" Cox: Irrepressible Democrat* (Detroit, 1959), pp. 93–95.
116. Jones to Seward, Feb. 1, 1865, Seward MSS.
117. Bilbo to Seward, Feb. 1, 1865, *ibid.*
118. Schell to F. W. Seward, Feb. 13, 1865, *ibid.*
119. New York *World*, Feb. 1, 1865.
120. Edward McPherson, *Political History of the United States of America during the Great Rebellion* (3rd ed., Washington, 1876), p. 590.
121. *Ibid.* Party lines were confused during the Civil War years. McPherson classifies with the Democrats all those generally acting with that party irrespective of the label under which they had been elected. The New York *Times*, Feb. 1, 1865, identifies the same sixteen as Democrats and added an additional name; Rhodes, however, analyzes the affirmative vote

as including 13 border-state men and 11 Democrats. *History of the United States*, V, p. 50.

122. John Ganson, Buffalo; Anson Herrick, New York City; Homer A. Nelson, Poughkeepsie; Moses F. Odell, Brooklyn; William Radforth, Yonkers; John B. Steele, Kingston. Only Odell had voted for the amendment the previous June.

123. Joseph Bailey, Alexander Coffroth, Archibald McAllister; Jesse Lazear was absent. Missouri gave two affirmative Democratic votes, those of James S. Rollins and Austin A. King. Of the additional such votes, one each came from Michigan, Connecticut, Ohio, Wisconsin, and Kentucky.

124. Abram Wakeman to Seward, Oct. 22, 1864, Seward MSS.

125. The exact political complexion of the *Intelligencer* in this period is somewhat obscure. Beginning as a Democratic organ, it had turned Whig, then pro-Bell; Joseph Gales, its longtime editor, died in 1860 and his partner, W. W. Seaton, retired December 31, 1864. The paper became a Johnson organ during his presidency, and in 1869 was classified as Democratic.

126. *See above*, footnote 67.

127. Blair to Johnson, June 16, 1865, Johnson MSS. Blair attempted to persuade Barlow and New York Democratic leaders to support the Thirteenth Amendment. Blair to Barlow, Dec. 20, 1864, Dec. 24, 1864, Jan. 15, 1865, Jan. 17, 1865, Barlow MSS.

128. Blair to Johnson, June 16, 1865, Johnson MSS.

129. George W. Julian, *Political Recollections, 1840 to 1872* (Chicago, 1884), p. 250.

130. Nicolay and Hay, *Abraham Lincoln*, X, pp. 84–85; Rhodes, *History of the United States*, V, p. 50; Randall and Current, *Lincoln the President*, p. 310; Carl Sandburg, *Abraham Lincoln: the War Years* (4 vols., New York, 1939), IV, pp. 7–9. If Professor Pomeroy is correct in believing that Charles Dana in retrospect confused Lincoln's interest in the admission of Nevada with his concern over the passage of the Thirteenth Amendment, Dana's account is another evidence of patronage promises. Pomeroy, "Lincoln, the Thirteenth Amendment and the Admission of Nevada," pp. 362–68; Dana, *Recollections*, p. 176.

131. Mallory, *Cong. Globe*, 38 Cong., 2 sess., p. 179 (Jan. 9, 1865).

132. New York *Times*, Oct. 10, 1865.

133. Cox, *Three Decades*, p. 329. Cox did not mention the incident in his recollections published in 1865; otherwise the two accounts are substantially the same.

134. *See above*, footnotes 87 and 88.

135. Bilbo to Johnson, Jan. 10, 1865, Johnson MSS.

136. Bilbo to Seward, Feb. 1, 1865, Seward MSS.

137. Nelson wrote Seward asking that the promise be kept; Nelson to Seward, July 29, 1865, *ibid.*

138. Bilbo to Seward, Feb. 1, 1865, *ibid.*

139. Chadbourne and Moore, *The Public Service*, II, Pt. 1, p. 151.

140. Nelson to Seward, Nov. 20, 1866, Seward MSS.

141. Carman and Luthin, *Lincoln and the Patronage*, pp. 125, 285–86; Randall and Current, *Lincoln the President*, pp. 44–45, 241; Oliver Carlson, *The Man Who Made News: James Gordon Bennett* (New York, 1942), p. 370.

142. New York *Herald*, Sept. 6, 1864, Sept. 9, 1864, Oct. 28, 1864, Oct. 29, 1864, Oct. 31, 1864, Nov. 7, 1864, Nov. 8, 1864.

143. Tanner, 'The Lobby,' p. 374.

CHAPTER 2

THE CONSERVATIVE OFFENSIVE

1. The recent work of Eric McKitrick, *Andrew Johnson and Reconstruction* (Chicago, 1960), is a major dissent, placing responsibility upon Johnson. For a careful analysis of Johnson historiography prior to 1959, *see* Willard Hays, "Andrew Johnson's Reputation," East Tennessee Historical Society, *Publications*, No. 31 (1959), pp. 1–31, No. 32 (1960), pp. 18–50.

2. For recent reappraisals of the Radicals, *see* David Donald, *Lincoln Reconsidered* (New York, 1956), pp. 103–27; Hans L. Trefousse, "Ben Wade and the Negro," *Ohio Historical Quarterly*, LXVIII (April, 1959), pp. 161–76; David Montgomery, "Radical Republicanism in Pennsylvania, 1866–1873," *Pennsylvania Magazine of History and Biography*, LXXXV (Oct., 1961), pp. 439–57; Ira V. Brown, "Pennsylvania and the Rights of the Negro, 1865–1887," *Pennsylvania History*, XXVIII (Jan., 1961), pp. 45–57, and his "William D. Kelley and Radical Reconstruction," *Pennsylvania Magazine of History and Biography*, LXXXV (July, 1961), pp. 316–29. Also relevant are Ralph Korngold, *Thaddeus Stevens: A Being Darkly Wise and Rudely Great* (New York, 1955); Fawn M. Brodie, *Thaddeus Stevens: Scourge of the South* (New York, 1959); and Benjamin P. Thomas and Harold M. Hyman, *Stanton: The Life and Times of Lincoln's Secretary of War* (New York, 1962).

The earlier hostile view of the Radicals owed much to the general approval which most historians gave to Johnson's program and to the widely accepted identification of his policy with that of Lincoln. Racist bias and economic determinism, a psychological interpretation of Civil War origins which in effect revived the "devil" role concept of anti-slavery extremists, together with a renewed interest in Johnson between 1927 and 1932 that resulted in a literature of near adulation, are other elements that help explain the unsympathetic treatment which Radicals have received.

3. *See below*, Chapters 9 and 10.

4. Speech of Oct. 31, 1868, in Baker, *Works of William H. Seward*, V, p. 544.

5. New York *Herald*, Feb. 12, 1865.

6. Horace Greeley, editor of the Radical paper the New York *Tribune;* David Dudley Field, outstanding member of the bar; George Opdyke, Mayor of New York City, 1862–1863; William Cullen Bryant, editor of the New York *Evening Post*.

7. Brummer, *Political History of New York State*, pp. 203–04, 290; Van Deusen, *Thurlow Weed*, pp. 301, 310; Alexander, *Political History of the State of New York*, III, p. 37.

8. For the 1864 political scene, *see* Randall and Current, *Lincoln the President*, Chapters 6, 7, and 10; Carmen and Luthin, *Lincoln and the Patronage*, Chapters 9 and 10; William F. Zornow, *Lincoln and the Party Divided* (Norman, Oklahoma, 1954); Brummer, *Political History of New York*, Chapters 14 and 15; David Donald, ed., *Inside Lincoln's Cabinet: The Civil War Diaries of Salmon P. Chase* (New York, 1954), pp. 23–33, Chapter 7.

9. Seward forwarded to President Lincoln this letter together with one from Case denying Weed's public accusations. Chase to Seward, May 30, 1864; Weed to F. W. Seward, June 2, 1864; Seward to Lincoln, June 4, 1864, Seward MSS.

10. Van Deusen, *Thurlow Weed*, pp. 312–16; Brummer, *Political History of New York*, pp. 384 ff.

11. New York *Herald*, Feb. 12, 1865.

12. The President was "dependent largely on the Seward-Weed influence in carrying New York State." Carman and Luthin, *Lincoln and the Patronage*, p. 279.

13. Raymond to Seward, Aug. 5, 1864; *also* his letters of June 21, 1864, Aug. 16, 1864, Aug. 18, 1864 (with Lincoln's endorsement); and Weed to Seward, Sept. 28, 1864, Oct. 14, 1864, Seward MSS.

14. Weed to Seward, Aug. 6, 1864, Aug. 10, 1864, Aug. 11, 1864; Schell to Seward, Aug. 26, 1864, *ibid*.

15. Letters to Seward from C. H. White, Sept. 1, 1864; Weed Parsons & Co., Printers, Sept. 6, 1864; Hugh McCulloch, Sept. 8, 1864; Wm. M. Evarts, Sept. 16, 1864; I. P. M. Epping, Sept. 30, 1864; I. N. Arnold, n.d., filed Sept. 30, 1864; I. W. Thompson,

n.d., erroneously filed July, 1864; "M.S." [?] n.d., received Oct. 6, 1864, *ibid.*

16. Abram Wakeman to Seward, Oct. 22, 1864, *ibid.*; and see above, Chapter 1, footnote 124.

17. Seward's letters to Geo. M. Fowle, June 8, 1865, J. W. Webb, Sept. 23, 1865, R. Schell, Oct. 12, 1866, *ibid.* Not Seward's letters, but rather those to him, furnish the evidence of his activity during the campaign.

18. Seward to Weed, Oct. 3, 1865, Weed MSS.

19. Simeon Draper, Abram Wakeman, James Kelly, respectively; Brummer, *Political History of New York*, pp. 394–95; Van Deusen, *Thurlow Weed*, pp. 310–11.

20. R. M. B. [Blatchford] to Seward, Dec. 10, 1864, Seward MSS.

21. Baker, ed., *Works of William H. Seward*, V, p. 504.

22. Seward's statement to the French government in 1862, New York *Herald*, Oct. 25, 1864.

23. I. P. M. Epping to Seward, Sept. 30, 1864, Seward MSS.

24. Letters respecting the peace mission of C. G. Baylor of Georgia, August through November, 1864, and Baylor to Seward, Jan. 14, 1865, *ibid.*

25. *See above*, Chapter 1, footnotes 116 and 117.

26. Bilbo to Seward, Jan. 23, 1865, Seward MSS.

27. New York *Herald*, Feb. 12, 1865.

28. Seward's letters to L. Laboulaye, Sept. 19, 1865, J. W. Webb, Aug. 9, 1865, Lord Lyons, Sept. 21, 1865, R. Balcom, Dec. 29, 1865, July 14, 1866, Seward MSS.

29. Baker, ed., *Works of William H. Seward*, V, pp. 513–14.

30. Bilbo to Seward, Feb. 1, 1865, Seward MSS.

31. Schell to F. W. Seward, Dec. 14, 1861, *ibid.*

32. Latham to Seward, Feb. 23, 1861, *ibid.*

33. *Cong. Globe*, 38 Cong., 2 sess., p. 171 (Jan. 9, 1865).

34. *Ibid.*, p. 526 (Jan. 31, 1865).

35. Mallory, *ibid.*, p. 180 (Jan. 9, 1865).

36. Kalbfleisch, *ibid.*, p. 528 (Jan. 31, 1865).

37. New York *Herald*, Jan. 15, 1865.

38. *Ibid.*, Feb. 2, 1865.

39. Though more Democratic than Republican, the *National Intelligencer* was somewhat ambiguous in its party affiliations. *See above*, Chapter 1, footnote 125.

40. Washington *National Intelligencer*, Jan. 27, 1865.

41. New York *Herald*, Feb. 12, 1865.

42. *Ibid.*

43. Carman and Luthin, *Lincoln and the Patronage*, Chapter 2.

44. Hogan to Johnson, June 19, 1865, Johnson MSS.

45. Seward to Lincoln, Aug. 13, 1864; Ward Hunt to Lincoln, Sept. 24, 1864; Hunt to Seward, Sept. 24, 1864, Seward MSS; Carman and Luthin, *Lincoln and the Patronage*, pp. 282–85.

46. Draft of MS, undated, Gideon Welles MSS, New York Public Library.

47. Chicago *Tribune*, Feb. 16, 1860.

48. *Ibid.*, May 16, 1860.

49. Barlow to S. F. Butterworth, March 22, 1865, Barlow MSS.

50. Barlow to M. Blair, May 10, 1864, *ibid.*

51. Barlow to M. Blair, Feb. 11, 1865, *ibid.*

52. This reaction was reflected both in private letters and in the public press. For examples, letters to Seward from A. de Gasparin, May 1, 1865, John Reid, May 14, 1865, G. Herman, June 19, 1865, Seward MSS; New York *Tribune*, April 17, 1865.

53. New York *Times*, April 25, 1865, May 13, 1865.

54. Campbell to Weed, May 1, 1865, Weed MSS.

55. *Diary of Gideon Welles* (Howard K. Beale, ed., 3 vols., New York, 1960), II, pp. 304, 307; New York *Times*, May 13, 1865.

56. Weed to Seward, May 11, 1865, May 12, 1865, Seward MSS.

57. For example, *Diary of Gideon Welles*, III, pp. 66, 492; "Recollections of President Johnson and his Cabinet," undated, Welles MSS.

58. Weed to Seward, May 23, 1865, Seward MSS; *see also* D. Morrison to Weed, March 31, 1866, Weed MSS.

59. New York *Times*, May 6, 1865, May 7, 1865.

60. *Ibid.*, June 7, 1865, June 8, 1865.

61. *Ibid.*, June 8, 1865.

62. New York *Herald*, May 19, 1865.

63. *Ibid.*, June 4, 1865.

64. *Ibid.*, July 10, 1865.

65. C. Vann Woodward, *Reunion and Reaction: The Compromise of 1877 and the End of Reconstruction* (New York, 1951). For the attitude of Tennessee's former Whigs toward party reorganization, *see* Thomas B. Alexander, "Whiggery and Reconstruction in Tennessee," *Journal of Southern History*, XVI (Aug., 1950), p. 298.

66. H. W. Hilliard to Seward, Aug. 1, 1865; Seward to Hilliard, Aug. 10, 1865; Seward to W. H. Boyce, Aug. 10, 1865; Seward to W. Woodbridge, Sept. 25, 1865, Seward MSS.

67. Weed to Seward, May 29, 1865, *ibid.*

68. Seward to Weed, June 1, 1865, Weed MSS.

69. Weed to Seward, Sept. 23, 1865, Seward MSS.

70. Weed to Seward, Sept. 12, 1865, *ibid.*

71. New York *Times*, June 12, 1865.

72. Seward to Webb, Aug. 9, 1865, Seward MSS.
73. Seward to Webb, Sept. 23, 1865. Seward apparently regretted his outburst and wrote two days later a friendly letter, *ibid.*
74. New York *World*, Aug. 18, 1865.
75. W. A. Darling to Seward, Aug. 25, 1865, with notation "returned from the President," Seward MSS.
76. McCulloch to Johnson, Aug. 23, 1865, Sept. 12, 1865, with W. E. Chandler to McCulloch, Sept. 11, 1865, Johnson MSS.

CHAPTER 3

THE BLAIRS AND THE DEMOCRACY

1. Barlow to W. H. Wadsworth, April 15, 1865; Barlow to M. Blair, April 15, 1865, Barlow MSS.
2. Barlow to M. Blair, April 21, 1865, April 29, 1865, *ibid.*
3. Barlow to T. G. Pratt, June 8, 1865, *ibid.*
4. Johnson's reply to an Illinois delegation, New York *Times*, April 19, 1865; Johnson's remarks at an interview with citizens of Indiana, April 15, 1865; Edward McPherson, *Political Manual for 1866* (Washington, 1866), pp. 44–47.
5. H. C. Page to Johnson, April 21, 1865, Johnson MSS.
6. Bancroft to Johnson, April 26, 1865, *ibid.*
7. H. Brewster to Johnson, May 5, 1865, *ibid.*
8. J. Tiegler to Johnson, May 15, 1865, *ibid.*
9. Hogan to Johnson, May 17, 1865, *ibid.*
10. Morgan to Johnson, Sept. 4, 1865, *ibid.*
11. Dixon to Johnson, May 5, 1865, *ibid.*
12. Green to Johnson, June 25, 1865, *ibid.*
13. Seymour to Johnson, Sept. 8, 1865, *ibid.*
14. New York *Herald*, July 29, 1865.
15. Dickinson to Johnson, Aug. 19, 1865, Aug. 21, 1865, Johnson MSS.
16. Croswell to Dickinson, Aug. 10, 1865, *ibid.*
17. Steele to Johnson, July 30, 1865, *ibid.*
18. New York *Herald*, May 12, 1865.
19. Blair to Barlow, May 1, 1864, May 4, 1864, May 11, 1864, May 27, 1864; Barlow to Blair, May 3, 1864, May 10, 1864, May 19, 1864, Barlow MSS.
20. Blair to Barlow, Oct. 15, 1864, *ibid.*
21. Blair to Barlow, Dec. 20, 1864, n.d. [ca. Dec. 24, 1864], Jan. 7, 1865, Jan. 12, 1865, *ibid.*
22. Blair to Barlow, Jan. 7, 1865, *ibid.*
23. Blair to Barlow, Feb. 9, 1865, *ibid.*

24. Barlow to Blair, Feb. 11, 1865, *ibid.;* and *see above,* Chapter 1, fotnotes 109, 110, and 127.
25. Barlow to Blair, Feb. 21, 1865, Barlow MSS.
26. New York *Herald,* May 12, 1865; William E. Smith, *The Francis Preston Blair Family in Politics* (2 vols., New York, 1933), II, pp. 327–29, 335, 343, 344, 346, 348, 360.
27. Geo. McClellan to Barlow, March 27, 1865, May 30, 1865; Barlow to McClellan, April 21, 1865, June 8, 1865; Barlow to Blair, April 21, 1865, Barlow MSS.
28. G. W. Childs to F. P. Blair, April 17, 1865, Johnson MSS.
29. Smith, *The Francis Preston Blair Family,* II, pp. 335, 338, 345, 348, 358.
30. Blair to Barlow, July 16, 1865, Barlow MSS.
31. F. P. Blair to Johnson, Aug. 1, 1865, Johnson MSS.
32. H. Reed to Blair, June 26, 1865, *ibid.*
33. W. A. Dudley to Blair, June 23, 1865; M. C. Johnson to Blair, Aug. 21, 1865, *ibid.*
34. F. P. Blair to M. Blair, June 22, 1865, *ibid.* Montgomery cynically interpreted Stanton's attack on General Sherman as a calculated effort to ingratiate himself with Johnson by destroying a "supposed rival of Johnson for the succession"; Blair to Barlow, April 28, 1865, Barlow MSS.
35. F. P. Blair to Johnson, Aug. 1, 1865, Johnson MSS.
36. Blair to Barlow, June 14, 1865, Barlow MSS.
37. Cox to Barlow, Aug. 13, 1865, *ibid.*
38. Barlow to Blair, April 15, 1865, *ibid.*
39. Blair to Barlow, April 18, 1865, *ibid.*
40. Montgomery's brother Frank also visited at Barlow's home in June. Barlow to Geo. McClellan, June 8, 1865, *ibid.*
41. Barlow to Blair, May 10, 1865, May 16, 1865, *ibid.;* June 15, 1865, July 19, 1865, Johnson MSS. (A copy of each of the later two letters is in the Barlow MSS; the originals were submitted by Blair to the President.)
42. Shipman to Barlow, July 12, 1865, July 22, 1865, Barlow MSS.
43. Shipman to Barlow, Aug. 12, 1865, *ibid.*
44. Blair to Barlow, May 13, 1865, May 25, 1865, June 14, 1865, *ibid.*
45. Blair to Barlow, July 8, 1865, *ibid.*
46. Barlow to Shipman, Aug. 22, 1865, *ibid.*
47. Shipman to Barlow, Aug. 26, 1865, *ibid.*
48. Shipman to Barlow, Sept. 9, 1865, *ibid.*
49. Two letters, Shipman to Barlow, both dated Sept. 13, 1865, *ibid.* The text of Johnson's speech is in the New York *Herald,* Sept. 12, 1865.
50. Barlow to M. Blair, June 10, 1865, Barlow MSS.

51. Barlow to M. Blair, July 19, 1865, Johnson MSS.
52. Barlow to M. Blair, June 10, 1865, Barlow MSS.
53. Blair to Barlow, June 14, 1865, *ibid.*
54. Blair to Barlow, June 15, 1865, *ibid.*
55. Blair to Barlow, June 14, 1865, June 15, 1865, *ibid.*
56. Barlow to Blair, July 24, 1865, Johnson MSS. Taylor's own account indicates that he saw the President on a number of occasions but does not indicate the nature of their discussions except in reference to Taylor's request to visit Jefferson Davis. Richard Taylor, *Destruction and Reconstruction: Personal Experiences of the Late War* (New York, 1879), pp. 239–46.
57. Barlow to Blair, Sept. 11, 1865, *ibid.*
58. New York *Herald*, July 20, 1865.
59. New York *World*, July 27, 1865.
60. *Ibid.*, Aug. 1, 1865.
61. *Ibid.*, Aug. 7, 1865.
62. Pratt to Barlow, Aug. 16, 1865, Barlow MSS.
63. Barlow to Pratt, Aug. 17, 1865, Johnson MSS.
64. Barlow to Pratt, Aug. 21, 1865, *ibid.*
65. Pratt to Barlow, Aug. 22, 1865, Barlow MSS.
66. Ch. Mason to Black, June 14, 1865, Black MSS, Library of Congress.
67. Black to Blair, July 15, 1865, Johnson MSS.
68. Blair to Black, Aug. 31, 1865, Black MSS.
69. Blair to Black, Aug. 5, 1865, Aug. 31, 1865, *ibid.*
70. Barlow to Pratt, Aug. 21, 1865, Johnson MSS. Richmond did go to Washington for an interview with the President shortly after the Democratic convention, but public notice of the visit was held to a minimum. Springfield *Republican*, Sept. 29, 1865; New York *Herald*, Sept. 28, 1865.
71. Barlow to Tilden, two letters, both dated Aug. 31, 1865, Tilden MSS, New York Public Library.
72. Barlow to Shipman, Sept. 11, 1865, Barlow MSS. Johnson's negotiations with the Democratic leaders cannot be explained away on the assumption that he merely listened while they spoke. Gideon Welles may have been correct in noting that the President had a habit of silently listening which was often mistaken for consent; but the nature of the references to the President's statements reported in private letters, together with the obvious persistence of New York leaders in their effort to obtain a commitment that could not be misunderstood, preclude such an explanation in respect to the series of conferences which preceded the endorsement of the President by the state Democratic convention.

Johnson gave assurances, but this fact should not be read as a political capitulation to the Democracy. For the President's independent political objective, *see below*, Chapters 4 and 5.

73. Barlow to Blair, Sept. 11, 1865, Johnson MSS; Barlow to Pratt, Sept. 11, 1865; Barlow to Houston, Sept. 12, 1865, Barlow MSS.
74. Reprinted in New York *Tribune*, Aug. 29, 1865.
75. Barlow to Shipman, Sept. 11, 1865, Barlow MSS.
76. *Ibid.*
77. Blair to Johnson, June 16, 1865, Johnson MSS.
78. New York *Times*, July 14, 1865; New York *World*, July 13, 1865, Aug. 28, 1865, Sept. 13, 1865, Oct. 3, 1865, Oct. 4, 1865; Smith, *The Francis Preston Blair Family*, II, pp. 340–43.
79. Blair to Barlow, July 8, 1865, July 11, 1865, July 16, 1865; Barlow to Shipman, July 11, 1865, July 19, 1865, Barlow MSS; Barlow to Blair, July 19, 1865, Johnson MSS.
80. Letters to Seward from J. W. Forney, July 22, 1865, J. M. Scovil, July 29, 1865, Weed, Sept. 12, 1865, Seward MSS.
81. Seward to Weed, July 22, 1865, Weed MSS.
82. Seward to John Bigelow, July 1, 1865, Seward MSS.

CHAPTER 4
THE NEW YORK BATTLE

1. Blair to Barlow, Sept. 13, 1865, Barlow MSS.
2. Barlow to R. Houston, Oct. 3, 1865, *ibid.*
3. New York *Herald*, Aug. 15, 1865; *Diary of Gideon Welles*, II, p. 386.
4. New York *World*, Aug. 19, 1865.
5. New York *Herald*, Aug. 17, 1865.
6. G. W. Blunt to Fox, Sept. 29, 1865, Gideon Welles MSS, Library of Congress.
7. New York *Herald*, Aug. 16, 1865; New York *World*, Aug. 18, 1865.
8. New York *Herald*, Aug. 16, 1865.
9. *Ibid.*, Aug. 22, 1865, Aug. 24, 1865, Sept. 2, 1865, Sept. 14, 1865.
10. *Ibid.*, July 10, 1865, Aug. 16, 1865; New York *World*, Aug. 15, 1865, Oct. 7, 1865; E. D. Webster to Seward, Aug. 14, 1865, Seward MSS.
11. Weed to Seward, Nov. 11, 1865, Seward MSS.
12. Weed to Seward, May 27, 1865, *ibid.*

13. New York *World*, Oct. 7, 1865, Oct. 18, 1865.
14. New York *Herald*, April 19, 1866.
15. Barlow to R. Houston, Oct. 3, 26, 28, 1865, Barlow MSS.
16. R. Houston to Barlow, Nov. 1, 1865, *ibid.*
17. New York *Herald*, Sept. 14, 1865.
18. Weed to Seward, Nov. 4, 1865, Nov. 11, 1865, Seward MSS.
19. Albany *Argus*, reprinted in New York *Tribune*, Nov. 22, 1865.
20. New York *Tribune*, Aug. 19, 1865.
21. New York *World*, July 18, 1865, July 27, 1865; New York *Times*, July 16, 1865.
22. Letter of John B. Haskins, reprinted in New York *Tribune*, Sept. 22, 1865.
23. New York *Herald*, Aug. 24, 1865.
24. New York *World*, Sept. 8, 1865, Sept. 9, 1865.
25. New York *Herald*, Sept. 9, 1865.
26. New York *Times*, Sept. 8, 1865.
27. New York *World*, Sept. 9, 1865.
28. New York *Times*, Sept. 9, 1865, Sept. 11, 1865; New York *World*, Sept. 12, 1865, Sept. 15, 1865.
29. Henry Wilson to Raymond, Sept. 12, 1865, Henry J. Raymond MSS, New York Public Library; Greeley to Chase, Oct. 23, 1865, Horace Greeley MSS, New York Public Library.
30. Blair to Barlow, Sept. 15, 1865, Barlow MSS.
31. Weed to Morgan, Sept. 18, 1865, Edwin D. Morgan MSS, New York State Library.
32. New York *Times*, Sept. 11, 1865.
33. *Ibid.*, Sept. 21, 1865.
34. Jms. Kelly to Seward, Nov. 9, 1865, Seward MSS.
35. Weed to Seward, Sept. 23, 1865, *ibid.*
36. Weed to Seward, Sept. 30, 1865, *ibid.*
37. New York *Herald*, Oct. 4, 1865.
38. Chandler to H. J. Raymond, Oct. 20, 1865, George Jones MSS.
39. Barlow to Taylor, Oct. 21, 1865, Barlow MSS.
40. *Ibid.*
41. Taylor to Barlow, Oct. 25, 1865, *ibid.*
42. Shipman to Barlow, Oct. 23, 1865, *ibid.*
43. Barlow to Shipman, Oct. 25, 1865, *ibid.*
44. The quotations and summary of the *World*'s position in this paragraph and the paragraphs following are from the paper's editorials of the following dates: Sept. 12, 21, 22, 23, 25, 26, 27, 29; Oct. 2, 3, 4, 6, 7, 14, 17, 18, 26; Nov. 16, 1865.
45. *See* footnote above.
46. *See* footnote 44 above.

47. Blair's speech, as reported in New York *Times*, Oct. 19, 1865. For speeches of Slocum and Van Buren, *see ibid.*, Oct. 5, 1865, Oct. 6, 1865.

48. New York *World*, Sept. 18, 1865. For the Democratic position on the Connecticut referendum on Negro suffrage, *see ibid.*, Sept. 13, 1865, Oct. 3, 1865, Oct. 4, 1865.

49. The summary of the *Times*' position, in this paragraph and the four following, are from the paper's editorials of the following dates: Sept. 21, 23, 27, 29, 30; Oct. 3, 10, 13, 15, 16, 17, 18, 21, 23, 24, 25; Nov. 2, 3, 4, 6, 7, 1865; also Weed's letter published Oct. 3, 1865, and Raymond's campaign speech in Albany, printed Oct. 15, 1865.

50. *See* footnote above.

51. New York *Tribune*, Oct. 7, 1865.

52. *Ibid.*, Oct. 20, 1865.

53. Compare the *Tribune* editorials of Oct. 7, 1865 and Oct. 18, 1865 with those of Oct. 23, 1865 and Oct. 26, 1865.

54. *Ibid.*, Oct. 21, 24, 25, 26, 28, 30, 31; Nov. 1, 4, 6, 7, 1865.

55. Speech at Cooper Institute, printed in New York *Times*, Oct. 19, 1865; Smith, *The Francis Preston Blair Family*, II, pp. 344–46.

56. *Mr. Seward at Auburn in 1865* (pamphlet, n.d., n.p.), Seward MSS.

57. Shipman to Barlow, Oct. 23, 1865, Barlow MSS.

58. Weed to Seward, Nov. 3, 1865, Seward MSS.

59. R. B. Minturn to Weed, Nov. 3, 1865 (on behalf of himself and Samuel G. Ward), Weed to Seward, Nov. 3, 1865, *ibid.*

60. Telegrams, Weed to Seward, Nov. 7, 1865, *ibid.*

61. Geo. Babcock to E. D. Webster, Nov. 11, 1865, *ibid.*

62. The total votes cast for Secretary of State were 26,172 fewer than in 1863, 85,983 more than in 1861.

63. New York *Times*, Nov. 8, 1865.

64. Raymond's speech at Albany, *ibid.*, Oct. 15, 1865.

65. *Ibid.*, Oct. 16, 1865.

66. *Ibid.*, Oct. 17, 1865.

67. *Ibid.*, Oct. 24, 1865.

68. *Ibid.*, Nov. 10, 1865.

69. *Ibid.*, Nov. 14, 1865.

70. New York *World*, Nov. 10, 1865, Nov. 11, 1865.

71. Barlow to Jms. Hughes, Nov. 8, 1865, Barlow to H. D. Bacon, Nov. 10, 1865, Barlow to Blair, Nov. 8, 1865, Barlow MSS.

72. Barlow to R. Houston, Nov. 15, 1865, *ibid.*

73. Barlow to Jms. Hughes, Nov. 16, 1865, *ibid.*

74. Blair to Barlow, Nov. 12, 1865, Nov. 18, 1865, *ibid.*

75. New York *Evening Post*, Nov. 27, 1865.

76. New York *World*, Nov. 28, 1865.

CHAPTER 5

THE MAN WITH TWO COATTAILS

1. For example, *see* New York *Herald*, April 23, 1865, May 2, 1865, May 19, 1865, June 19, 1865, Aug. 23, 1865, Sept 15, 1865.
2. *Ibid.*, May 14, 1865, Aug. 20, 1865, Sept. 20, 1865.
3. *Ibid.*, Sept. 15, 1865.
4. *Ibid.*, April 27, 1865.
5. *Ibid.*, May 25, 1865, July 10, 1865, Aug. 8, 19, 22, 28, 1865, Sept. 2, 9, 19, 1865.
6. *Ibid.*, Oct. 4, 1865, Oct. 9, 1865.
7. *Ibid.*, Nov. 9, 10, 16, 1865.
8. Johnson to Bennett, Oct. 6, 1865, Johnson MSS.
9. Bennett to Johnson, Oct. 15, 1865, *ibid.*
10. H. Calkin to Marble, Jan. 22, 1867, Marble MSS.
11. Wikoff to Johnson, July 30, 1865, Aug. 21, 1865, Oct. 26, 1865; Bennett to Johnson, Aug. 26, 1865; Phillips to Johnson, Oct. 26, 1865, Johnson MSS.
12. W. Rives to Bennett, Feb. 19, 1866, *ibid.*
13. New York *Herald*, Aug. 13, 1865.
14. *Ibid.*, May 19, 1865, Aug. 29, 1865, Sept. 11, 1865, Dec. 10, 1865, Dec. 13, 1865.
15. *Ibid.*, Sept. 9, 1865, Sept. 14, 1865.
16. *Ibid.*, Aug. 13, 1865.
17. Italics added. *Ibid.*, Sept. 23, 1865.
18. *Ibid.*, May 24, 1865, June 7, 1865, Aug. 9, 1865, Aug. 31, 1865, Sept. 15, 1865.
19. *Ibid.*, June 19, 1865.
20. *Ibid.*, June 21, 1865.
21. *Ibid.*, June 21, 23; July 7, 10, 18; Aug. 9, 22, 1865, Feb. 26, 1866.
22. *Ibid.*, Aug. 7, 1865.
23. *Ibid.*, May 20, 1865.
24. *Ibid.*, Aug. 20, 1865.
25. *Ibid.*, Sept. 13, 14, 16, 1865.
26. *Ibid.*, Jan. 7, 28, 30, 1866.
27. *Ibid.*, Nov. 6, 1865; *see also* Aug. 3, 1865, Aug. 20, 1865.
28. *Ibid.*, Dec. 7, 1865.
29. *Ibid.*, Oct. 4, 1865.
30. *Ibid.*, Dec. 11, 1865.
31. *Ibid.*, Dec. 13, 1865.
32. *Ibid.*, Dec. 17, 1865.
33. *Ibid.*, May 17, 1866.

34. We do not wish to be misunderstood as suggesting that Bennett framed Johnson's policy; the President's decisions were his own. We believe it is clear, however, that the opinion of the *Herald* was one of the elements upon which the President based his assessment of the political scene. For Johnson's close attention to the paper's editorial position, *see* footnotes 8 through 12 above and 60 below; *see also* Chapter 9, footnote 29.

35. M. A. Sono to Johnson, Sept. 29, 1865, Johnson MSS.

36. Dixon to Johnson, May 5, 1865, Sept. 26, 1865, *ibid.*

37. Chase to Johnson, May 12, 1865, *ibid.*

38. Green to Johnson, June 25, 1865, *ibid.*

39. Letters to Johnson from W. W. Boyce, July 12, 1865, A. Rich, July 14, 1865, J. S. Carlile, July 16, 1865, N. Ranny, July 21, 1865, Wm. Thorpe, Aug. 16, 1865, T. J. Rawls, Sept. 12, 1865, A. H. Kerr, Nov. 2, 1865, G. W. Jones, Nov. 5, 1865, *ibid.*

40. Dickinson to Johnson, Aug. 19, 1865, *ibid.*

41. Text of Johnson's speech, New York *Times*, March 20, 1865.

42. Robert W. Winston, *Andrew Johnson, Plebeian and Patriot* (New York, 1928), p. 339; see also George Fort Milton, *The Age of Hate: Andrew Johnson and the Radicals* (New York, 1930), pp. 635–39, and Jonathan T. Dorris, *Pardon and Amnesty under Lincoln and Johnson* (Chapel Hill, N.C., 1953), pp. 316, 354–56.

43. Springfield *Republican*, Oct. 13, 1865.

44. Winston, *Andrew Johnson*, p. 305; Johnson's speech to a delegation from Montana, Feb. 7, 1866, and his reply to a Virginia delegation, Feb. 10, 1866, revised clippings, Johnson MSS; *see below*, footnotes 59 through 62.

45. *Diary of Gideon Welles*, III, pp. 398, 454, 455.

46. Undated, Welles MSS, N.Y.P.L.

47. Entries for July 7, 8, 9, 1868, transcript of Col. W. G. Moore's shorthand diary, Johnson MSS.

48. Entries of Aug. 24, 1867, March 27, 1868; *see also* entry of Oct. 25, 1866, *ibid.*

49. Entry of Aug. 14, 1867, *ibid.*

50. *Ibid.*

51. Le Roy P. Graf, editor of the projected publication of the Andrew Johnson papers. After Lincoln's election, Johnson became the most influential patronage broker in Tennessee. In the use of this power, Johnson gave consideration to old party associates and to the building of a "Johnson Party" at the expense of consolidating former Whig and Bell Unionist influence behind the new Administration. See Graf's "Andrew Johnson and the Coming of the War," *Tennessee Historical Quarterly*, XIX (Sept., 1960), pp. 208, 214, 216–17, 220; *also* J. Milton Henry, "The

Revolution in Tennessee, February, 1861, to June, 1861," *ibid.*, XVIII (June, 1959), pp. 108–10, 117–19.

52. Winston, *Andrew Johnson*, pp. 119–20; L. D. Campbell to Weed, May 1, 1865, Weed MSS; Campbell to Johnson, May 8, 1865, Johnson MSS.

53. Winston, *Andrew Johnson*, p. 34.

54. For Vice-President Johnson's severity toward the South, *see* Charles A. Dana, *Recollections of the Civil War* (New York, 1899), pp. 269–70.

55. Winston, *Andrew Johnson*, 212 ff.

56. Clifton R. Hall, *Andrew Johnson, Military Governor of Tennessee* (Princeton, 1916), p. 170; for the election oath and the protest it evoked, see *Collected Works of Abraham Lincoln*, VIII, pp. 58–72; *also*, J. T. Dorris, "The Treatment of Confederates by Lincoln and Johnson," *Lincoln Herald*, LXI (Winter, 1959), p. 146.

57. New York *World*, Oct. 25, 1865; *see also* Sept. 18, 1865, Sept. 23, 1865, Oct. 13, 1865, Oct. 14, 1865, *ibid.*

58. Speech to a delegation from Montana, Feb. 7, 1866, revised clipping, Johnson MSS.

59. *Ibid.*; also Johnson's reply to a Virginia delegation, Feb. 10, 1866, revised clipping, *ibid.*

60. Sherman to Johnson, Feb. 11, 1866, *ibid.*

61. W. B. Phillips to Johnson, Feb. 23, 1866, *ibid.*

62. H. W. Hilliard to Johnson, Feb. 28, 1866, *ibid.*

63. Interview with George L. Stearns, Oct. 3, 1865, McPherson, *Political Manual for 1866*, p. 48. Johnson had long preferred to be the courted rather than the courtier; Graf, "Andrew Johnson and the Coming of the War," pp. 216–17.

64. Springfield *Republican*, Sept. 30, 1865.

65. Barlow to McClellan, Oct. 12, 1865, Barlow MSS.

66. Speech to a delegation from Montana, Feb. 7, 1866, revised clipping, Johnson MSS.

67. Reported in the New York *Herald*, Aug. 29, 1866.

68. Entry of July 3, 1868, transcript of Moore's diary, Johnson MSS.

69. Ewing to Wm. T. Sherman, Thomas Ewing MSS, Library of Congress.

70. A. G. M. Bumey [?] to Johnson, March 7, 1866, Johnson MSS.

71. Campbell to Johnson, May 8, 1865, *ibid.*; *see also* Campbell to Weed, May 1, 1865, Weed MSS.

72. Campbell to D. T. Patterson, Jan. 22, 1866; *see also* Campbell to Johnson, Jan. 19, 1866, Johnson MSS.

73. Campbell to Johnson, June 22, 1866, Aug. 21, 1866; H. S. Burnett to Johnson, March 24, 1866, *ibid.*

74. Watterson to Johnson, July 8, 1865, *ibid.*
75. Watterson to Johnson, Sept. 26, 1865, *ibid.*
76. Watterson to Johnson, Oct. 7, 1865, *ibid.*
77. Watterson to Johnson, Oct. 20, 1865, *ibid.*
78. V. [?] S. Harris to Watterson, Dec. 29, 1865, *ibid.; see also,* Martin Abbott, ed., "A Southerner Views the South, 1865: Letters of Harvey M. Watterson," *Virginia Magazine of History and Biography,* LXVIII (Oct., 1960), pp. 478–79.
79. Henry Watterson to Johnson, Dec. 7, 1865, *ibid.*
80. Joseph F. Wall, *Henry Watterson: Reconstructed Rebel* (New York, 1956), pp. 63–64.
81. R. S. Saunders to Johnson, Sept. 6, 1865, *see also* his letter of July 13, 1865, Johnson MSS.
82. Rousseau to Johnson, Sept. 11, 1865, *ibid.* Rousseau was an experienced politician, having served in both the Indiana and New York State legislatures.
83. East to Johnson, Sept. 23, 1865; G. W. Jones to Johnson, Nov. 5, 1865, *ibid.*
84. F. C. Dunnington to Robert Johnson, Dec. 11, 1865, *ibid.*
85. Letters to Johnson from M. Burns, Aug. 22, 1865, Sept. 2, 1865, S. Milligan, Aug. 22, 1865, Sept. 1, 1865, J. Keyes, Dec. 10, 1865, *ibid.*
86. Barlow to Houston, Oct. 28, 1865, Barlow MSS.
87. Houston to Barlow, Nov. 1, 1865, *ibid.*

CHAPTER 6

THE PROBLEM OF PATRONAGE

1. This is not, however, the view of Eric McKitrick, see *Andrew Johnson and Reconstruction,* pp. 377–94.
2. Rhodes, *History of the United States,* V, p. 621.
3. Appointment Records, Johnson MSS.
4. Three untitled pamphlets on appointments, *ibid.*
5. Report of interview with a New Hampshire delegation and speech at Philadelphia, New York *Herald,* Aug. 20, 1866, Aug. 29, 1866.
6. *See above,* Chapter 2, footnote 75 and Chapter 4, footnote 35.
7. A. Van Eyck to Maj. C. S. Jones, July 19, 1866, Johnston MSS.
8. J. A. Kasson to Blair, Aug. 28, 1866, *ibid.*
9. Letters to Weed from H. J. Raymond, June 8, 1866, E. J. Fowle, June 19, 1866, F. W. Seward, July 6, 1866, A. Hawley, July 15,

1866, D. C. Littlejohn, Aug. 8, 1866, W. H. Rice, Aug. 10, 1866, G. W. Ernst, Aug. 13, 1866, Oct. 2, 1866, E. H. Downs, Aug. 22, 1866, Sept. 24, 1866, H. A. Phillips, Aug. 23, 1866, J. W. Sherman, Aug. 23, 1866, A. Roggen, Aug. 30, 1866, V. W. Smith, Oct. 1, 1866, Oct. 21, 1866, C. A. Harrington, Oct. 2, 1866, W. S. Lincoln, Oct. 4, 1866, H. McCulloch, Oct. 11, 1866, J. W. Adams, Oct. 19, 1866, J. H. Kidd, Oct. 23, 1866, St. J. B. L. Skinner, Oct. 26, 1866, L. A. Spalding, Oct. 27, 1866, G. P. Eddy, Oct. 29, 1866, G. J. J. Barber, Nov. 1, 1866, Weed MSS.

10. Weed to Seward, Oct. 27, 1866, Seward MSS; *see also* Weed to Johnson, Oct. 2, 1866, Johnson MSS.

11. For examples, *see* letters to Johnson from A. R. Corbin, June 25, 1866, A. Smith, July 17, 1866, J. W. Hinkle, July 31, 1866, N. P. Sawyer, Aug. 20, 1866, Johnson MSS.

12. Johnson to D. M. Fleming, Oct. 14, 1866, *ibid.*

13. F. O'Byrne to Johnson, April 16, 1866; H. S. Burnett to Johnson, March 24, 1866, *ibid.*

14. Rice to Johnson, June 1, 1866, June 23, 1866, July 31, 1866, *ibid.*

15. Wm. Shipman to Barlow, April 8, 1866, Barlow MSS.

16. W. Power to Johnson, Aug. 2, 1866; J. G. Jones to Johnson, Sept. 22, 1866, Johnson MSS.

17. R. P. L. Baber to Johnson, March 30, 1866, *ibid.*

18. J. Smith to Johnson, May 1, 1866, *ibid.*

19. Morgan to Johnson, July 7, 1866, *ibid.*

20. R. W. Scott to Johnson, July 31, 1866, *ibid.*

21. E. Burke to Johnson, July 30, 1866; *see also* his letter of June 19, 1866, *ibid.*

22. A. R. Corbin to Johnson, June 25, 1866, *ibid.*

23. Morgan to G. Rowland, April 19, 1866, Morgan MSS.

24. J. F. Miller to D. T. Patterson, Nov. 10, 1865, Johnson MSS.

25. Barlow to J. Hughes, Dec. 21, 1865, *ibid.*

26. Springfield *Republican*, April 27, 1866, April 28, 1866.

27. Blair to Barlow, Nov. 18, 1865, Barlow MSS.

28. *See above*, Chapter 4, footnotes 3 through 12.

29. Blair to Johnson, Nov. 21, 1865, enclosing Cochrane to Blair, Nov. 19, 1865; Cochrane to Blair, Dec. 22, 1865; Bennett to Johnson, Feb. 1, 1865; Cochrane to Johnson, Feb. 4, 1866, Feb. 12, 1866; H. C. Page to Johnson, Dec. 22, 1865, April 10, 1866; E. Pierrepont to Johnson, March 13, 1866, March 24, 1866; C. G. Halpine to Johnson, March 21, 1866, Johnson MSS.

30. Barlow to Hughes, Dec. 6, 1865, Barlow MSS.

31. Hughes to Barlow, Dec. 7, 1865, *ibid.*

32. Barlow to Hughes, Dec. 9, 1865, *ibid.*

33. Barlow to R. Taylor, Dec. 9, 1865; Barlow to Hughes, Dec. 9, 1865, *ibid.*
34. Barlow to Hughes, Dec. 21, 1865, Johnson MSS.
35. Barlow to Hughes, Dec. 22, 1865, Dec. 26, 1865, Barlow MSS.
36. Barlow to Church, Jan. 2, 1866, Jan. 4, 1866, *ibid.*
37. Barlow to M. Blair, Jan. 18, 1866, *ibid.*
38. Barlow to Blair, Jan. 13, 1866, *ibid.*
39. Blair to S. J. Tilden, March 14, 1866, Tilden MSS.
40. Blair to Barlow, April 7, 1866, Barlow MSS.
41. The word may be "shake"; Montgomery Blair's handwriting was appalling, as Barlow complained and Blair acknowledged.
42. Blair to Barlow, Jan. 18, 1866, Feb. 12, 1866, Barlow MSS; Blair to Tilden, March 14, 1866, Tilden MSS.
43. Barlow to Van Buren, Jan. 11, 1866; Blair to Barlow, Jan. 18, 1866, Barlow MSS.
44. Haskins to Johnson, March 21, 1866, Johnson MSS.
45. Barlow to S. F. Butterworth, Jan. 31, 1866, Barlow MSS.
46. Haskins to Johnson, March 21, 1866, Johnson MSS.
47. Tilden to Blair, March 10, 1866, Blair MSS, Library of Congress.
48. Barlow to T. J. Barnett, Jan. 24, 1866; Barlow to J. Hughes, Dec. 22, 1865, Barlow MSS.
49. Barlow to J. T. Doyle, Jan. 30, 1866, *ibid.*
50. Tilden to Blair, March 10, 1866, Blair MSS; Barlow to R. Taylor, March 7, 1866; Blair to Barlow, April 7, 1866, Barlow MSS.
51. Draft, Blair to Johnson, April 9, 1866, Blair MSS; Blair to Johnson, April 11, 1866, Johnson MSS.
52. Weed to Seward, Nov. 13, 1865, Nov. 14, 1865, Jan. 29, 1866, Seward MSS; Weed to Morgan, Dec. 5, 17, 27, 1865, Morgan MSS; Raymond to Weed, Dec. 15, 1865, Weed MSS.
53. McCulloch to Johnson, Dec. 16, 1865, enclosing J. A. Stewart to McCulloch, Dec. 15, 1865; McCulloch to Johnson, Dec. 28, 1865, enclosing Godwin to McCulloch, Dec. 25, 1865; Godwin to Johnson, Dec. 25, 1865, Johnson MSS. War Democrat H. C. Page listed Bailey with the "committed" men who should be ruled out. Page to Johnson, Dec. 22, 1865, *ibid.*
54. Raymond to Weed, Dec. 15, 1865, Weed MSS.
55. Morgan to Weed, Dec. 15, 1865, Dec. 26, 1865, Morgan MSS.
56. Weed to Morgan, Dec. 17, 1865, *ibid.*
57. Barlow to Blair, Jan. 13, 1866, Barlow MSS.
58. E. Croswell to W. Radford, Feb. 19, 1866, Feb. 26, 1866, E. Pierrepont to Johnson, March 13, 1866, Johnson MSS.
59. Barlow to J. Van Buren, Jan. 11, 1866; Barlow to Blair, Jan. 13, 1866, Barlow MSS.

60. Forney to Johnson, Jan. 2, 1866, Johnson MSS.
61. Springfield *Republican*, Feb. 2, 1866. For an analysis of the reaction to the first veto and February 22nd speech, *see below*, Chapter 9.
62. Weed to Seward, Feb. 28, 1866, Seward MSS.
63. Weed to Seward, March 12, 1866, *ibid.;* Weed to Morgan, March 12, 1866, Morgan MSS.
64. Marble to Blair, March 10, 1866; Marble to [?], March 11, 1866, Marble MSS.
65. Weed to Seward, March 17, 1866, Seward MSS; for Barlow on Littlejohn *see* Barlow to J. Hughes, April 14, 1866, Barlow MSS.
66. Raymond to Weed, n.d. [*ca.* early April, 1866], Weed MSS; *see also* Morgan to Weed, April 4, 1866, Morgan MSS. Barlow deprecated Depew as well as Littlejohn; Barlow to J. Hughes, April 14, 1866, Barlow MSS.
67. Weed to Raymond, April 3, 1866, George Jones MSS.
68. Morgan to Weed, April 4, 1866; Weed to Morgan, April 6, 1866, Morgan MSS.
69. Weed to Seward, Jan. 29, 1866, Seward MSS; Morgan to Weed, Jan. 25, 1866, Weed MSS.
70. Barlow to M. Blair, Feb. 14, 1866, April 14, 1866, Barlow to J. Hughes, Feb. 14, 1866, April 14, 1866, Barlow MSS.
71. Blair to Tilden, March 14, 1866, Tilden MSS.
72. Van Dyck to Morgan, March 6, 1866, March 7, 1866; R. Morrow (of the President's staff) to Morgan, March 8, 1866; *see also* Morgan to Van Dyck, March 4, 1866, Morgan MSS.
73. Blatchford to Seward, March 30, 1866, Seward MSS.
74. Lane to Johnson, April 13, 1866, Johnson MSS. For other references to Davies, *see* Dixon to Johnson, March 31, 1866, April 12, 1866, April 13, 1866, *ibid.;* Weed to Seward, March 17, 1866, March 30, 1866, Seward MSS; Morgan to Weed, March 8, 1866, Morgan MSS.
75. New York *Herald*, Dec. 12, 1865, Dec. 30, 1865.
76. Weed to Seward, Dec. 27, 1865, Dec. 29, 1865, Seward MSS.
77. Springfield *Republican*, Feb. 2, 1866.
78. Blair to Johnson, April 11, 1866, Johnson MSS.
79. New York *Herald*, Dec. 15, 1865; [?] to Weed with Weed's notation, Jan. 18, 1866, Morgan MSS; Smythe to D. T. Patterson, March 20, 1866, Johnson, MSS.
80. J. A. Stewart to McCulloch, Dec. 15, 1865, Johnson MSS.
81. Barlow to J. Hughes, Dec. 21, 1865, *ibid.*
82. Smythe to Barlow, Nov. 18, 1865, Barlow MSS.
83. Barlow to Smythe, March 31, 1866, *ibid.*
84. Barlow to Blair, March 31, 1866, *ibid.*

85. Blair to Barlow, April 7, 1866, *ibid.*
86. Barlow to Blair, March 19, 1867, *ibid.*
87. Barlow to Blair, April 14, 1866; *see also* Barlow to J. Hughes, April 14, 1866, *ibid.*
88. Blair to Barlow, April 15, 1866, *ibid.*
89. Smythe to D. T. Patterson, March 20, 1866, Johnson MSS.
90. *See* letters to Johnson from Halpine, March 21, 1866, Huntington, March 27, 1866, Walker, March 30, 1866, April 14, 1866, R. Johnson, April 15, 1866; also Smythe to Johnson, April 13, 1866, *ibid.*
91. New York *Herald*, April 18, 1866, April 21, 1866; Weed to Morgan, April 19, 1866, April 22, 1866, Morgan MSS; Morgan to Weed, April 21, 1866, April 23, 1866, McCulloch to Weed, Sept. 10, 1866, Weed MSS; Weed to Seward, June 16, 1866, Raymond to Seward, Seward MSS. Reports had reached Seward of disparaging remarks made about him by Smythe, apparently in respect to Seward's drinking habits; Seward accepted Smythe's disavowal. Smythe to Seward, Dec. 27, 1865, *ibid.*
92. Morgan to Weed, April 21, 1866, April 23, 1866, Weed MSS; Weed to Morgan, April 22, 1866, Morgan MSS.
93. Smythe to Barlow, Sept. 8, 1864, Barlow MSS.
94. New York *Herald*, April 25, 1866.
95. W. S. Huntington to Johnson, March 27, 1866, Johnson MSS.
96. New York *Herald*, April 18, 19, 21, 1866. The Brooklyn postmaster, a self-designated Radical, had commended the appointment to the Kings County Union League! G. B. Lincoln to Johnson, April 21, 1866, Johnson MSS.
97. Smythe to Johnson, April 19, 1866, Johnson MSS.
98. New York *Herald*, May 15, 1866.
99. Morgan to Weed, May 5, 1866, Weed MSS.
100. Smythe to E. Cooper (of the President's staff), July 16, 1866, Johnson MSS.
101. R. B. Warren to Johnson, Feb. 26, 1866, *ibid.*
102. J. A. Martin to Johnson, Aug. 4, 1866, *ibid.*

CHAPTER 7

RESTORATION, RECONSTRUCTION, AND CONFUSION

1. New York *World*, Nov. 22, 1865.
2. Barlow to Taylor, Nov. 22, 1865, Barlow MSS. For Taylor, *see* Chapter 3, footnote 56.

3. New York *Tribune*, Nov. 13, 1865; see also Oct. 7, 1865.
4. New York *Herald*, Nov. 28, 1865.
5. Springfield *Republican*, Dec. 5, 1865.
6. Newspaper clippings on Annual Message, 1865, Scrapbook, Johnson MSS. The clippings are not always completely identified, hence those cited below are in some instances but partially identified.
7. Brooklyn *Daily Union*, Dec. 8, 1865, *ibid.*
8. Baltimore *Evening Transcript*, *ibid.*
9. Pittsburgh *Commercial*, Dec. 6, 1865, *ibid.*
10. St. Louis *Democrat*, Dec. 6, 1865; St. Louis *Evening News*, Dec. 6, 1865, *ibid.*
11. Compare Lancaster *Intelligencer*, Dec. 6, 1865, and reprint from *Daily South Carolinian*, Dec. 7, 1865, with Vicksburg *Herald*, Dec. 12, 1865, and reprint from Louisville *Democrat*, *ibid.*
12. Lancaster *Intelligencer*; Petersburgh [Va.] *Daily Index*; Doylestown *Democrat*, *ibid.*
13. [Portland, Me.] *Eastern Argus*, *ibid.*
14. Brooklyn *Daily Union*, *ibid.*
15. New York *Atlas*; Chicago *Tribune*; St. Louis *Republican*, *ibid.*
16. LaFayette [Ind.] *Daily Journal*; Fort Smith *New Era*; Cincinnati *Daily Gazette*, *ibid.*
17. New York *Sun*; Port Royal *New South*, *ibid.*
18. Memphis *Appeal*, *ibid.*
19. New York *Sun*, *ibid.*
20. Concord [N.H.] *Democrat*; [Augusta, Me.] *Kennebec Journal*; New York *Evening Post*; Brooklyn *Daily Union*; Philadelphia *Press and Times*; Philadelphia *Daily Chronicle*; Philadelphia *North American*; Chicago *Republican*; St. Louis *Democrat*; Atchison *Daily Champion*, *ibid.*
21. [Boston] *Right Way*; Lancaster *Intelligencer*; Chicago *Tribune*; Milwaukee *Sentinel*; Memphis *Appeal*; Norfolk *Post*; Richmond *Times*; Iowa City *State Press*, *ibid.*
22. Clarksburg [W. Va.] *National Telegram*; [Augusta, Me.] *Port Kennebec Journal*; New York *Evening Post*; New York *Times*; Philadelphia *Inquirer*; Philadelphia *Press and Times*; Washington *National Republican*; Philadelphia *North American*; Cincinnati *Daily Gazette*, *ibid.*
23. New York *Evening Post*; Doylestown *Democrat*; Milwaukee *News*; Milwaukee *Free Press*; Montgomery *Ledger*, *ibid.*
24. Annual Message, Dec. 4, 1865, McPherson, *Political Manual for 1866*, pp. 64–65.
25. Messages, Johnson MSS. For identification of the Seward draft, see John and LaWanda Cox, "Andrew Johnson and His Ghost

Writers," *Mississippi Valley Historical Review*, XLVIII (Dec., 1961), p. 461.

26. William A. Dunning, *Essays on the Civil War and Reconstruction* (New York, 1904), pp. 103–104.

27. McPherson, *Political Manual for 1866*, pp. 64–65.

28. Italics added. *Ibid.*, p. 65.

29. Johnson to B. G. Humphrey, Nov. 17, 1865, Johnson MSS.

30. Springfield *Republican*, Nov. 18, 1865.

31. Revised clipping, Johnson MSS, also in McPherson, *Political Manual for 1866*, p. 58; A. K. McClure's report of an interview, New York *Times*, Nov. 14, 1865.

32. Lafayette [Ind.] *Daily Journal*, clippings on Annual Message, Scrapbook, Johnson MSS.

33. Speech at Framington, Mass., reported in New York *World*, July 10, 1865.

34. New York *Herald*, Sept. 29, 1865, Oct. 30, 1865, Nov. 2, 1865, Nov. 6, 1865; New York *World*, Oct. 10, 1865, Oct. 26, 1865, Nov. 1, 1865, Nov. 9, 1865.

35. New York *World*, Nov. 3, 1865.

36. New York *Times*, Nov. 8, 1865.

37. Reprint of Forney letter, New York *Tribune*, Nov. 7, 1865.

38. New York *Times*, Nov. 14, 1865.

39. New York *Tribune*, Oct. 31, 1865.

40. *Ibid.*, Oct. 31, 1865, Nov. 4, 1865; New York *World*, Oct. 26, 1865; Springfield *Republican*, Oct. 26, 1865; New York *Herald*, Oct. 26, 1865; New York *Times*, Nov. 3, 1865.

41. New York *Times*, Nov. 30, 1865, Jan. 29, 1865; New York *Herald*, Nov. 18, 1865.

42. Springfield *Republican*, Nov. 14, 1865.

43. Of the many accounts, the most authoritative is that of Benjamin B. Kendrick, *The Journal of the Joint Committee of Fifteen on Reconstruction* (New York, 1914), pp. 139–43.

44. Springfield *Republican*, Oct. 21, 1865, Oct. 26, 1865, Nov. 28, 1865, Dec. 4, 5, 9, 1865.

45. *Ibid.*, Nov. 22, 1865, Nov. 23, 1865; New York *Evening Post*, Nov. 30, 1865; New York *Times*, Nov. 9, 13, 20, 1865; and *see above*, footnotes 13, 16, 20.

46. *See above*, Chapter 4.

47. Hartford (weekly) *Connecticut Courant*, Feb. 10, 1866.

48. C. Day to Welles, Feb. 15, 1866, A. E. Burr to Welles, March 12, 1866, Welles MSS, L. C.; New Haven *Palladium*, Feb. 15, 1866; Hartford *Evening Press*, Feb. 15, 1866.

49. N. D. Sherry to W. Dennison, Feb. 14, 1866, Johnson MSS.

50. *Diary of Gideon Welles*, II, p. 433.

51. Revised clipping, Johnson MSS, also in McPherson, *Political Manual for 1866*, p. 58.
52. Hartford *Daily Post*, Feb. 15, 1866.
53. *Ibid.*, Feb. 17, 1866.
54. Washington *National Intelligencer*, Feb. 19, 1866; editorial and also reprint from Hartford correspondent of Boston *Advertiser*, New Haven *Daily Register*, March 12, 1866.
55. Hartford *Evening Press*, Feb. 19, 20, 21, 23, 28, 1866, March 1, 1866, report of Hawley's speech in issue of March 3, 1866.
56. Hawley to Welles, Feb. 26, 1866, Welles MSS, L. C.
57. Welles to W. A. Croffut, March 15, 1866, *ibid.*
58. *Diary of Gideon Welles*, II, p. 452.
59. *Ibid.*, pp. 455–56.
60. For the Democratic version, *see* New Haven *Daily Register*, March 27, 1866, April 2, 1866; for a Republican version *see* Hartford correspondent, New York *Times*, March 31, 1866. Probably neither was an accurate report of just what Hawley had said on the occasion; the one oversimplified his response and the other may have overelaborated it.
61. New Haven *Daily Register*, March 19, 1866.
62. *Ibid.*, March 20, 1866 and March 21, 1866.
63. M. A. Osborn to Welles, March 11, 1866, A. E. Burr to Welles, March 12, 1866, Welles MSS, L. C.
64. *Diary of Gideon Welles*, II, pp. 452–53, 454.
65. Barlow to T. G. Pratt, March 16, 1866, Barlow MSS.
66. Hawley to Welles, March 17, 1866, Welles MSS, L. C.
67. *Diary of Gideon Welles*, II, p. 457.
68. *Ibid.*, pp. 457–60.
69. Hawley to Welles, March 22, 1866, Welles to Hawley, March 24, 1866, Welles MSS, L. C.
70. For the Democratic view of Republican Hawley's interview, *see* New Haven *Daily Register*, March 23, 1866 and March 27, 1866; compare New Haven *Palladium*, March 22, 1866 and March 23, 1866. For the E. H. Owen and W. Griswold [Republican] interview, compare New Haven *Palladium*, March 22, 1866, March 23, 1866, with New Haven *Daily Register*, March 22, 1866. For James F. Babcock's visit with Johnson, *see* the New Haven *Daily Register*, March 24, 1866, and the New Haven *Palladium*, March 24, 1866; and for his and F. W. Smith's public letter, *ibid*. The Hartford correspondent of the New York *Times*, March 31, 1866, gave two versions of the meeting between Johnson and A. E. Burr and C. M. Ingersoll [Democrats]; see also New Haven *Daily Register*, March 26, 1866, and New Haven *Palladium*, March 24, 1866. For conflicting accounts of

James T. Pratt's [Republican] visit with the President, *see* Hartford *Evening Press*, March 29, 1866, and New Haven *Daily Register*, March 29, 1866.

71. Hartford *Evening Press*, March 24, 1866.

72. *Ibid.*, March 26, 1866, March 31, 1866.

73. *Ibid.*, March 24, 1866.

74. *Ibid.*, March 28, 1866.

75. *Diary of Gideon Welles*, II, pp. 454, 461–62, 465; Babcock to Weed, April 16, 1866, Weed MSS; Babcock to Welles, July 12, 1866, Welles MSS, L. C. In the latter letter, Babcock wrote: "We made a great mistake here in not electing English. . . . The President was right in that thing and I was wrong."

76. Springfield *Republican*, March 26, 1866.

77. Johnson to Huntington, March 27, 1866, Johnson MSS: *see also* Huntington to Johnson March 27, 1866, March 28, 1866, *ibid.*; New Haven *Daily Register*, March 27, 1866; Babcock to Welles, March 29, 1866, Welles MSS, L.C.

78. Hartford *Evening Press*, March 27, 1866.

79. A. E. Burr to Welles, April 27, 1866, Welles MSS, L.C.

CHAPTER 8

JOHNSON AND THE NEGRO

1. *National Anti-Slavery Standard*, Dec. 9, 1865, clippings on Annual Message, Scrapbook, Johnson MSS.

2. *Liberator*, Dec. 15, 1865, *ibid.*

3. Brooklyn *Daily Union*, Dec. 8, 1865, *ibid.*

4. Lloyd P. Stryker, *Andrew Johnson: A Study in Courage* (New York, 1936), Chapter 5; Winston, *Andrew Johnson*, pp. 134, 142, 145, 266. See also, Graf, "Andrew Johnson and the Coming of the War," p. 215.

5. New York *Tribune*, April 22, 1865.

6. Nashville speech, June 9, 1864, McPherson, *Political Manual for 1866*, p. 46, footnote; *Collected Works of Abraham Lincoln*, VIII, pp. 216–17; Milton Lomask, *Andrew Johnson: President on Trial* (New York, 1960), pp. 16–17, 24–26; Milton, *Age of Hate*, pp. 136–37.

7. New York *World*, Sept. 18, 1865.

8. McPherson, *Political Manual for 1866*, pp. 50–51.

9. "Gorham" to Johnson, June 3, 1865, Johnson MSS.

10. Watterson to Johnson, June 20, 1865, *ibid.*

11. Entry of April 9, 1868, transcript of Moore's diary, *ibid.*

12. McPherson, *Political Manual for 1866*, p. 51; *see also* report of Johnson's interview with colored clergymen, New York *Herald*, May 12, 1865.
13. McPherson, *Political Manual for 1866*, p. 55.
14. Mitchell to Johnson, Nov. 21, 1865, Johnson MSS; *see also* Mitchell to Seward, Sept. 14, 1865, and his printed pamphlet *Brief on Emigration and Colonization and Report in Answer to a Resolution of the Senate* (Washington, 1865), both in Seward MSS.
15. Compare Howard K. Beale, *The Critical Year: A Study of Andrew Johnson and Reconstruction* (New York, 1930), pp. 180–81.
16. Report of interview, New York *Herald*, June 25, 1865.
17. Welles to Sumner, June 30, 1865, Welles MSS, L.C.
18. *See above*, Chapter 4, footnote 48.
19. C. D. Warner to Welles, Sept. 20, 1865, including clipping from Hartford *Times* of Sept. 19, 1865; W. A. Croffut to Welles, Sept. 20, 1865; Welles to Croffut, Sept. 22, 1865; Welles to Warner, Sept. 22, 1865; Welles MSS, L.C.
20. Interview of Oct. 3, 1865, McPherson, *Political Manual for 1866*, pp. 48–49. This appeared in the press of Oct. 23, 1865.
21. New York *Tribune*, Oct. 23, 1865; New York *World*, Oct. 24, 1865.
22. Watterson to Johnson, June 27, 1865, Johnson MSS.
23. Letters to Johnson from C. D. McLean, June 29, 1865, Watterson, July 8, 1865, J. E. Brown, July 24, 1865, J. B. Steedman, Aug. 15, 1865, W. Conner, Sept. 13, 1865, also A. G. Mackey to C. Schurz, July 23, 1865, M. C. Johnson to M. Blair, Aug. 21, 1865, *ibid.*
24. J. C. Bradley to Johnson, Nov. 15, 1865, *ibid.*
25. McPherson, *Political Manual for 1866*, p. 6. Note that Mississippi's rejection of the President's recommendation of limited Negro suffrage, discussed below, preceded the December message.
26. Johnson to Sharkey, Aug. 15, 1865, Johnson MSS.
27. Sharkey to Johnson, Aug. 20, 1865, *ibid.*
28. Johnson to Sharkey, Aug. 21, 1865, *ibid.*
29. Johnson to Sharkey, Aug. 25, 1865, *ibid.*; New York *Herald*, Aug. 26, 1865.
30. Sharkey to Johnson, Aug. 28, 1865, Johnson MSS.
31. Johnson to Sharkey, Nov. 1, 1865, *ibid.*
32. Humphreys to Johnson, Nov. 16, 1865, *ibid.*
33. Johnson to Humphreys, Nov. 17, 1865, *ibid.*
34. McPherson, *Political Manual for 1866*, pp. 20, 31.
35. In early September, Johnson had been quoted as recommending Negro suffrage on the basis of literacy to a Louisianan with the

argument that "there were not five hundred negroes in Louisiana that can stand this test, but it will be doing justice and will stop northern clamor." A month later, he was reported as telling an Alabaman that "political rights, such as suffrage, sitting on juries, &c are not expected to be conferred on them at this time." Springfield *Republican*, Sept. 9, 1865, Oct. 9, 1865; *see also* Oct. 17, 1865.

36. Campbell to Johnson, Nov. 16, 1865, Johnson MSS.
37. W. B. Phillips to Johnson, Nov. 24, 1865, with clipping from *Herald* enclosed, *ibid.*
38. McPherson, *Political Manual for 1866*, pp. 114–15.
39. New York *Times*, Jan. 22, 1866.
40. G. C. Smith to Johnson, Jan. 20, 1866, Johnson MSS.
41. McPherson, *Political Manual for 1866*, pp. 51–52.
42. Kendrick, *Journal of the Joint Committee on Reconstruction*, pp. 41, 51, 199; Joseph B. James, *The Framing of the Fourteenth Amendment* (Urbana, 1956), pp. 37, 46, 60.
43. R. P. L. Baber to Johnson, March 29, 1866, Johnson MSS.
44. McPherson, *Political Manual for 1866*, pp. 52–55.
45. R. R. French to Johnson, Feb. 8, 1866, Johnson MSS.
46. P. Ripley to Marble, Feb. 8, 1866, Marble MSS.
47. New York *Times*, Aug. 19, 1865; *see also* Aug. 18, 1865, Aug. 26, 1865.
48. *Ibid.*, Aug. 29, 1865.
49. *Ibid.*, Sept. 14, 1865.
50. *Ibid.*, Sept. 21, 1865.
51. *Ibid.*, Oct. 3, 13, 15, 1865.
52. Jackson *Daily News*, Nov. 14, 1865, clipping enclosed in R. S. Donaldson to J. W. Weber, Nov. 17, 1865, Johnson MSS; New York *Times*, Oct. 5, 8, 11, 1865. After the President's telegrams of Nov. 17, 1865, one to elected Governor Humphreys and the other to Provisional Governor Sharkey, expressly mentioning Negro testimony, the Mississippi legislature did yield a circumscribed right of testimony but only as part of a general act that included harsh and discriminating provisions against the Negro in respect to the ownership and leasing of lands and the enforcement of labor contracts. For the act, *see* McPherson, *Political Manual for 1866*, p. 31.
53. Speech of Raymond reported in New York *Times*, Oct. 15, 1865.
54. New York *Times*, Oct. 23, 1865.
55. *Ibid.*, Nov. 6, 1865.
56. *Ibid.*, Nov. 7, 1865, Nov. 8, 1865.
57. New York *Herald*, Sept. 8, 1865.

58. Italics added. New York *World*, Sept. 21, 1865, Oct. 21, 1865.

59. Italics added. New York *Herald*, Oct. 12, 15, 31, 1865.

60. Springfield *Republican*, Nov. 3, 1865; *see also* B. C. Truman to W. C. Browning (of the President's staff), Nov. 9, 1865, Johnson MSS.

61. Springfield *Republican*, Nov. 15, 1865, Nov. 18, 1865.

62. W. W. Boyce to F. P. Blair, Oct. 17, 1865, letters to Johnson from J. C. Bradley, Oct. 13, 1865, Nov. 15, 1865, A. H. Wilson, Oct. 25, 1865, H. Kennedy, Nov. 23, 1865, R. J. Powell, Nov. 26, 1865, F. G. Clark, Dec. 4, 1865, and A. S. Wallace to W. H. Seward, Dec. 25, 1865, Johnson MSS; letters to Seward from M. G. Dobbins, Nov. 11, 1865, B. J. Sanford, Nov. 23, 1865, P. Moller, n.d., rcd. Nov. 29, 1865, I. J. Stiles, Dec. 9, 1865, T. Cottman, Dec. 11, 1865, A. Dockery to R. I. Powell [?] Nov. 13, 1865, Seward to Dobbins, Nov. 21, 1865, Sewad to Cottmann, Dec. 11, 1865, Seward MSS; M. Howard to Welles, Nov. 13, 1865, Dec. 2, 1865, Dec. 16, 1865, Welles MSS, L.C.

63. W. W. Holden to Johnson, Oct. 17, 1865; Johnson to Holden, Oct. 18, 1865; R. J. Powell to Johnson, Nov. 26, 1865; Johnson to Holden, Nov. 27, 1865, (N.C.); James Johnson to Johnson, Oct. 27, 1865; Johnson to James Johnson, Oct. 28, 1865, (Ga.); O. P. Morton to Johnson, Oct. 31, 1865, Johnson to W. L. Sharkey, Nov. 1, 1865, (Miss.); Johnson to B. J. Perry, Oct. 28, 1865, Oct. 31, 1865, (S.C.); draft telegram with eleven signatures, to L. E. Parsons and B. Fitzpatrick, Sept. 19, 1865, (Ala.), Johnson MSS.

64. Seward to W. Marvin, Nov. 20, 1865, Seward MSS.

65. George R. Bentley, *History of the Freedmen's Bureau* (Philadelphia, 1955). pp. 66–67.

66. Swayne to O. O. Howard, Sept. 28, 1865, Oct. 2, 1865; Howard to Swayne, Oct. 19, 1865, Records of the Bureau of Refugees, Freedmen, and Abandoned Lands, War Records Office, National Archives.

67. Parsons to Johnson, Sept. 13, 1865, Johnson MSS.

68. Parsons to Johnson, Sept. 23, 1865; *see also* Parsons to Johnson, Sept. 28, 1865, *ibid.* From Watterson, who was on hand lobbying with convention leaders, there came word that they were ready to do anything believed to be indispensable for restoration; Watterson made no mention of freedmen's rights. Watterson to Johnson, Sept. 26, 1865, *ibid.*

69. Johnson to Parsons, Oct. 3, 1865, *ibid.*

70. J. [?] P. Pryor to Johnson, Oct. 10, 1865, A. J. Fletcher to Johnson, Nov. 20, 1865, *ibid.*

71. Johnson to A. J. Fletcher, Dec. 9, 1865, *ibid.*
72. Reported in New York *Herald,* Oct. 14, 1865.
73. Copy of law of Jan. 25, 1866, with endorsement, C. B. Fisk to O. O. Howard; *see also* Fisk to Howard, Dec. 19, 1865, Freedmen's Bureau Records.
74. Howard to W. W. Holden, O. O. Howard MSS, Bowdoin College Library; Howard to Assistant Commissioners, Sept. 6, 1865; Howard to C. B. Fisk, Sept. 9, 1865; Howard to B. J. Perry, Oct. 21, 1865; W. Swayne to L. E. Parsons, July 29, 1865; Swayne to Howard, Aug. 4, 7, 14, 28, 1865, Sept. 29, 1865; W. L. Sharkey to S. Thomas, Sept. 18, 1865; Thomas to Howard, Sept. 21, 22, 23, 29, 1865, Nov. 13, 1865; Thomas to T. J. Wood, Nov. 23, 1865; F. H. Peirpoint to O. Brown, Oct. 7, 1865; Freedmen's Bureau Records.
75. W. Swayne to Howard, Nov. 28, 1865; B. K. Johnston to E. Bamberger, with endorsement of R. S. Donaldson, Nov. 16, 1865; S. Thomas to Howard, Nov. 21, 1865, Dec. 13, 1865; F. D. Sewall report of inspection, April 5, 1866, *ibid*; Bentley, *History of the Freedmen's Bureau,* pp. 67–68.
76. New York *Herald,* Oct. 15, 1866. *See also* Governor O. O. Morton's message, in W. H. Schlater (of the President's staff) to Johnson, Nov. 12, 1865, Johnson MSS, and Lyman Trumbull as reported in New York *Times,* Dec. 20, 1865.
77. McPherson, *Political Manual for 1866,* p. 23; for newspaper controversy over Seward's interpretation *see* New York *World,* Nov. 18, 1865, New York *Tribune,* Nov. 17, 1865.
78. Italics added. McPherson, *Political Manual for 1866,* p. 23.
79. *Ibid.,* pp. 21, 25; New York *Times,* Dec. 17, 1865. Compare Howard D. Hamilton, *Legislative and Judicial History of the Thirteenth Amendment* (Ph.D. dissertation, University of Illinois, 1950, University Microfilms, Ann Arbor, Michigan), pp. 55–57.
80. S. Thomas to O. O. Howard, Dec. 13, 1865, M. S. Hopkins to J. Johnson, Feb. 28, 1866, Freedmen's Bureau Records.
81. New York *World,* Aug. 28, 1865; New York *Herald,* Aug. 20, 1865.
82. Compare Washington correspondent, Springfield *Republican,* Nov. 18, 1865, and C. B. Fisk's report of presidential interview in *ibid.,* Nov. 23, 1865, with New York *World,* Sept. 13, 1865, New York *Herald,* Sept. 14, 1865, Sept. 21, 1865, Nov. 19, 1865, report of President's letter to W. L. Sharkey in Springfield *Republican,* Oct. 18, 1865, and B. F. Perry to D. E. Sickles, Dec. 7, 1865, Freedmen's Bureau Records.

CHAPTER 9

THE PRESIDENT DECLARES WAR

1. Cox to Marble, Feb. 20, 1866, Marble MSS.
2. Dawes to wife, Feb. 20, 1866, Henry L. Dawes MSS, Library of Congress.
3. *Ibid.*, Feb. 22, 1866.
4. New York *Herald*, March 28, 1866.
5. Columbia [Penna.] Democrat, clippings on Freedmens' Bureau veto, Scrapbook, Johnson MSS.
6. "J. C." to Marble, Dec. 2, 1865, Marble MSS.
7. Seymour to Blair, Jan. 3, 1866, Blair MSS.
8. *See above*, Chapter 4.
9. Enclosed in M. Ryerson to Seward, Feb. 15, 1866, Seward MSS.
10. Campbell to Johnson, Jan. 19, 1866, Johnson MSS.
11. Campbell to D. L. Patterson, Jan. 22, 1866, *ibid.*
12. Springfield *Republican*, Feb. 2, 1866.
13. Chicago *Tribune*, Feb. 13, 1866; S. S. Cox to Marble, Feb. 20, 1866, Marble MSS.
14. Washington *National Intelligencer*, Feb. 15, 1866.
15. New York *World*, Feb. 12, 1866, Jan. 25, 1866.
16. Cochrane to Johnson, Feb. 4, 1866, Johnson MSS.
17. Bates to Johnson, Feb. 10, 1866, *ibid.*
18. J. H. Brinton to Johnson, enclosed in Brinton to T. B. Florence, Feb. 14, 1866, *ibid.*
19. Cochrane to Johnson, Jan. 23, 1866, *ibid.*
20. *Ibid.*
21. Cochrane to Johnson, Feb. 4, 1866, Bennett to Johnson, Feb. 1, 1866, *ibid.*
22. Letters to Johnson from Greeley, Jan. 28, 1866, Pendleton, Jan. 28, 1866, Richmond, Jan. 31, 1866, Tilden, Feb. 1, 1866, Schell, Feb. 2, 1866, *ibid.*
23. New York *Times*, Feb. 6, 1866.
24. B. Rush to Johnson, Jan. 20, 1866; Cochrane to Johnson, Jan. 23, 1866; Memorial from Hamilton, Ohio, Jan. 23, 1866; W. Patton to Johnson, Jan. 30, 1866, Johnson MSS.
25. P. Ripley to Marble, Feb. 8, 1866, Marble MSS.
26. T. T. Davis to Johnson, Feb. 17, 1866, Johnson MSS; M. Ryerson to Seward, Feb. 15, 1866, Seward MSS.
27. New York *World*, Jan. 29, 1866.
28. New York *Herald*, Feb. 17, 1866.

29. W. Rives (of the President's staff) to J. G. Bennett, Jr., Feb. 19, 1866, Johnson MSS.

30. T. E. Bramlette to Johnson, Feb. 12, 1866; *see also* letters to Johnson from J. Hughes, Jan. 17, 1866, L. H. Rousseau, Jan. 17, 1866, A. G. Hodges, Jan. 20, 1866, J. W. Graham, Feb. 6, 1866, C. O. Faxon, Feb. 17, 1866, and Johnson to Hughes, Jan. 19, 1866, *ibid.*

31. J. L. Helm to Johnson, Feb. 17, 1866; *see also* W. Dudley to M. Blair, Feb, 19, 1866, *ibid.*

32. J. L. Helm to Johnson, Feb. 20, 1866, *ibid.* For an examination of charges against the Bureau and of the reasons for southern hostility, see John and LaWanda Cox, "General O. O. Howard and the 'Misrepresented Bureau,'" *Journal of Southern History*, XIX (Nov., 1953), pp. 427–56.

33. Columbus [Ga.] *Sun*, Feb. 9, 1866, quoting letter of Governor J. L. Orr of South Carolina to the President, Jan. 19, 1866.

34. Columbia [S.C.] *Phoenix*, Feb. 25, 1866, with letter of Perry, Feb. 16, 1866.

35. Columbus [Ga.] *Sun*, Jan. 10, 1866, Feb. 1, 2, 11, 1866, with quotations from Chicago *Tribune*, Cincinnati *Gazette*, Macon *Telegram*, and Philadelphia *Ledger*, respectively.

36. P. Ripley to Marble, Feb. 8, 1866, Marble MSS.

37. Cox, "Andrew Johnson and His Ghost Writers," pp. 462–65.

38. *Andrew Johnson and Reconstruction*, pp. 285–87.

39. *See above*, Chapter 5, footnotes 55 and 56.

40. *See above*, Chapter 2, footnotes 17 and 18.

41. *Diary of Gideon Welles*, II, p. 435.

42. Cox, "Andrew Johnson and His Ghost Writers." Three of the other four drafts for the veto were identified as those of Secretary Welles, Senator Doolittle, and Senator Cowan.

43. McPherson, *Political Manual for 1866*, p. 71.

44. Johnson's treatment of the civil rights-states' rights issue was evasive. See Cox, "Andrew Johnson and His Ghost Writers," pp. 466–67.

45. After military defeat, Seward expected that in response to a judicious policy of mingled pressure and persuasion the rebel states would return to a genuine allegiance to the Union. *Mr. Seward at Auburn in 1865*, p. 7.

46. New York *Daily News*, Feb. 23, 1866.

47. *Ibid.*

48. New York *Herald*, Feb. 23, 1866.

49. *Mass Meeting of the Citizens of New York Held at the Cooper Institute, February 22d, 1866, to Approve the Principles An-*

nounced in the Message of Andrew Johnson, President of the United States (pamphlet, New York 1866), pp. 12–21.

50. New York *Tribune,* Feb. 23, 1866.

51. Compare New York *Herald* of Feb. 23, 1866, and Feb. 24, 1866.

52. New York *World,* Feb. 23, 1866.

53. *Ibid.,* Feb. 24, 1866.

54. *Ibid.,* Feb. 26, 1866.

55. Weed to Morgan, Feb. 26, 1866, Morgan MSS.

56. Wakeman to Seward, Feb. 19, 1866, Seward MSS.

57. Weed to Seward, Feb. 20, 1866, *ibid.*

58. *Mass Meeting at Cooper Institute,* p. 3. An elaborately prepared copy of the call and the resolutions is also in the Johnson MSS under date of Feb. 28, 1866.

59. *Before the Meeting; or Behind the Scenes: A Political Extravaganza; Characters by Wm. H. Seward, Thurlow Weed, Richard Schell & Co.*

60. New York *Tribune,* Feb. 23, 1866.

61. New York *World,* Feb. 23, 1866.

62. New York *Evening Post,* Feb. 23, 1866.

63. New York *Herald,* Feb. 24, 1866.

64. New York *Times,* Feb. 24, 1866.

65. *The Diary of George Templeton Strong, IV: Post-War Years, 1865–1875* (ed., Allan Nevins and M. H. Thomas, New York, 1952), p. 70.

66. *Mass Meeting at Cooper Institute,* pp. 7–12.

67. Seward to Morgan, Feb. 23, 1866, Morgan MSS; Seward to F. W. Seward, Feb. 23, 1866, Seward to Johnson, Feb. 23, 1866, Johnson MSS.

68. Dix to Johnson, March 2, 1866, Johnson MSS.

69. Tilden to Blair, March 10, 1866, Blair MSS.

70. *See above,* Chapter 6, footnotes 29, 33, 34, 47, 51, 75, 77, 78.

71. Weed to Seward, March 21, 1866; *see also* Weed to Seward March 17, 1866, Seward MSS.

72. These generalizations are based primarily upon the letters-received file of the Johnson MSS, Feb. 23, 1866 to March 26, 1866.

73. Andrew to Blair, March 18, 1866, Johnson MSS. For a perceptive account of Andrew's position, *see* McKitrick, *Andrew Johnson and Reconstruction,* pp. 217–38.

74. Barlow to Blair, April 9, 1866, quoting a recent letter from McClellan. General McClellan's one condition was that Johnson turn out Stanton. *See also* Barlow to Blair, July 16, 1866, Barlow MSS.

75. Seward to Johnson, Feb. 23, 1866; Weed to Johnson, Feb. 23, 1866, Johnson MSS.
76. M. Perry to Seward, Feb. 23, 1866, Seward MSS.
77. New York *Evening Post,* reprinted in Philadelphia *Evening Telegraph,* clippings on Freedmen's Bureau veto, Scrapbook, Johnson MSS.
78. *See* Chapter 7, footnote 77.
79. Washington *Chronicle,* Feb. 17, 1866.
80. The principal source for the conclusions and quotations in this and the following paragraph is the extensive collection of newspaper clippings on the Freedmen's Bureau veto in the presidential Scrapbook, Johnson MSS.
81. New York *Herald,* Feb. 26, 1866.
82. New York *World,* March 1, 1866.
83. Springfield *Republican,* March 1, 1866; *see also* Feb. 28, 1866.
84. Morgan to Weed, March 8, 1866, Morgan MSS.
85. Dawes to wife, March 16, 1866, Dawes MSS.
86. Howard K. Beale reached the conclusion that the veto lost Johnson few friends. *The Critical Year,* p. 84.
87. Phillips to Sumner, March 24, 1866, Charles Sumner MSS, Houghton Library of the Harvard College Library.
88. Kendrick, *Journal of the Joint Committee on Reconstruction,* pp. 252–55; McKitrick, *Andrew Johnson and Reconstruction,* pp. 339–43; James, *Framing of the Fourteenth Amendment,* pp. 94–97.
89. James, *Framing of the Fourteenth Amendment,* p. 96. On the desire for conciliation following the veto, see McKitrick, *Andrew Johnson and Reconstruction,* pp. 298–306.

CHAPTER 10

CIVIL RIGHTS:
THE ISSUE OF RECONSTRUCTION

1. There was also some opposition to the Civil Rights Bill from Republican Conservative leaders. Senator Cowan urged a veto on the ground that otherwise "they" would be able to claim power to do anything, including granting the right of suffrage. Cowan to Johnson, March 23, 1866, Johnson MSS. Secretary Welles prepared a five-page argument against the bill; see Cox "Andrew Johnson and His Ghost Writers," pp. 474, 477.
2. Morgan to Johnson, March 19, 1866, Johnson MSS.

3. Blair to Johnson, March 18, 1866, *ibid.*

4. Beecher to Johnson, March 17, 1866, *ibid.*

5. Cox to Johnson, March 22, 1866, *ibid.*

6. Weed to Seward, March 25, 1866, *ibid.*

7. The note is filed under date of March 27, 1866, *ibid.*

8. *See* Cox, "Andrew Johnson and His Ghost Writers," pp. 474–77, 479.

9. Messages, Johnson MSS.

10. The official message was a slightly edited composite of three working papers, Seward's, Henry Stanbery's, and Secretary Welles'. Cox, "Andrew Johnson and His Ghost Writers," pp. 473–77.

11. This passage appeared in no one of the three drafts.

12. In these points, the message followed Stanbery's draft.

13. This passage appeared in no one of the three drafts. For the text of the official message, we have used McPherson, *Political Manual for 1866,* pp. 74–78.

14. Morgan to I. Sherman, April 2, 1866, Morgan MSS.

15. Morgan to H. H. Van Dyck, March 31, 1866, *ibid.*

16. Morgan to Seward, March 26, 1866; *see also* his two notes of March 2, 1866, Seward MSS.

17. Endorsement on Morgan to Seward, March 26, 1866, *ibid.*

18. W. G. Moore (of the President's staff) to Seward, March 26, 1866, *ibid.*

19. *Diary of Gideon Welles,* II, pp. 463–64.

20. Morgan to R. Balcom, April 3, 1866; *see also* Morgan to Weed, April 4, 1866, Morgan MSS.

21. Weed to Morgan, April 6, 1866, *ibid.*

22. Morgan to Weed, April 8, 1866, Weed MSS.

23. Morgan to J. Jay, May 16, 1866; *see also* Morgan to G. Dawson, May 19, 1866, Morgan to H. H. Van Dyck, May 19, 1866, Morgan MSS.

24. *Cong. Globe,* 39 Cong., 2 sess., p. 1761 (April 4, 1866).

25. New York *Herald,* March 17, 1866.

26. *Ibid.,* March 28, 1866.

27. Dawes to wife, March 31, 1866, Dawes MSS. Dawes voted to override the veto.

28. Some devoted advocates of civil rights for the freedmen, notably John Bingham, questioned the constitutional basis for the Civil Rights Act. Bingham voted against the bill for that reason, and is generally recognized as the father of the civil rights provisions of section one of the Fourteenth Amendment.

29. *See* McKitrick, *Andrew Johnson and Reconstruction,* pp. 350–52, 356–57.

30. Even after the vetoes, there was much sentiment for conciliation. Especially after the formulation of what was to become the Fourteenth Amendment, there was hope that Johnson might give the moderates an alternative to opposition. See Thomas Ewing, Jr., to his father, April 12, 1866, Ewing MSS; *Diary of Gideon Welles,* II, p. 527; New York *Times,* June 14, 1866, June 15, 1866.
31. Cowan to Johnson, March 23, 1866, Johnson MSS.
32. Cochrane to Johnson, Jan. 23, 1866.
33. Baber to Johnson, March 29, 1866, Johnson MSS; Baber to Doolittle, Feb. 28, 1866, March 29, 1866, James R. Doolittle MSS, Historical Society of Wisconsin; Baber to Seward, March 30, 1866, Johnson MSS.
34. Houston to Johnson, April 5, 1866, Johnson MSS.
35. W. A. Newell to Johnson, April 9, 1866, *ibid.* Evidence of popular support for civil rights legislation can be found in other private papers as well. For example, General O. O. Howard, head of the Freedmen's Bureau, received a letter from an associate who was at the time in New York City. It read: "You may be sure the veto of the Civil Rights Bill stirred up even the old conservatives of this city. Mr. Raymond had letters from many, stopping the Times, whom he had not anticipated would turn against him. Will you get a new Bureau Bill. I hope so and think it can be done. There is no mistake as to the reaction among *the people,* and the President must yield." J. W. Alvord to Howard, April 17, 1866, Howard MSS.
36. J. Warren to Seward, Feb. 24, 1866, Seward MSS.
37. E. G. Cook to Seward, April 20, 1866, *ibid.*
38. F. Vinton [?] to Morgan, April 7, 1866, Morgan MSS.
39. S. Osgood to Morgan, April 18, 1866, *ibid.*
40. O. D. Swan to Morgan, May 3, 1866, *ibid.*
41. H. Day to Morgan, May 8, 1866, *ibid.*
42. Springfield *Republican,* March 28, 1866.
43. *Ibid.,* April 4, 1866.
44. Clipping, Scrapbook, Johnson MSS.
45. Clipping, *ibid.*
46. These generalizations are based primarily upon the extensive press clippings on the Civil Rights veto, *ibid.*
47. Before the opening of Congress in December, 1865, Schuyler Colfax, Speaker of the House, made a speech which was widely regarded as a statement of majority Republican opinion. He abjured any inflexibility of policy, spoke warmly of what the President had already accomplished in securing commitments from the southern states, but made clear that some additional assurances were considered necessary. The first of these, and

indeed the only one that was substantive, was that "the Declaration of Independence be recognized as the law of the land" by the protection of the freedmen in their rights of person and property including the right to testify. He made no mention of suffrage for the Negro nor of any punitive action against the South. For text of speech, see New York *Times*, Nov. 19, 1865.

48. Clipping from a Buffalo paper, March 29, 1866, Scrapbook, Johnson MSS.

49. Chicago *Evening Journal*, March 28, 1866, *ibid.*

50. *See* Stanley Coben, "Northeastern Business and Radical Reconstruction: A Re-examination," *Mississippi Valley Historical Review*, XLVI (June, 1959), pp. 67–90; Robert P. Sharkey, *Money, Class and Party: An Economic Study of Civil War and Reconstruction* (Baltimore, 1959); Irwin Unger, "Business Men and Specie Resumption," *Political Science Quarterly*, LXXIV (March, 1959), pp. 46–70. Howard K. Beale's study made much of economic issues, but his findings showed that they had not been central to the political campaign of 1866. Johnson's failure to make them such, Beale considered "a fatal error in political judgment." *The Critical Year*, p. 299.

51. Letters in the Johnson MSS indicate this support, see those of August Belmont, March 24, 1866, A. J. Drexel, May 3, 1866, Alexander T. Stewart, June 18, 1866; also reports of business support in the letters of W. G. Smith, March 2, 1866 (Buffalo), J. B. Hussey, March 3, 1866 (New York), W. J. Hilton, March 7, 1866 (Albany), R. B. Carnahan, March 16, 1866 (Pittsburgh), G. W. Morgan, July 14, 1866 (Ohio), D. S. Seymour, Nov. 8, 1866 (Troy).

52. In the Tilden MSS there are printed letters outlining the arrangements, including a seating chart for the dinner, and itemizing the expenses with assessments. Tilden's share of the cost was $145.38. Smythe, Johnson's appointee as Collector of the Port, feared the plans for Johnson's New York visit would give the impression that "a *few* are to get hold of you" and advised the President to stop at the Fifth Avenue Hotel, rather than Delmonico's to "give '*the people*'" a better opportunity to see him. Smythe to Johnson, Aug. 25, 1866, Johnson MSS.

53. New York *Times*, Sept. 2, 1866.

54. Wilson to Johnson, March 3, 1866, Johnson MSS.

55. McKitrick, *Andrew Johnson and Reconstruction*, p. 19, footnote 2.

56. The roll call came on a motion to table the resolution. McPherson, *Political Manual for 1866*, pp. 110–111.

57. *Ibid.*, p. 109.

58. *Ibid.*, p. 113; compare the vote p. 81.

59. On the meaning of "Radical," compare McKitrick, *Andrew Johnson and Reconstruction,* pp. 53–67. The Chicago *Tribune,* the leading Radical newspaper, had some revealing comments. Before the Republican convention of 1860, it identified the "more radical" wing of the party as a body of men "somewhat in advance of the party's creed," zealous, honest and possibly impractical, who recognized that they had no power to interfere with slavery in the states but still hoped "that the election of a Republican President will in some way tend to the crippling of the institution they hate." In 1866, the *Tribune* defined as the vestige of slavery "all discrimination against freedmen." Until these be removed, it held that the South would not be at peace with itself or with the North. Chicago *Tribune,* Feb. 6, 1860, Feb. 16, 1860, and clipping on Freedmen's Bureau veto, Scrapbook, Johnson MSS.

60. *See* the quotations cited above, footnotes 5, 6, 32, 43.

61. Kendrick, *Journal of the Joint Committee on Reconstruction,* pp. 251–52.

62. T. Barry to Grider, March 8, 1866, Johnson MSS.

63. *State and Union,* April 5, 1866, Scrapbook, *ibid.*

64. *Constitutional Union,* March 28, 1866, *ibid.*

65. Clipping on Civil Rights veto, *ibid.*

66. Boylestown *Democrat,* Feb. 27, 1866, *ibid.*

67. Wayne County [Ohio] *Democrat, ibid.*

68. *See above,* Chapter 8.

69. Portland *Press,* Scrapbook, Johnson MSS.

70. For the texts of the messages we have used McPherson, *Political Manual for 1866.*

71. *See above,* Chapter 3, footnotes 29, 30, 31; Chapter 5, footnotes 18, 21, 22, 25; Chapter 10, footnote 3.

72. *Diary of Gideon Welles,* II, p. 369.

73. *Ibid.,* p. 374.

74. Springfield *Republican,* Sept. 30, 1865.

75. *Diary of Gideon Welles,* II, p. 431.

76. *Ibid.,* p. 394.

77. James L. Sellers, "James R. Doolittle," *Wisconsin Magazine of History,* XVII (Dec., 1933), 176; (March, 1934), pp. 287–88, 293, 302–03.

78. Doolittle to Johnson, Sept. 9, 1865, Johnson MSS.

79. J. C. G. Kennedy to Doolittle, March 9, 1866; notes for speech, March or April 1866, Doolittle MSS.

80. Doolittle to wife, Mary, Nov. 11, 1866, *ibid.*

81. Sellers, "James R. Doolittle," *Wisconsin Magazine of History* XVIII (Sept., 1934), pp. 26–27.

82. Messages, Johnson MSS. See Cox, "Andrew Johnson and His Ghost Writers," p. 463.
83. Cowan to Johnson, March 23, 1866, Johnson MSS.
84. McPherson, *Political Manual for 1866*, p. 80.
85. Quoted in B. J. Pershing, "Senator Edgar A. Cowan, 1861–1867," *Western Pennsylvania Historical Magazine*, IV (Oct., 1921), pp. 229–30.
86. *Ibid.*
87. *Speech of Hon. Edgar Cowan of Pennsylvania on Executive Appointments and Removals, Delivered in the Senate of the United States, May 9, 1866* (pamphlet, Washington, 1866), p. 13.
88. Dixon to Johnson, Oct. 8, 1865, Johnson MSS.
89. Mark Howard, *Despotic Doctrines Declared by the United States Senate Exposed; and Senator Dixon Unmasked* (pamphlet, Hartford, 1863), p. 8.
90. From the Toledo *Commercial*, in Ellen Ewing Sherman, comp., *Memorial of Thomas Ewing of Ohio* (New York, 1873), p. 123.
91. Ewing MSS.
92. Speech in reply to a toast, published in *An Appeal to the Senate to Modify its Policy and Save from Africanization and Military Despotism the States of the South*, printed by order of the National Democratic Resident Committee (pamphlet, Washington, 1868).
93. Messages, Johnson MSS. See Cox, "Andrew Johnson and His Ghost Writers," pp. 475, 477–79.
94. *Diary of Gideon Welles*, III, p. 4.
95. Charles Warren, *The Supreme Court in United States History* (rev. ed., 3 vols., Boston, 1937), II, p. 603.
96. J. G. Randall and David Donald, *The Civil War and Reconstruction* (Boston, 1961), p. 24. Maurice G. Baxter, *Orville H. Browning: Lincoln's Friend and Critic* (Bloomington, Indiana, 1957), pp. 19–20, 67–69.
97. For Browning's wartime position, see Baxter, *Orville H. Browning*, pp. 119–20, 141–43, 148.
98. National Union Club Documents, *Speeches of Hon. Edgar Cowan, Hon. Jas. R. Doolittle, Hon. Hugh McCulloch, Letter of Hon. O. H. Browning and an Address by a Member of the Club; also the Condition of the South: A Report of Special Commissioner B. F. Truman* (pamphlet, Washington, 1866), pp. 21–22; *Diary of Gideon Welles*, II, pp. 534, 638.
99. Baxter, *Orville H. Browning*, pp. 228, 245–56.
100. Joseph Schafer, "Alexander W. Randall," *Dictionary of American Biography*, XV, pp. 344–45.

101. *Ibid.;* H. A. Tenney and David Atwood, *Memorial Record of the Fathers of Wisconsin* (Madison, 1880), pp. 134–35.

102. Clark S. Matteson, *The History of Wisconsin* (Milwaukee, 1892), p. 303.

103. *Diary of Gideon Welles,* II, pp. 534, 608–09, 617–18, 628, III, pp. 64, 83.

104. Hugh McCulloch, *Men and Measures of Half a Century: Sketches and Comment* (New York, 1889), p. 518.

105. Mobile *Times,* Oct. 24, 1865, reprinted in New York *Herald,* Nov. 2, 1865.

106. *Diary of Gideon Welles,* III, p. 4.

107. *Ibid.,* II, p. 394.

108. McCulloch, *Men and Measures,* p. 381; *Diary of Gideon Welles,* II, pp. 531, 534.

109. McCulloch, *Men and Measures,* pp. 515–18.

110. Campbell to Johnson, Aug. 21, 1865, Johnson MSS.

111. Campbell to Johnson, Jan. 22, 1866, *ibid.*

112. Campbell to Johnson, May 1, 1866, *ibid.*

113. The possible importance of the death of his wife was suggested to us by Professor Glyndon G. Van Deusen, who has a very special knowledge of the Seward MSS.

114. *See above,* Chapter 2, footnote 28.

115. *Diary of Gideon Welles,* III, p. 4.

116. *Ibid.,* II, pp. 534–35, 608–10. In the Seward MSS are two documents, one of which suggests that between the overriding of the Civil Rights veto and the call for the Philadelphia Convention, Seward was trying to obtain a reasonable compromise on an amendment; the other indicates an unyielding position on the part of the President during the same period. The first is a copy of House Bill #543, for restoring the states lately in insurrection, submitted by Stevens for the Committee on Reconstruction April 30, 1866. In his own hand, Seward made changes and additions that would have softened the proposal but left intact the provisions for protecting civil rights. The second is a copy dated May 28, 1866, of the constitutional amendment suggested the previous January by the President that provided only for representation according to voters and direct taxation based on the value of property. On its reverse side is noted the following:

"No amendment to the Constitution, or laws passed by Congress, as conditions precedent to the admission by Congress of loyal Representatives.

"Representation from the several States should be left where the Constitution now places it.

"No committals to any plan or proposition which may be made, while incomplete, and before thorough consideration by the President." Note particularly the first statement. It is in marked contrast to Seward's proposal on the April bill that when any state should ratify the amendment, its senators and representatives would be admitted (after taking the required oaths of office.)

117. Messages, Johnson MSS. See Cox, "Andrew Johnson and His Ghost Writers," p. 461.

118. Beale, *The Critical Year*, pp. 400–02.

119. Welles says that Seward's endorsement of the message in cabinet meeting was "formal not from the heart, but yet not against it." *Diary of Gideon Welles*, II, p. 628.

120. Letters of criticism from old friends, some written in anger, more in sorrow, are preserved in the Seward MSS. See letters to Seward from J. Warren, Feb. 24, 1866, C. C. Royce, March 10, 1866, I. A. Gates, April 16, 1866, July 17, 1866, E. G. Cook, April 20, 1866, A. Conkling, May 4, 1866, L. M. Bond, May 24, 1866, R. Balcom, July 13, 1866, W. G. Bacon, July 16, 1866, D. C. Gamble, July 18, 1866, G. Hall, July 19, 1866, S. M. Hopkins, July 22, 1866, J. Henderson, July 27, 1866, C. L. Wood, July 29, 1866, and G. Dawson to F. W. Seward, July 14, 1866, July 18, 1866, Seward to Ryerson, April 30, 1866, Seward to Conkling, May 7, 1866, Seward to Balcom, July 14, 1866, Seward to Hopkins, July 25, 1866. The coldness of life-long friends broke Weed. Sarah Pellet to Seward, March 6, 1869, Seward MSS.

121. A. F. Kinnaird to Weed, Dec. 30, 1865, Weed MSS.

122. Unidentified member of the House of Representatives, quoted in C. L. Wood to Seward, July 29, 1866, Seward MSS. For Seward's public position in May, see his Corning Hall, Auburn, speech, draft, and printed copy, *ibid*.

The failure of the Philadelphia Convention to organize a third party did not indicate that this goal was abandoned. One reason for postponement was the desire to win support from Republican ranks, which was essential to victory and also to the creation of a new party that would be more than a rejuvenation of the Democratic party under another label. Republicans were saying that no idea could be "more crazy than that of getting up a new Union party. There was nothing to be furnished from the Republican side but leaders, and the Democrats are not such d——d fools as to supply all the rank and file" without demanding leadership also. Unidentified member of the House of Representatives, quoted in C. L. Wood to Seward, July 29, 1866, *ibid*.

Raymond's curiously contradictory account of his interview with Johnson prior to the Philadelphia Convention is of interest in this connection. While Raymond opposed a third party and the President agreed that the convention should not attempt to organize one, Raymond yet reported his impression that the President was eager to gain a foothold in the South and to lay the foundation for a *"National"* party that would absorb the Democratic party of the North and West and all of the Union party except the Radicals. Raymond commented that this seemed to him a desirable object! "Extracts from the Journal of Henry J. Raymond (edited by his son), Fourth Paper: The Philadelphia Convention of 1866," *Scribner's Monthly*, XX (June, 1880), pp. 276–77; *see also* John A. Krout, "Henry J. Raymond on the Republican Caucuses of July, 1866," *American Historical Review*, XXXIII (July, 1928), p. 839.

123. This fact is clearly evident from the correspondence in the Barlow MSS.

124. Even so restrained a man as John Sherman wrote in early July, 1866: "I almost fear he [Johnson] contemplates civil war." J. Sherman to W. T. Sherman, July 8, 1866, *The Sherman Letters, Correspondence Between General and Senator Sherman from 1837–1891* (Rachel Sherman Thorndike, ed., New York, 1894), p. 276.

125. Italics added. Draft, Seward to Seymour, Oct. 14, 1868, Seward MSS.

126. *See above*, Chapter 4, footnote 49, and Chapter 8, footnotes 47 through 56.

127. New York *Times*, March 26, 1866.

128. *See above*, footnotes 22 and 23.

129. New York *Times*, July 30, 1866, June 15, 1866, and McKitrick *Andrew Johnson and Reconstruction*, p. 358.

130. Raymond's letter to the committee requesting him to run again for Congress, Sept. 15, 1866, in Augustus Maverick, *Henry J. Raymond and the New York Press* Hartford, 1870), pp. 175–84. *See also* Raymond's address of February, 1866, at Cooper Institute, in *ibid.*, pp. 175–84.

131. *Diary of Gideon Welles*, II, pp. 534, 618; III, p. 251.

132. "Extracts from the Journal of Henry J. Raymond: The Philadelphia Convention," pp. 278–79; McKitrick, *Andrew Johnson and Reconstruction*, p. 411.

133. Edward McPherson, *Handbook of Politics for 1868* (Washington, 1869), p. 241. Raymond drafted the resolutions after hearing those proposed by William B. Reed of Pennsylvania, Governor Sharkey of Mississippi, and Senator Cowan, all of which he

considered too prosouthern. "Extracts from the Journal of Henry J. Raymond: The Philadelphia Convention," p. 278.

134. Maverick, *Henry J. Raymond*, p. 189. See also Raymond's address to the convention in *The Proceedings of the National Union Convention Held at Philadelphia, August 14, 1866* (pamphlet, n.p., n.d.), pp. 12–13.

135. Raymond to R. Balcom, July 17, 1866, in Maverick, *Henry J. Raymond*, pp. 173–74.

136. New York *Times*, Oct. 11, 1866, Nov. 12, 1866.

137. J. Sherman to W. T. Sherman, May 16, 1865, April 23, 1866, *The Sherman Letters*, pp. 251, 270; see also John Sherman, *Recollections of Forty Years in the House, Senate and Cabinet: an Autobiography* (2 vols., Chicago, 1895), I, pp. 364, 366–67, 369.

138. J. Sherman to W. T. Sherman, Oct. 26, 1866, *The Sherman Letters*, p. 278.

139. *Diary of Gideon Welles*, II, p. 448. For Trumbull's repudiation of the President after the Civil Rights veto, *see above*, footnote 24.

For Grimes, see William Salter, *The Life of James W. Grimes, Governor of Iowa, 1854–1858 and Senator of the United States, 1859–1869* (New York, 1876), pp. 75, 392; F. I. Herriott, "James W. Grimes versus the Southrons," *Annals of Iowa*, XV (July, 1926), pp. 325–27; Fred B. Lewellen, "Political Ideas of James W. Grimes," *Iowa Journal of History and Politics*, XLII (Oct., 1944), pp. 383–95.

For Fessenden, *see* Francis Fessenden, *Life and Public Services of William Pitt Fessenden* (2 vols., Boston and New York, 1907), I, pp. 283–87, II, pp. 29–32, 34–35, 65–66, 314–15; and William A. Robinson, "William Pitt Fessenden," *Dictionary of American Biography*, VI, pp. 348–50.

For Trumbull, *see* Horace White, *The Life of Lyman Trumbull* (Boston, 1913), p. 277; *also* Arthur H. Robertson, *The Political Career of Lyman Trumbull* (M. A. Thesis, University of Chicago, 1910), pp. 37–39, 56, 59, 75. Robertson's study indicates that Trumbull's prewar view of the race problem included colonization and the conviction that Negroes could not be placed upon an equal social or political position with whites. However, by the winter of 1865–66, there can be no doubt of Trumbull's deep sense of national responsibility for the freedmen nor of his sincerity in fighting to secure for them equal rights, short of suffrage and officeholding.

140. George H. Porter, *Ohio Politics During the Civil War Period* (New York, 1911), pp. 210–13; Homer C. Hockett, "Jacob Dolson Cox," *Dictionary of American Biography*, IV, pp. 476–

78; Jacob Dolson Cox, *Military Reminiscences of the Civil War* (2 vols., New York, 1900), I, pp. 157–63; James Rees Ewing, *Public Services of Jacob Dolson Cox* (Ph.D. dissertation, Johns Hopkins University, 1902), pp. 8, 14–15; William C. Cochran, *General Jacob Dolson Cox: Early Life and Military Services* (pamphlet, Oberlin, Ohio, 1901), pp. 10–13.

141. Cox to Johnson, March 22, 1866, Johnson MSS.

142. Cox to Johnson, June 21, 1866, *ibid.*

143. Ewing, *Public Services of Jacob Dolson Cox*, p. 15.

144. Printed in William Dudley Foulke, *Life of Oliver P. Morton* (2 vols., Indianapolis, 1899), I, p. 449.

145. *Ibid.*, pp. 434, 455; James, *Framing of the Fourteenth Amendment*, pp. 29, 200. *See also* Governor Morton's message of November, 1865, in W. H. Schlater (of the President's staff) to Johnson, Nov. 12, 1865, Johnson MSS.

146. Foulke, *Life of Oliver P. Morton*, I, pp. 466–67; McKitrick, *Andrew Johnson and Reconstruction*, pp. 309–10.

147. Compare Beale, *The Critical Year*, pp. 106–107, 121–22, 178, 180, 184–86.

148. *See above*, footnotes 4–9, 20–23, 27, 31–49.

149. McPherson, *Handbook of Politics for 1868*, p. 102.

150. Compare McKitrick, *Andrew Johnson and Reconstruction*, p. 443.

151. New York *Herald*, Sept. 19, 1866.

152. Cox to Marble, Oct. 9, 1866, Marble MSS. *See also* Barlow to R. Taylor, Oct. 26, 1866, Barlow MSS.

153. Barlow to R. Johnson, Oct. 24, 1866, Barlow MSS.

154. Barlow to T. J. Barnett, Sept. 27, 1866, *ibid.*

155. Browning to W. H. Benneson and H. V. Sullivan, Oct. 13, 1866, printed in New York *Times*, Oct. 24, 1866. *See also* the earlier public statement of Democratic and Conservative members of Congress to the effect that the "dignity and equality of the States" must be preserved, including "the exclusive right of each State to control its own domestic concerns"; published in the New York *Herald*, July 4, 1866.

156. Professor Beale erroneously assumed that Seward's unidentified draft message had been prepared by Johnson and had reflected his views. *The Critical Year*, pp. 400–403.

157. Doolittle to Browning, Nov. 8, 1866, Doolittle MSS; *see also* James, *Framing of the Fourteenth Amendment*, p. 178, and McKitrick, *Andrew Johnson and Reconstruction*, pp. 464–65, especially footnote 38.

158. Weed to Seward, Nov. 24, 1866, Seward MSS. By the end of February, Weed was apprehensive of congressional reconstruction

proposals and uncertain of the best presidential tactics; Weed to Seward, Feb. 21, 1867, *ibid.*

159. P. W. Bartley to Johnson, Nov. 9, 1866, Johnson MSS.

160. S. Smith to Johnson, Nov. 10, 1866, *ibid.*

161. T. S. Seybolt to Johnson, Nov. 8, 1866, F. A. Aiken to Johnson, Nov. 26, 1866, *ibid.*

162. New York *Times,* Oct. 31, 1866, Nov. 3, 9, 12, 17, 19, 1866, Dec. 4, 27, 31, 1866.

163. *Diary of Gideon Welles,* III, p. 78.

164. *Ibid.,* p. 232.

165. New York *Times,* Nov. 14, 1867; McKitrick, *Andrew Johnson and Reconstruction,* p. 498.

166. *See above,* Chapter 5, pp. 95–106.

167. Of the 65 votes which Johnson obtained on the first ballot for the presidential nomination of the Democratic party in 1868, all but four were from southern delegates. Charles H. Coleman, *The Election of 1868: The Democratic Effort to Regain Control* (New York, 1933), pp. 164, 208.

168. J. Sherman to W. T. Sherman, July 8, 1866, *The Sherman Letters,* p. 276. For Trumbull's reaction *see Cong. Globe,* 39 Cong., 1 sess., p. 1761 (April 4, 1866); and C. H. Ray to M. Blair, April 10, 1866, enclosure in Blair to Johnson, April 15, 1866, Johnson MSS. A digest and explanation of the bill, unsigned, but in Trumbull's handwriting, is in the Johnson MSS; see Cox, "Andrew Johnson and His Ghost Writers," p. 473.

169. Fessenden to Morgan, June 26, 1867, Morgan MSS. The distrust, of course, involved party as well as principle. By mid-1866, it was widely believed that Johnson intended to bring the Democracy back into national power and ascendancy, and that he had deliberately sought to wreck the party that had elected him.

BIBLIOGRAPHY

THE MATERIALS FOR RECONSTRUCTION HISTORY ARE EXTENSIVE, and for them there are available to the scholar a number of useful guides. Hence we have decided against the inclusion of a comprehensive bibliography. Footnote citations indicate most of the sources we have used. We thought, however, that the reader might find useful a selected bibliography of materials published since January, 1953, which are both significant and pertinent to this study.

SELECTED PUBLICATIONS, 1953 AND AFTER

Basler, Roy P. and others, eds. *Collected Works of Abraham Lincoln.* 9 vols. New Brunswick, N.J., 1953–55.

Baxter, Maurice G. *Orville H. Browning: Lincoln's Friend and Critic.* Bloomington, Indiana, 1957.

Beale, Howard K., ed. *Diary of Gideon Welles.* 3 vols. New York, 1960.

Bentley, George R. *History of the Freedmen's Bureau.* Philadelphia, 1955.

Bickel, Alexander M. "The Original Understanding and the Segregation Decision," *Harvard Law Review,* LXIX (Nov., 1955), pp. 1–65.

Briefs for Appellants and for the United States on Reargument, *Brown v. Board of Education of Topeka*, in the Supreme Court of the United States, October Term, 1953.

Brodie, Fawn M. *Thaddeus Stevens: Scourge of the South*. New York, 1959.

Brown, Ira V. "Pennsylvania and the Rights of the Negro, 1865–1887," *Pennsylvania History*, XXVIII (Jan., 1961), pp. 45–57.

Brown, Ira V. "William D. Kelley and Radical Reconstruction," *Pennsylvania Magazine of History and Biography*, LXXXV (July, 1961), pp. 316–29.

Coben, Stanley. "Northeastern Business and Radical Reconstruction: A Re-examination," *Mississippi Valley Historical Review*, XLVI (June, 1959), pp. 67–90.

Cox, John H. and LaWanda. "Andrew Johnson and His Ghost Writers: An Analysis of the Freedmen's Bureau and Civil Rights Veto Messages," *Mississippi Valley Historical Review*, XLVIII (Dec., 1961), pp. 460–79.

Cox, John H. and LaWanda. "General O. O. Howard and the 'Misrepresented Bureau,'" *Journal of Southern History*, XIX (Nov., 1953), pp. 427–56.

Cox, LaWanda. "The Promise of Land for the Freedmen," *Mississippi Valley Historical Review*, XLV (Dec., 1958), pp. 413–40.

Donald, David, ed. *Inside Lincoln's Cabinet: The Civil War Diaries of Salmon P. Chase*. New York, 1954.

Donald, David. *Lincoln Reconsidered*. New York, 1956.

Fishel, Leslie H., Jr. "Northern Prejudice and Negro Suffrage, 1865–1870," *Journal of Negro History*, XXXIX (Jan., 1954), pp. 8–26.

Franklin, John Hope. *Reconstruction After the Civil War*. Chicago, 1961.

Graf, Le Roy P. "Andrew Johnson and the Coming of the War," *Tennessee Historical Quarterly*, XIX (Sept., 1960), pp. 208–21.

Hays, Willard. "Andrew Johnson's Reputation," East Tennessee Historical Society, *Publications*, No. 31 (1959), pp. 1–31, No. 32 (1960), pp. 18–50.

Henry, J. Milton. "The Revolution in Tennessee, February, 1861, to June, 1861," *Tennessee Historical Quarterly*, XVIII (June, 1959), pp. 99–119.

James, Joseph B. *The Framing of the Fourteenth Amendment*. Urbana, Ill., 1956.

James, Joseph B. "Southern Reaction to the Proposal of the Fourteenth Amendment," *Journal of Southern History*, XXII (Nov., 1956), pp. 477–97.

Jellison, Charles A. *Fessenden of Maine: Civil War Senator*. Binghamton, N.Y., 1962.

Johnson, Andrew. *Presidential Papers.* Microfilm, 55 reels. Library of Congress, Photoduplication Service, Washington, D.C., 1961.

Kelly, Alfred H. "The Fourteenth Amendment Reconsidered: The Segregation Question," *Michigan Law Review,* LIV (June, 1956), pp. 1049–86.

Korngold, Ralph. *Thaddeus Stevens: A Being Darkly Wise and Rudely Great.* New York, 1955.

Krug, Mark M. "On Rewriting the Story of Reconstruction in the United States History Textbooks," *Journal of Negro History,* XLVI (July, 1961), pp. 133–53.

Lomask, Milton. *Andrew Johnson: President on Trial.* New York, 1960.

McKitrick, Eric. *Andrew Johnson and Reconstruction.* Chicago, 1960.

Montgomery, David. "Radical Republicanism in Pennsylvania, 1866–1873," *Pennsylvania Magazine of History and Biography,* LXXXV (Oct., 1961), pp. 439–57.

Randall, J. G. and Richard N. Current. *Lincoln the President: Last Full Measure.* New York, 1955.

Randall, J. G. and David Donald. *The Civil War and Reconstruction.* Boston, 1961.

Rawley, James A. "Senator Morgan and Reconstruction," *New York History,* XXXIV (Jan., 1953), pp. 27–53.

Riddleberger, Patrick W. "The Break in the Radical Ranks: Liberals vs. Stalwarts in the Election of 1872," *Journal of Negro History,* XLIV (April, 1959), pp. 136–57.

Riddleberger, Patrick W. "The Making of a Political Abolitionist: George W. Julian and the Free Soilers, 1848," *Indiana Magazine of History,* LI (Sept., 1955), pp. 221–36.

Riddleberger, Patrick W. "The Radicals' Abandonment of the Negro during Reconstruction," *Journal of Negro History,* XLV (April, 1960), pp. 88–102.

Scroggs, Jack B. "Southern Reconstruction: A Radical View," *Journal of Southern History,* XXIV (Nov., 1958), pp. 407–29.

Sharkey, Robert P. *Money, Class and Party: An Economic Study of Civil War and Reconstruction.* Baltimore, 1959.

Shortreed, Margaret. "The Anti-Slavery Radicals, 1840–1868," *Past and Present,* No. 16 (Nov., 1959), pp. 65–87.

Sproat, John G. "Blueprint for Radical Reconstruction," *Journal of Southern History,* XXIII (Feb., 1957), pp. 25–44.

Thomas, Benjamin P. and Harold M. Hyman. *Stanton: The Life and Times of Lincoln's Secretary of War.* New York, 1962.

Trefousse, Hans L. "Ben Wade and the Negro," *Ohio Historical Quarterly,* LXVIII (April, 1959), pp. 161–72.

Unger, Irwin. "Business Men and Specie Resumption," *Political Science Quarterly*, LXXIV (March, 1959), pp. 46–70.

Weisberger, Bernard A. "The Dark and Bloody Ground of Reconstruction Historiography," *Journal of Southern History*, XXV (Nov., 1959), pp. 427–47.

Woodward, C. Vann. "Equality: America's Deferred Commitment," *American Scholar*, XXVII (Autumn, 1958), pp. 459–72.

Zoellner, Robert H. "Negro Colonization: The Climate of Opinion Surrounding Lincoln, 1860–1865," *Mid-America*, XLII (July, 1960), pp. 131–50.

INDEX

287

Richmond, Dean, 26, 27, 33, 47, 57, 59–60, 62–6, 73, 91, 92, 100, 114, 115, 120, 176, 247*n*
Richmond Regency, 47
Richmond *Republic*, 48
Robinson, Lucius, 72
Rockland (Me.) *Democrat and Free Press*, 206
Rollins, James S., 240*n*
Rousseau, L. H., 104, 150, 254*n*

Schell, Augustus, 176
Schell, Richard, 9, 13–15, 17, 18, 19, 24–5, 28, 35, 40, 176, 187
Schenck, Robert C., 161
Seward, Frederick, 11, 24–5, 28, 36, 40, 189
Seward, William H., 3, 30, 32, 33–4, 35–6, 37, 38, 45, 46, 47–8, 51, 61, 91, 97, 99, 105, 108, 114, 149, 167, 170, 171, 177, 197–200, 203, 204, 219, 220–3, 228, 230, 258*n*, 268*n*, 271*n*
   and the Blairs, 53–4, 59, 66–7, 117
   for compromise, 169–71, 180–92 *passim*, 197–200, 203, 276–7*n*
   discretion in correspondence of, 4, 36, 38–9, 48, 180
   and drafts of presidential messages, 135–6, 138, 180–3, 197–8, 207, 230
   and Johnson, 44–9 *passim*, 135, 180–3 *passim*, 197, 220–3
   in New York 1865 election, 70, 71, 82–4, 87
   and patronage grants, 109–28 *passim*
   position on slavery, 4, 220–1, 222
   as pro-amendment lobbyist, 6–30 *passim*, 39–40, 41
   on Reconstruction, 220–3 *passim*
   see also Weed, Thurlow
Seymour, Horatio, 16, 19, 21, 65, 96, 126, 174

Sharkey, William L., 156–8
Sherman, John, 191, 225, 231, 278*n*
Sherman, William T., 8, 99, 246*n*
Shipman, William D., 57–9, 74, 83, 115, 124
slavery, *see* Thirteenth Amendment
Slocum, Henry W., 72, 116
Smythe, Henry A., 123–6 *passim*, 258*n*
South
   admission and basis of representation for, 30, 62, 68, 75, 132–7, 139–43, 157, 158, 178, 182, 183, 206, 228, 276–7*n*
   and Blair family, 54–67 *passim*, 195–6
   conciliatory policies toward the, 17, 24, 30, 37–8, 41–2, 43, 46, 51, 58, 75, 129–35, 143, 156–9, 177–80, 183, 195, 202
   and Johnson, 60, 102–4, 125–6, 129–34, 135–41, 145, 151–71 *passim*, 162–3, 166–7, 177–9, 193–4, 195, 202, 209, 231, 281
   and Seward, 30, 47, 167, 170, 221, 268*n*
Speed, James, 42–3
Springfield *Republican*, 96, 122, 130, 141, 142, 175, 193, 206, 214–15
   see also Bowles, Samuel
Stanbery, Henry, 218, 219, 271*n*
Stanton, Edwin M., 26, 47, 51, 56, 59, 74, 83, 114, 176–7, 222, 246*n*, 269*n*
states rights, 51, 56, 64, 76, 78–9, 97–8, 136, 139, 154, 156, 160–1, 183–4, 202, 212, 214
   linked with the Thirteenth Amendment, 5–6, 20, 168, 170, 198–9, 280*n*
Stearns, George L., 155, 156, 159
Stebbins, Henry G., 119, 120
Steedman, James B., 176
Steele, John B., 53, 240

Atheneum Paperbacks

STUDIES IN AMERICAN NEGRO LIFE

THE ADAMS PAPERS

THE NEW YORK TIMES BYLINE BOOKS

Atheneum Paperbacks

HISTORY—AMERICAN

Atheneum Paperbacks

HISTORY

HISTORY—ASIA

ECONOMICS AND BUSINESS

Atheneum Paperbacks

LAW AND GOVERNMENT

DIPLOMACY AND INTERNATIONAL RELATIONS

Atheneum Paperbacks

Atheneum Paperbacks

Atheneum Paperbacks

THE WORLDS OF NATURE AND MAN

LITERATURE AND THE ARTS